# How We Got the
# NEW TESTAMENT

*Text, Transmission, Translation*

STANLEY E. PORTER

**Baker Academic**
*a division of Baker Publishing Group*
Grand Rapids, Michigan

© 2013 by Stanley E. Porter

Published by Baker Academic
a division of Baker Publishing Group
P.O. Box 6287, Grand Rapids, MI 49516-6287
www.bakeracademic.com

Printed in the United States of America

Library of Congress Cataloging-in-Publication Data
Porter, Stanley E., 1956–
    How we got the New Testament : text, transmission, translation / Stanley E. Porter.
        pages cm. — (Acadia studies in Bible and theology)
    Includes bibliographical references and index.
    ISBN 978-0-8010-4871-5 (pbk.)
        1. Bible. New Testament—History. I. Title.
BS2315.P67  2013
225.4′86—dc23                                                           2013021059

Unless otherwise indicated, Scripture quotations are from the King James Version of the Bible.

Scripture quotations labeled TNIV are from the Holy Bible, Today's New International Version®. TNIV®. Copyright © 2001, 2005 by Biblica, Inc.™ Used by permission of Zondervan. All rights reserved worldwide. www.zondervan.com

13   14   15   16   17   18   19          7   6   5   4   3   2   1

To Lionel Pye, Burt Hamilton, Nina Thomas,
and all of my other colleagues at McMaster Divinity College
who kept the college running smoothly
while I was temporarily medically incapacitated.

Thank you.

God is good.

# Contents

Preface  ix
Abbreviations  xiii

**Introduction**  1

1. **The Text of the New Testament**  9

   Introduction  9
   Is There a Text of the Greek New Testament? Or, What Is the
   Goal of Textual Criticism?  12
   The History of the Printed Greek Text of the
   New Testament  36
   Bart Ehrman and *Misquoting Jesus*  65
   Eclectic or Single Manuscript?  72
   Conclusion  76

2. **The Transmission of the New Testament**  77

   Introduction  77
   The Manuscripts of the Greek New Testament  79
   A Reconstructed History of the Transmission of the Greek
   New Testament before the Major Codexes  84
   The Major Codexes  124

Minuscules and Lectionaries   138

A Proposal regarding Textual Transmission of the Greek
New Testament   141

Conclusion   146

3.  The Translation of the New Testament   147

Introduction   147

The History of Translation of the New Testament   148

Major Issues in Translation of the New Testament   173

Conclusion   209

Conclusion   211

Index of Ancient Sources   214

Index of Modern Authors   219

# Preface

I was honored to have been invited to offer these lectures on October 20–22, 2008, at Acadia Divinity College in Wolfville, Nova Scotia, as the Hayward Lecturer for that year. I wish to thank those responsible for this invitation, especially my good friend Dr. Craig Evans, along with the rest of the faculty at Acadia Divinity College. I was honored not only to give these lectures but also to be invited to preach in the morning worship service in Manning Memorial Chapel on October 22 on the campus of Acadia University. Danny Zacharias was also a great help in managing the technical logistics. I enjoyed the opportunity to talk less formally with a number of students.

I have previously been a part of the Hayward Lectures at Acadia Divinity College, the first time in 2002 responding to the major set of lectures by Professor I. Howard Marshall, and the second time in 2006 as a contributor to a volume on the origins of the Bible. The first was published as "Hermeneutics, Biblical Interpretation, and Theology: Hunch, Holy Spirit, or Hard Work?" in *Beyond the Bible: Moving from Scripture to Theology*, by I. Howard Marshall, with essays by Kevin J. Vanhoozer and Stanley E. Porter, Acadia Studies in Bible and Theology (Grand Rapids: Baker Academic, 2004), 97–127. The second was published as "Paul and the Process of Canonization," in *Exploring the Origins of the Bible: Canon Formation in Historical, Literary, and Theological Perspective*, edited by Craig A. Evans and Emanuel Tov, Acadia Studies in Bible and Theology (Grand Rapids:

Baker Academic, 2008), 173–202. I have made some use of this second paper in another form in chapter 2 on the transmission of the New Testament in this volume.

Those two occasions were very profitable times, as I was fortunate to engage in interesting discussion of these topics and to enjoy tremendous hospitality in the company of both colleagues and students. I wish to thank several of the students of Acadia Divinity College with whom I spoke after delivering my paper in 2006 for prompting me to think further about the topic of formation of the Pauline canon. It is largely because of their prompting, as well as the encouragement of Craig Evans, that I chose this set of topics for my lectures in 2008. I was pleased to be able to return to Wolfville to offer these lectures on particular issues arising within the broader topic of how we got the New Testament. I have broken the topic down into three subfields to bring together several areas that are not always considered in concert in treatment of this broad topic. Matters of textual criticism have been brought once more to the fore on the basis of some recent work by those who have raised doubts about the nature and reliability of the text of the New Testament, including questioning the viability of an original or autograph text. The question of how the New Testament has been transmitted continues to be a subject of widespread and intense debate, as there are so many different theories of the dark or tunnel period before the assembling of our major codexes. The subject of translation may seem the most far-fetched in relation to the other two topics. However, from almost the advent of Christianity the New Testament has been translated into other languages, and so translation itself is a part of the transmission process of the New Testament text. Most of us who use the Bible use it in a translated form, so I thought it wise to say some things about the nature of the translation process and how it affects the New Testament that we use.

All of my Hayward experiences have been rewarding, as they have offered me opportunities to pursue a number of different areas of research. This latest experience provided the occasion for me to further pursue a topic of abiding personal interest and to make a number of proposals that I have not seen in print before. The audiences at all of these events were gracious in their responses and probing in their questions. The manuscript that I prepared in advance of the lectures was too long for delivery in its entirety, so I needed to abridge the individual presentations. This volume includes the complete lectures, essentially as they were prepared, but corrected and enhanced as they benefited from constructive comments and suggestions by those who heard and responded to them, and as I have had further occasion to think more about these important topics. My hope is that they will be as rewarding to read as they have been to research, deliver, and write.

I wish to thank Dr. Craig Evans for his suggestions on making the lectures into a book; Nathan Hui for reading the manuscript and making some suggestions; Hughson Ong for helping to correct and revise the manuscript; and my friends at Baker, Jim Kinney and James Ernest, for their patience and steadfast encouragement.

# Abbreviations

## General

| | | | |
|---|---|---|---|
| ad loc. | at the place discussed | ibid. | in the same source |
| c. | circa | i.e. | that is |
| cf. | compare | n(n). | note(s) |
| chap(s). | chapter(s) | n.s. | new series |
| e.g. | for example | p(p). | page(s) |
| esp. | especially | pl. | plural |
| ET | English translation | repr. | reprint |
| etc. | and the rest | rev. | revised |
| fasc(s). | fascicles | v(v). | verse(s) |

## Ancient Texts, Text Types, and Versions

LXX    Septuagint

## Modern Editions

NA²⁵    *Novum Testamentum Graece.* Edited by Eberhard Nestle, Erwin
Nestle, and Kurt Aland. 25th revised edition. Stuttgart: Württem-
bergische Bibelanstalt, 1963

NA²⁶    *Novum Testamentum Graece.* Edited by [E. Nestle and E. Nestle],
Kurt Aland, Matthew Black, Carlo M. Martini, Bruce M. Metzger,

and Allen Wikgren. 26th revised edition. Stuttgart: Deutsche Bibelgesellschaft, 1979

NA²⁷   *Novum Testamentum Graece.* Edited by [E. Nestle and E. Nestle],
Barbara Aland, Kurt Aland, Johannes Karavidopoulos, Carlo M.
Martini, and Bruce M. Metzger. 27th revised edition. Stuttgart:
Deutsche Bibelgesellschaft, 1993

NA²⁸   *Novum Testamentum Graece.* Edited by [E. Nestle and E. Nestle],
Barbara Aland, Kurt Aland, Johannes Karavidopoulos, Carlo M.
Martini, and Bruce M. Metzger. 28th edition. Stuttgart: Deutsche
Bibelgesellschaft, 2012

UBS⁴   *The Greek New Testament.* Edited by Barbara Aland, Kurt Aland,
Johannes Karavidopoulos, Carlo M. Martini, and Bruce M.
Metzger. 4th revised edition. Stuttgart: Deutsche Bibelgesellschaft/
United Bible Societies, 1993

## Modern Versions

| | | | |
|---|---|---|---|
| ESV | English Standard Version | NKJV | New King James Version |
| HCSB | Holman Christian Standard Bible | NLT | New Living Translation |
| | | NRSV | New Revised Standard Version |
| NASB | New American Standard Bible | | |
| NET | New English Translation | RSV | Revised Standard Version |
| NIV | New International Version | TNIV | Today's New International Version |

## Papyri

| | | | |
|---|---|---|---|
| P.Aberd. | Aberdeen Papyri | P.Lond.Christ. | British Museum Papyri |
| P.Amh. | Amherst Papyri | | |
| P.Barcelona | Barcelona Papyrus | P.Merton | Merton Papyri |
| | | P.Oxy. | Oxyrhynchus Papyri |
| P.Berl. | Berlin Papyri | | |
| P.Bodmer | Bodmer Papyri | P.Ryl. | John Rylands Library Papyri |
| P.Chester Beatty | Chester Beatty Papyri | PSI | Papyri of the Società Italiana |
| P.Egerton | Egerton Papyri | P.Vindob. | National Library Papyrus Collection |
| P.Köln | Kölner Papyri | | |

## Apostolic Fathers

*1–2 Clem.*        *1–2 Clement*

## Greek and Latin Works

### Cicero

*Att.*     *Epistulae ad Atticum*
*Fam.*    *Epistulae ad familiares*

### Eusebius

*Hist. eccl.*    *Historia ecclesiastica*
                 *(Ecclesiastical History)*
*Praep. ev.*    *Praeparatio evangelica*
                 *(Preparation for the*
                 *Gospel)*
*Vit. Const.*    *Vita Constantini (Life*
                 *of Constantine)*

### Irenaeus

*Haer.*    *Adversus haereses (Against*
           *Heresies)*

### Josephus

*Ag. Ap.*    *Against Apion*
*Ant.*       *Jewish Antiquities*

### Justin

*1 Apol.*    *Apologia i (First Apology)*

### Philo

*Moses*    *On the Life of Moses (De*
           *vita Mosis)*

### Tertullian

*Marc.*     *Adversus Marcionem*
            *(Against Marcion)*
*Praescr.*  *De praescriptione hae-*
            *reticorum (Prescription*
            *against Heretics)*

## Secondary Sources

| | |
|---|---|
| AB | Anchor Bible |
| *AcOr* | *Acta orientalia* |
| ANF | Ante-Nicene Fathers |
| *AngJT* | *Anglican Journal of Theology* |
| ANRW | *Aufstieg und Niedergang der römischen Welt: Geschichte und Kultur Roms im Spiegel der neueren Forschung.* Edited by H. Temporini and W. Haase. Berlin, 1972– |
| ANTF | Arbeiten zur neutestamentlichen Textforschung |
| APVG | Archiv für Papyrusforschung und verwandte Gebiete |
| ASBT | Acadia Studies in Bible and Theology |

| | |
|---|---|
| ASP | American Studies in Papyrology |
| *BASP* | *Bulletin of the American Society of Papyrologists* |
| *BBC* | *Bulletin of the Bezan Club* |
| *BBR* | *Bulletin for Biblical Research* |
| BETL | Bibliotheca ephemeridum theologicarum lovaniensium |
| *Bib* | *Biblica* |
| BIS | Biblical Interpretation Series |
| BLUW | Beiträge zur Leipziger Universitäts- und Wissenschaftsgeschichte |
| BSNA | Biblical Scholarship in North America |
| *BT* | *The Bible Translator* |
| BZNW | Beihefte zur Zeitschrift für die neutestamentliche Wissenschaft |
| CBET | Contributions to Biblical Theology and Exegesis |
| *CBQ* | *Catholic Biblical Quarterly* |
| ConBNT | Coniectanea neotestamentica or Coniectanea biblica: New Testament Series |
| CSCO | Corpus scriptorum christianorum orientalium. Edited by I. B. Chabot et al. Paris, 1903– |
| CTL | Cambridge Textbooks in Linguistics |
| *CurBS* | *Currents in Research: Biblical Studies* |
| *DBCI* | *Dictionary of Biblical Criticism and Interpretation.* Edited by S. E. Porter. London, 2007 |
| *DNTB* | *Dictionary of New Testament Background.* Edited by C. A. Evans and S. E. Porter. Downers Grove, 2000 |
| *DPL* | *Dictionary of Paul and His Letters.* Edited by G. F. Hawthorne and R. P. Martin. Downers Grove, 1993 |
| GRM | Graeco-Roman Memoirs |
| HBT | History of Bible Translation |
| HSCL | Harvard Studies in Comparative Literature |
| HTB | Histoire du texte biblique |
| *HTR* | *Harvard Theological Review* |
| ITL | International Theological Library |
| *JBL* | *Journal of Biblical Literature* |
| *JETS* | *Journal of the Evangelical Theological Society* |
| *JGRChJ* | *Journal of Greco-Roman Christianity and Judaism* |
| *JÖB* | *Jahrbuch der österreichischen Byzantinistik* |
| JSNTSup | Journal for the Study of the New Testament: Supplement Series |
| JSPSup | Journal for the Study of the Pseudepigrapha: Supplement Series |

| | |
|---|---|
| JTS | *Journal of Theological Studies* |
| KAV | Kommentar zu den Apostolischen Vätern |
| LHBOTS | Library of Hebrew Bible and Old Testament Studies |
| LNTS | Library of New Testament Studies |
| LTCH | Literature of Theology and Church History |
| MJTM | *McMaster Journal of Theology and Ministry* |
| MNTS | McMaster New Testament Studies |
| MPÖN | Mitteilungen aus der Papyrussammlung der Österreichischen Nationalbibliothek (Papyrus Erzherzog Rainer) |
| MTS | Marburger theologische Studien |
| NovTSup | Novum Testamentum Supplements |
| NTGF | New Testament in the Greek Fathers |
| NTM | New Testament Monographs |
| NTOA | Novum Testamentum et Orbis Antiquus |
| NTS | *New Testament Studies* |
| NTTS | New Testament Tools and Studies |
| NTTSD | New Testament Tools, Studies, and Documents |
| OPIAC | Occasional Papers of the Institute for Antiquity and Christianity |
| OTM | Oxford Theological Monographs |
| OTS | Old Testament Studies |
| PL | Patrologia latina [= Patrologiae cursus completus: Series latina]. Edited by J.-P. Migne. 217 vols. Paris, 1844–1864 |
| PSt | Pauline Studies |
| RB | *Revue biblique* |
| RBL | *Review of Biblical Literature* |
| SBG | Studies in Biblical Greek |
| SBLAB | Studies in Biblical Literature Academia Biblica |
| SBLSymS | Society of Biblical Literature Symposium Series |
| SBLTCS | Society of Biblical Literature Text-Critical Studies |
| SD | Studies and Documents |
| SNTSMS | Society for New Testament Studies Monograph Series |
| SPap | Université de Paris IV Paris-Sorbonne série "Papyrologie" |
| SPP | Studien zur Palaeographie und Papyruskunde |
| ST | Studies in Theology |
| STR | Studies in Theology and Religion |
| TENTS | Texts and Editions for New Testament Study |
| TS | Texts and Studies |
| TynBul | *Tyndale Bulletin* |
| UBSMS | United Bible Societies Monograph Series |

| VCSup | Vigiliae christianae Supplements |
| WBC | Word Biblical Commentary |
| WUNT | Wissenschaftliche Untersuchungen zum Neuen Testament |
| ZNW | *Zeitschrift für die neutestamentliche Wissenschaft und die Kunde der älteren Kirche* |
| ZPE | *Zeitschrift für Papyrologie und Epigraphik* |

# Introduction

It may seem more than a little presumptuous to address the question "How did we get the New Testament?" in a book that comes out of a conference held at Acadia Divinity College. Suggesting this topic sounds something like the proverbial taking of coals to Newcastle. After all, what more can possibly be said about where the New Testament came from than has been said at Acadia by Acadians and related people? Even previous Hayward Lectures at Acadia have addressed topics related to the question of how we got the New Testament. I myself was a participant in one of these previous discussions.[1] In spite of these warning signs, I must confess that I have been interested in the origins of the New Testament for a considerable length of time, including (at least) the dimensions of its text, its transmission, and its translation. Thus, the selection of these topics is not foreign to me, but rather is a further extension and consolidation of work begun earlier, and in some ways brought to fruition first in these lectures and now in this book.

I became intensely interested in the text of the New Testament through research in papyrology and epigraphy. For further exploration of the topic and as a potential resource for readers, I include a list

1. Stanley E. Porter, "Paul and the Process of Canonization," in *Exploring the Origins of the Bible: Canon Formation in Historical, Literary, and Theological Perspective*, ed. Craig A. Evans and Emanuel Tov, ASBT (Grand Rapids: Baker Academic, 2008), 173–202.

of works in this area that I have published, alone and with others, as an indication of the kind of work that stands behind this book.[2] As I began to examine documents and edit and comment upon manuscripts, I became increasingly aware of the need for New Testament scholars to have greater firsthand acquaintance with the primary artifacts of our profession. Each manuscript has its own characteristics, features, and contribution to make to our understanding of the New Testament text. New Testament textual artifacts, whether papyrus or parchment manuscripts, are the realia of our discipline and must be examined for the contribution that each makes as an artifact in its own right, not simply as a repository of variant readings.[3] As a result of my interest in manuscripts—a highlight of which has been the opportunity to identify and first publish (along with my wife, Wendy) a sixth-century New Testament papyrus of the book of Acts and a

2. See esp. Stanley E. Porter and Wendy J. Porter, *New Testament Greek Papyri and Parchments: New Editions*, 2 vols., MPÖN n.s. 29, 30 (Berlin: de Gruyter, 2008); see also Stanley E. Porter, "Is ἀμβιτεύειν Really ἐμβατεύειν (*P. Oxy.* XVII 2110.15)?" *BASP* 27 (1990): 45–47; "The Argument of Romans 5: Can a Rhetorical Question Make a Difference?" *JBL* 110 (1991): 655–77; "P.Oxy. 744.4 and Colossians 3:9," *Bib* 73 (1992): 565–67; "Artemis Medeia Inscription Again," *ZPE* 93 (1992): 219–21; "The Greek Papyri of the Judaean Desert and the World of the Roman East," in *The Scrolls and the Scriptures: Qumran Fifty Years After*, ed. Stanley E. Porter and Craig A. Evans (JSPSup 26; Sheffield: Sheffield Academic Press, 1997), 293–316; "The Rhetorical Scribe: Textual Variants in Romans and Their Possible Rhetorical Purpose," in *Rhetorical Criticism and the Bible*, ed. Stanley E. Porter and Dennis L. Stamps, JSNTSup 195 (Sheffield: Sheffield Academic Press, 2002), 403–19; "Textual Criticism in the Light of Diverse Textual Evidence for the Greek New Testament: An Expanded Proposal," in *New Testament Manuscripts: Their Texts and Their World*, ed. Thomas J. Kraus and Tobias Nicklas, TENTS 2 (Leiden: Brill, 2006), 305–37; Stanley E. Porter and Matthew Brook O'Donnell, "The Implications of Textual Variants for Authenticating the Words of Jesus," in *Authenticating the Words of Jesus*, ed. Bruce Chilton and Craig A. Evans, NTTS, vol. 28, no. 1 (Leiden: Brill, 1999), 97–133; "The Implications of Textual Variants for Authenticating the Activities of Jesus," in *Authenticating the Activities of Jesus*, ed. Bruce Chilton and Craig A. Evans, NTTS, vol. 28, no. 2 (Leiden: Brill, 1998), 121–51; Stanley E. Porter, "Manuscripts, Greek New Testament" and "Textual Criticism," *DNTB* 670–78, 1210–14; Stanley E. Porter and Wendy J. Porter, "Acts of the Apostles 1, 1–5 and 1, 7–11 (P.Harrauer 2)," in *Wiener Papyri: Als Festgabe zum 60. Geburtstag von Hermann Harrauer (P. Harrauer)*, ed. Bernhard Palme (Vienna: Holzhausen, 2001), 7–14, with plate; Stanley E. Porter, "Textual Criticism and Oldest Gospel Manuscripts," in *Encyclopedia of the Historical Jesus*, ed. Craig A. Evans (London: Routledge, 2008), 640–44.

3. A recent work that makes this point acutely well is Thomas J. Kraus, *Ad fontes: Original Manuscripts and Their Significance for Studying Early Christianity; Selected Essays*, TENTS 3 (Leiden: Brill, 2007).

sixth-century papyrus of the Christian poet Romanos Melodus[4]—I also developed an intense interest in the transmission of the text. I became interested not only in the texts important for Christianity but also in how were they transmitted to us. Again, I provide a list of studies that stand behind my work here and helped to generate my interest in the subject.[5] Dealing with manuscripts, some older and

4. Porter and Porter, "Acts of the Apostles," reprinted and amended in Porter and Porter, *Papyri and Parchments*, no. 8, 1:28–32; Stanley E. Porter and Wendy J. Porter, "P. Vindob. G 26225: A New Romanos Melodus Papyrus in the Vienna Collection," *JÖB* 52 (2002): 135–48, with plate. The edition that my wife and I published of Austrian National Library Suppl. Gr. 106 was also apparently the first edition of this manuscript to be published (see Porter and Porter, *Papyri and Parchments*, no. 24, 1:94–102).

5. See esp. Stanley E. Porter, *The Grammarian's Rebirth: Dead Languages and Live Issues in Current Biblical Study* (London: Roehampton Institute, 1996); "The Greek Apocryphal Gospels Papyri: The Need for a Critical Edition," in *Akten des 21. Internationalen Papyrologenkongresses, Berlin, 13.–19.8.1995*, ed. Bärbel Kramer et al., APVG 3 (Stuttgart: Teubner, 1997), 2:795–803; Richard J. Bauckham and Stanley E. Porter, "Apocryphal Gospels," *DNTB* 71–78; Stanley E. Porter, "POxy II 210 as an Apocryphal Gospel and the Development of Egyptian Christianity," in *Atti del XXII Congresso Internazionale di Papirologia, Firenze, 23–29 agosto 1998*, ed. Isabella Andorlini et al. (Florence: Istituto Papirologico "G. Vitelli," 2001), 2:1095–108 (now recognized as the standard critical edition of this manuscript in Andrew Bernhard, *Other Early Christian Gospels: A Critical Edition of the Surviving Greek Manuscripts*, LNTS 315 [London: T&T Clark, 2006], 100); "Developments in the Text of Acts before the Major Codices," in *The Book of Acts as Church History: Text, Textual Traditions and Ancient Interpretations* [= *Apostelgeschichte als Kirchengeschichte: Text, Texttraditionen und antike Auslegungen*], ed. Tobias Nicklas and Michael Tilly, BZNW 120 (Berlin: de Gruyter, 2003), 31–67 (abstract, 423–24); "Why So Many Holes in the Papyrological Evidence for the Greek New Testament?" in *The Bible as Book: The Transmission of the Greek Text*, ed. Scot McKendrick and Orlaith A. O'Sullivan (London: British Library Publications and Oak Knoll Press, 2003), 167–86; "Apocryphal Gospels and the Text of the New Testament before AD 200," in *The New Testament Text in Early Christianity: Proceedings of the Lille Colloquium, July 2000* [= *Le texte du Nouveau Testament au début du christianisme: Actes du colloque de Lille, juillet 2000*], ed. C.-B. Amphoux and J. K. Elliott, HTB 6 (Lausanne: Éditions du Zèbre, 2003), 235–58; "When and How Was the Pauline Canon Compiled? An Assessment of Theories," in *The Pauline Canon*, ed. Stanley E. Porter, PSt 1 (Leiden: Brill, 2004), 95–127; "Pericope Markers in Some Early Greek New Testament Manuscripts," in *Layout Markers in Biblical Manuscripts and Ugaritic Tablets*, ed. Marjo C. A. Korpel and Josef M. Oesch, Pericope 5 (Assen: Van Gorcum, 2005), 161–76; "Textual Criticism in the Light of Diverse Textual Evidence for the Greek New Testament: An Expanded Proposal," in Kraus and Tobias, *New Testament Manuscripts*, 305–37; "The Use of Hermeneia and Johannine Manuscripts," in *Akten des 23. Internationalen Papyrologenkongresses, Wien, 22.–28. Juli 2001*, ed. Bernhard Palme, Papyrologica Vindobonensia 1 (Vienna: Verlag der Österreichischen Akademie der Wissenschaften, 2007), 573–80; "The Influence of Unit Delimitation on Reading and Use of Greek

some younger, makes one aware of the passing on of the tradition and the means by which this was done. In dealing with individual biblical manuscripts, therefore, I have tried to be attentive to their place within the larger tradition. This tradition includes not only the other New Testament manuscripts but also apocryphal texts and other documents that may inform our understanding, even though they are not part of the New Testament itself. A natural result of such interest in text and transmission is interest in translation of the New Testament. These two disciplines are not usually linked together in study of contemporary translations.[6] My interest in the process of

---

Manuscripts," in *Method in Unit Delimitation*, ed. Marjo C. A. Korpel, Josef M. Oesch, and Stanley E. Porter, Pericope 6 (Leiden: Brill, 2007), 44–60; "Pericope Markers and the Paragraph: Textual and Linguistic Considerations," in *The Impact of Unit Delimitation on Exegesis*, ed. Raymond de Hoop, Marjo C. A. Korpel, and Stanley E. Porter, Pericope 7 (Leiden: Brill, 2008), 175–95; "Fragmente unbekannter Evangelien auf Papyrus" (with Thomas J. Kraus), "Der Papyrus Egerton 2 (P.Egerton 2/P.Lond. Christ 1)," "Der Papyrus Köln VI 255 (P.Köln VI 255)," "Der Papyrus Berolinensis 11710 (P.Berl. 11710)," "Rylands Apokryphes Evangelium (?) (P.Ryl. III 464)" (with Wendy J. Porter), "Der Papyrus Oxyrhynchus II 210 (P.Oxy. II 210)," all in *Antike christliche Apokryphen in deutscher Übersetzung*, vol. 1, part 1, *Evangelien und Verwandtes*, ed. Christoph Markschies and Jens Schröter, 7th ed. (Tübingen: Mohr Siebeck, 2012), 353–56, 360– 65, 366–67, 368–69, 377–78, 387–89; "Early Apocryphal Gospels and the New Testament Text," in *The Early Text of the New Testament*, ed. Charles E. Hill and Michael J. Kruger (Oxford: Oxford University Press, 2012), 350–69; "Early Apocryphal Non-Gospel Literature and the New Testament," *JGRChJ* 8 (2011–2012): 192–98; "What Do We Know and How Do We Know It? Reconstructing Christianity from Its Earliest Manuscripts" and "Recent Efforts to Reconstruct Early Christianity on the Basis of Its Papyrological Evidence," in *Christian Origins and Greco-Roman Culture: Social and Literary Contexts for the New Testament*, ed. Stanley E. Porter and Andrew W. Pitts, TENTS 9 (Leiden: Brill, 2013), 41–70, 71–84.

6. Stanley E. Porter, "The Contemporary English Version and the Ideology of Translation," in *Translating the Bible: Problems and Prospects*, ed. Stanley E. Porter and Richard S. Hess, JSNTSup 173 (Sheffield: Sheffield Academic Press, 1999), 18–45; "Mark 1.4, Baptism and Translation," in *Baptism, the New Testament and the Church: Historical and Contemporary Studies in Honour of R. E. O. White*, ed. Stanley E. Porter and Anthony R. Cross, JSNTSup 171 (Sheffield: Sheffield Academic Press, 1999), 81–98; "New Testament Versions, Ancient," *DNTB* 745–48; "Modern Translations," in *The Oxford Illustrated History of the Bible*, ed. John Rogerson (Oxford: Oxford University Press, 2001), 134–61; "Eugene Nida and Translation," *BT* 56, no. 1 (2005): 8–19; "Language and Translation of the New Testament," in *The Oxford Handbook of Biblical Studies*, ed. John W. Rogerson and Judith M. Lieu (Oxford: Oxford University Press, 2006), 184–210; "Translations of the Bible (Since the KJV)," in *DBCI*, 362–69; "Assessing Translation Theory: Beyond Literal and Dynamic Equivalence," in *Translating the New Testament: Text, Translation, Theology*, ed. Stanley E. Porter and Mark J. Boda, MNTS (Grand Rapids: Eerdmans, 2009), 117–45; Stanley E.

translation and the resulting numerous translations has developed along two lines, one concerned with translations of the New Testament into English and the other concerned with early bilingual manuscripts, usually with Coptic as the other language. I have come to appreciate that translation is one of the most important tools for textual transmission that we have had in the history and development of the New Testament, along with its being a primary avenue for the fulfillment of the mission of the church. Despite my interest, however, I am still wary of the fact that many others have said something about all of these topics before me.

These previous attempts might constitute a good-enough reason to avoid this broader subject and choose another, one that perhaps has had less recent exposure or has had its paths less well trodden. However, the topic of the origins of the New Testament continues to attract preternatural and, I would even say, unmerited and unfair attention in diverse quarters. The Jesus Seminar, along with some others, has raised the question of whether the church in fact has the correct canon of authoritative Scriptures. Some connected with the Jesus Seminar believe that there are other books not included in the New Testament that should be incorporated instead. One prime example, labeled by those of the Jesus Seminar as the "Fifth Gospel," is the *Gospel of Thomas*.[7] The question for them is not only which books belong in the canon, but also what the very nature of the canon is and whether it should be revisited and even reopened. Without directly addressing these claims here, I indirectly address the question through tracing the early transmission of the New Testament. One of the major issues in Dan Brown's novel *The Da Vinci Code* revolves around the origin of the New Testament.[8] He claims that, essentially, the Roman emperor Constantine brought the New Testament into being in the fourth century when, by sheer capricious assertion, he

---

Porter and Matthew Brook O'Donnell, "Comparative Discourse Analysis as a Tool in Assessing Translations Using Luke 16:19–31 as a Test Case," in Porter and Boda, *Translating the New Testament*, 185–99; "Translation, Exegesis, and 1 Thessalonians 2.14–15," *BT* 64, no. 1 (2013): 82–98.

7. See Robert W. Funk, Robert Hoover, and the Jesus Seminar, *The Five Gospels: What Did Jesus Really Say? The Search for the Authentic Words of Jesus* (New York: HarperOne, 1996). The study of the *Gospel of Thomas* has become an industry of its own. Very little will be said about it below.

8. Dan Brown, *The Da Vinci Code* (New York: Doubleday, 2003).

selected among a host of possible works, especially numerous gospels, the ones that should be included in our Bible.[9] In a distinctly Canadian contribution, Tom Harpur's *The Pagan Christ*[10] wants to go even further and question not only the nature of the documents of the New Testament but also the events that lie behind them. Harpur claims that Jesus never existed and that the major theological ideas of Christianity, and Judaism as well, came from Egyptian religion.[11] I am sure that there are even more far-fetched and sensational claims being made, although this is somewhat hard to imagine, and even harder to fathom.

The more circumscribed question of how we got the New Testament is the topic that I want to address here. Even the more specific question of how we got the New Testament is more problematic than it at first appears. By the title of this book, *How We Got the New Testament*, do I mean to address how we got the New Testament that we use today? Do I mean the English or some other translation that most of us use in our everyday reading of the Bible, or do I mean the Greek New Testament that we (unfortunately, sometimes too occasionally) refer to if we are students of the text? Do I mean to ask how we got the New Testament when it was first assembled in ancient times, or do I mean to ask how the documents that went into that New Testament came about? These are a lot of questions, and I hope to say at least something about each of them, as well as some others, over the course of the following three substantive chapters.

I have divided the topic into three manageable parts. The first chapter is concerned with the text of the New Testament. Here I begin with the question of what we are trying to do in talking about the text of the New Testament. I will then examine briefly the history of development of the printed Greek text that we do have. Then I will consider a couple of proposals regarding this text, including Bart

9. Stanley E. Porter, "The Da Vinci Code, Conspiracy Theory, and the Biblical Canon," *MJTM* 6 (2003–2005): 49–80. *The Da Vinci Code* also became its own minor industry, which generated numerous responses, the occasional one even making a substantive contribution to the discussion.

10. Tom Harpur, *The Pagan Christ: Recovering the Lost Light* (Toronto: Thomas Allen, 2004). Since then, Harpur has continued his theme in *Water into Wine: An Empowering Vision of the Gospels* (Toronto: Thomas Allen, 2007).

11. See Stanley E. Porter and Stephen J. Bedard, *Unmasking the Pagan Christ: An Evangelical Response to the Cosmic Christ Idea* (Toronto: Clements, 2006).

Ehrman's contentions in his book *Misquoting Jesus*[12] and a proposal regarding the merits of using a manuscript text rather than an eclectic text of the New Testament.     *Chapter 2 - textual transmission*

The subject of textual transmission is the topic of the second chapter. In many ways this topic is directly related to the larger and more diffuse issue of canonical formation, although I will try not to get too directly involved in this debate,[13] but will instead confine myself to the issues of transmission of the Greek New Testament. A few of the topics that I will touch upon in this area include factors related to where the various New Testament documents originated and how they were gathered together and where, and how they then became part of what we would now recognize as the Greek New Testament.

My third chapter concerns the translation of the New Testament. ③ *Translation* Early Christians were well familiar with a translated Bible, as they (along with most Jews of the first century) used the Septuagint, the Greek translation of the Hebrew Scriptures. It is not surprising that early on the New Testament was translated into other languages, a process that continues to this very day.[14] The vast majority of those who read the New Testament do so in translation, and so translation of the New Testament is part of its transmission, and it is appropriate to address the question of how translation relates to the text and transmission of the Greek New Testament. Bible translation theory involves a number of approaches that are worth articulating. These approaches constitute the major focus of the third chapter, as I explore their different points of engagement with the text, the varying purposes for which they might be made, and their potential use and applicability in future translational work.

At the end of this summary of the book's contents, let me make clear who my intended audience is. I hope that some things in this

12. Bart D. Ehrman, *Misquoting Jesus: The Story behind Who Changed the Bible and Why* (San Francisco: HarperSanFrancisco, 2005). In chapter 1 I will say more about such claims as this title implies, but in the meantime I must say that publishers who issue books with such sensational titles should be ashamed of themselves. Unfortunately, more and more publishers are solely focusing upon the bottom line—profit from sales. The quality and academic rigor of publications are clearly falling.

13. For my take on these larger issues, see Stanley E. Porter, "Canon: New Testament," in *The Oxford Encyclopedia of the Books of the Bible*, vol. 1, ed. Michael D. Coogan (Oxford: Oxford University Press, 2011), 109–20.

14. See M. Paul Lewis, ed., *Ethnologue: Languages of the World*, 16th ed. (Dallas: SIL International, 2009), which recounts the state of the languages of the world.

book will challenge my fellow scholars, and I think that I do present some ideas worth consideration by them. These include my perspective on the use of a single-manuscript text of the New Testament, the early formation of the bulk of the New Testament, and how the constraints of translation theory can be broadened—among possibly several others. Nevertheless, I conceive of my audience for this book as being similar to the audience that originally heard these lectures—an inquisitive and generally well-educated and thinking Christian audience, ideally though not necessarily with some formal theological education, that wishes to learn more about the New Testament and where it came from. I do not deny that portions of this book may require the reader to pay close attention—especially in chapter 1, where a number of people are mentioned and make short appearances in the discussion—but my hope is that the topic will be sufficiently engaging to propel the reader forward. While many of these individual topics could well constitute the material for a full set of lectures or a monograph in their own right, I attempt to bring them all together into a whole, so that at the conclusion we can appreciate more fully the means by which we got the New Testament.

# 1

# The Text of the New Testament

## Introduction

A. T. Robertson, the great Greek grammarian as well as textual critic and general student of the New Testament,[1] tells the following story about John Brown of Haddington, Scotland. Born in 1722, John Brown was the son of common and ordinary parents, although they had an interest in learning. His father, a weaver by winter and a salmon fisherman during the summer, taught himself to read so that he could read Christian books. In the area where John grew up, local schooling was not always available, so he accumulated only a few months of formal education. Nevertheless, these rare experiences excited his interest in learning, and he read whatever he could, even starting to learn Latin. Unfortunately, John's father died when the boy was eleven, as did his mother not long after. The orphaned John, however, was soon adopted by a Christian family. A sickly child, he was converted to Christian faith when he was twelve years old, and he became a shepherd. His

---

1. Among his many works, see esp. (for this volume) A. T. Robertson, *A Grammar of the Greek New Testament in the Light of Historical Research*, 4th ed. (Nashville: Broadman, 1934); *An Introduction to the Textual Criticism of the New Testament* (London: Hodder & Stoughton, 1925). He also wrote thirty other volumes on a range of topics in New Testament studies.

adoptive father could not read, so John spent many days reading to his new parent. John also borrowed Latin books and spent time improving his Latin, and during his two-hour lunch break he often visited his local minister, who gave him Latin exercises. John graduated to Greek next. Greek was not as well known as Latin, and so he tackled this language on his own. He borrowed a Greek New Testament and, using his Latin grammar book and a copy of the works of the Roman poet Ovid, figured out the Greek alphabet and its sounds. John then started to learn Greek vocabulary by comparing short words to those in his English Bible. He began learning Greek grammar by comparing the Greek endings with those in Latin.

One day, at the age of sixteen, John Brown heard that a bookstore in St. Andrews, Scotland, twenty-four miles away, had a copy of the Greek New Testament for sale. He very much wanted to have one of his own. He left his sheep with a friend and made the trek by foot to the city, walking throughout the entire night, so that he arrived the next morning in St. Andrews, where he found the bookstore of one Alexander McCulloch. He entered the shop, likely with some trepidation, and asked the no-doubt surprised shopkeeper for a Greek New Testament. Here was this slight, roughly clothed, barefoot young man asking for a Greek New Testament. "What would *you* do wi' that book? You'll no can read it," the bookstore owner said. "I'll try to read it," John humbly replied. There happened to be some professors who had entered the shop, and they heard this short conversation. One of the professors, probably Francis Pringle, professor of Greek at the university, asked the bookstore owner to fetch the Greek New Testament. Tossing it on the counter, he said, "Boy, if you can read that book, you shall have it for nothing."

No doubt there was a lightness in John Brown's step as he walked all the way back from St. Andrews that day, new Greek New Testament tucked under his arm. He had eagerly taken up the book, read out a passage to the amazement of everyone there, including Pringle, and turned and walked out the door, his prize firmly in his grasp. By the afternoon of the same day, John was back tending his flock while reading from his Greek New Testament. However, the story does not end there.

Some other young men became jealous of this shepherd who was becoming an accomplished scholar. These young men were studying for the ministry in the area, and one of them accused John of having gotten his knowledge from the devil. John treated such accusations as a joke because, after all, he knew what hard work had gone into gaining such knowledge. Not only did he know Latin and Greek, but he also taught himself Hebrew. His increased knowledge led to increased suspicion, with even his own pastor agreeing that witchcraft explained John's knowledge. After five years of such unfounded accusations, the elders of his church unanimously voted a certificate of full membership for John, although his pastor refused to sign it. John continued to learn while supporting himself as a peddler, soldier, schoolmaster, and then preacher and divinity student, and eventually as a pastor, professor of theology, and scholar. John Brown published in 1769 *A Dictionary of the Holy Bible*, only the second Bible dictionary ever published, and one that stayed in print until 1868. Brown's *The Self-Interpreting Bible*, first published in 1778, was last published in 1919.[2]

As Robertson states in his mammoth grammar of the Greek New Testament,

> There is nothing like the Greek New Testament to rejuvenate the world, which came out of the Dark Ages with the Greek Testament in its hand. Erasmus wrote in the Preface to his Greek Testament about his own thrill of delight: "These holy pages will summon up the living image of His mind. They will give you Christ Himself, talking, healing, dying, rising, the whole Christ in a word; they will give Him to you in an intimacy so close that He would be less visible to you if He stood before your eyes." The Greek New Testament is the New Testament. All else is translation.[3]

Robertson eloquently expresses the centrality of the Greek New Testament for all New Testament study and appreciation. This centrality comprises the first consideration of this series of studies on the topic of how we got the Greek New Testament. In the course of these three chapters I will deal with three specific subtopics: the text, its transmission, and its translation. I begin with the text of the Greek New Testament. But which Greek New Testament is Robertson talking about? In the course of this chapter I will consider this question,

---

2. The above story is taken from A. T. Robertson, *The Minister and His Greek New Testament* (London: Hodder & Stoughton, 1923), 103–8, with supplements from the Wikipedia entry on John Brown. ! ?
3. Robertson, *Grammar of the Greek New Testament*, xix.

along with tracing the history of the development of our modern text of the Greek New Testament. I will also examine in some detail one recent challenge to the integrity of our Greek New Testament and will, finally, make my own suggestion regarding which Greek New Testament we should consider using today.

## Is There a Text of the Greek New Testament? Or, What Is the Goal of Textual Criticism?

There has been much recent discussion about the original text of the Greek New Testament. After a number of years in which textual studies have been relatively quiet, there is renewed interest in the text of the New Testament and whether we indeed can come close to identifying or reconstructing the original. As a result, some recent scholarship has attempted to question the traditional opinion regarding the original text and its recoverability. In this section I will examine the traditional opinion, scrutinize some recent counterproposals, and then offer some opinion on this recent debate.[4]

### Traditional Opinion

The traditional opinion of the purpose of textual criticism of the Greek New Testament is, ideally, to find the original autograph that

4. Throughout this book I employ standard abbreviations and terminology used to identify various manuscripts and their characteristics. Lists and descriptions of these terms can be found in most books on textual criticism and similar books. For ease of reference, I use 𝔓 with a number for papyrus manuscripts (manuscripts written on prepared papyrus strips, an early form of paper), as in 𝔓⁵⁶; a number starting with 0 and/or letter for codex majuscule manuscripts (manuscripts written on parchment in majuscule, or uppercase, letters in an early book form), often with a name attached, as in Codex Vaticanus (03 B); a number for minuscules (manuscripts written in lowercase ligatured, or connected, handwriting), as in 1079; and numbers for lectionaries. See Kurt Aland and Barbara Aland, *The Text of the New Testament: An Introduction to the Critical Editions and to the Theory and Practice of Modern Textual Criticism*, trans. Erroll F. Rhodes, 2nd ed. (Grand Rapids: Eerdmans, 1989), 280. For recent surveys of textual criticism, see Eckhard J. Schnabel, "Textual Criticism: Recent Developments," in *The Face of New Testament Studies: A Survey of Recent Research*, ed. Scot McKnight and Grant R. Osborne (Grand Rapids: Baker Academic, 2004), 59–75; Scott D. Charlesworth, "The Gospel Manuscript Tradition," in *The Content and Setting of the Gospel Tradition*, ed. Mark Harding and Alanna Nobbs (Grand Rapids: Eerdmans, 2010), 28–61.

the author wrote. Failing that, the purpose is to work back through the manuscript evidence to arrive at the earliest form of the text and then, through principles of textual criticism, to posit or reconstruct what the original text must have been. This has been the motivating principle of textual criticism from earliest times to the present. In somewhat of a whirlwind tour through the work of textual critics of the last five hundred years, I will cite a number of significant voices on this topic because I will be returning to some of their work in subsequent discussion.[5]

Desiderius Erasmus (1466–1536), the Renaissance humanist and the first to publish a Greek New Testament, appends at the end of his Greek New Testament the statement that it was "with regard to the Greek truth" (ad Graecam veritatem), believing, apparently, that he had published as close to the original Greek text as he could.[6]

The nineteenth century was an age of textual criticism, and the opinion of the major critics of the day is unanimous. Samuel Tregelles (1813–1875), a "common man" like John Brown, writing in 1844, defines textual criticism as the means "by which we know, on grounds of ascertained certainty, the actual words and sentences of that charter [the Bible] in the true statement of its privileges, and in the terms in which the Holy Ghost gave it."[7] J. Scott Porter (1801–1880 [no relation, so far as I know]), the then well-known biblical scholar,

5. I cite these scholars roughly in chronological order according to their major works that I cite on the topic of textual criticism. I do not attempt to cite all textual critics, and, because of the nature of this work, I confine myself to those whose works are in English, either originally or through translation. A relatively complete listing of introductions to textual criticism is provided in Bruce M. Metzger and Bart D. Ehrman, *The Text of the New Testament: Its Transmission, Corruption, and Restoration*, 4th ed. (New York: Oxford University Press, 2005), 345–48.

6. Robertson, *Introduction to the Textual Criticism*, 18–19. We know now, of course, that Erasmus could have done better, on the basis of what we know about the manuscripts available even then (such as Codex Vaticanus [03 B ]); nevertheless, he did the best he could within the confines of knowledge at the time. Erasmus apparently did know of Vaticanus, and through intermediaries he consulted the manuscript on a few isolated points, but he did not use it in any thorough or systematic way. See Stephen Pisano, "The Text of the New Testament," in *Prolegomena*, accompanying volume to *Bibliorum sacrorum Graecorum Codex Vaticanus B: Bibliothecae Apostolicae Vaticanae Codex Vaticanus Graecus 1209* (Vatican: Istituto Poligrafico e Zecca dello Stato, 1999), 29.

7. Samuel P. Tregelles, *An Account of the Printed Text of the Greek New Testament, with Remarks on Its Revision upon Critical Principles* (London: Samuel Bagster,

writing in 1848 in one of the first books on textual criticism, states that textual criticism is that area of learning that treats ancient writings, especially the Bible, "of the means which may be applied for ascertaining the true text."[8] Constantin Tischendorf (1815–1874), the man who discovered and published the now famous Codex Sinaiticus (01 א [about which I will say more in what follows]) as well as numerous other manuscripts, and whose eighth edition of the Greek New Testament still constitutes one of the most important sources of text-critical information in its textual apparatus,[9] says that he determined to devote himself "to the textual study of the New Testament, and attempted, by making use of all the acquisitions of the last three centuries, to reconstruct, if possible, the exact text, as it came from the pen of the sacred writers."[10] B. F. Westcott (1825–1901) and F. J. A. Hort (1828–1892), who published the most important hand edition of the Greek New Testament for the English-speaking world, write of their first Greek edition of 1881, "This edition is an attempt to present exactly the original words of the New Testament, so far as they can now be determined from surviving documents."[11] Frederick Scrivener (1813–1891), one of Westcott and Hort's most intelligent critics and editor of the fifth-century Codex Bezae (05 D), says of textual criticism that "it aims at bringing back that text, so far as may be, to the condition in which it stood in the sacred autographs; at removing all spurious additions, if such be found in our present printed copies; at restoring whatsoever may have been lost or corrupted or accidentally changed in the lapse of eighteen hundred years."[12] The theologian Benjamin Warfield (1851–1921) says that textual criticism involves a

---

1854), viii. Tregelles spent his career as an ironworker, but he devoted his "spare" time to textual criticism.

8. J. Scott Porter, *Principles of Textual Criticism, with Their Application to the Old and New Testaments* (London: Simms & M'Intyre, 1848), 9.

9. Constantin Tischendorf, *Novum Testamentum Graece*, 8th ed., 2 vols. (Leipzig: Giesecke & Devrient, 1869–1872). The third volume, *Prolegomena*, was written by Caspar René Gregory and published after Tischendorf's death (Leipzig: Hinrichs, 1894).

10. Constantin Tischendorf, *When Were Our Gospels Written? An Argument, with a Narrative of the Discovery of the Sinaitic Manuscript* (London: Religious Tract Society, 1896), 15.

11. Brooke Foss Westcott and Fenton John Anthony Hort, *The New Testament in the Original Greek* (Cambridge: Macmillan, 1882), 2:1.

12. Frederick Henry Ambrose Scrivener, *A Plain Introduction to the Criticism of the New Testament*, 3rd ed. (Cambridge: Deighton, Bell, 1883), 5.

process of examining documents "with a view to discovering from them whether and wherein it has become corrupted, and of proving them to preserve it or else restoring it from their corruptions to its originally intended form."[13] Finally, although others could be cited, Eberhard Nestle (1851–1913), a German scholar and developer of the Nestle Greek New Testament, which is still the basis of the standard critical edition (the so-called Nestle-Aland), writes, "The task [of textual criticism] is to exhibit what the original writer intended to communicate to his readers, and the method is simply that of tracing the history of the document in question back to its beginning, if, and in so far as, we have the means to do so at our command."[14]

If the nineteenth century reflects a common critical opinion of the task of textual criticism, most of the twentieth century is not much different. Frederic Kenyon (1863–1952), editor of many papyri, including $\mathfrak{P}^{45}$,[15] and director and principal librarian of the British Museum and Library, writing in 1901, states, "The province of Textual Criticism is the ascertainment of the true form of a literary work, as originally composed and written down by its author."[16] Alexander Souter (1873–1949), editor of the Oxford Classical Texts Greek New Testament,[17] writes, "Textual criticism seeks, by the exercise of knowledge and trained judgment, to restore the very words of some original document which has perished, and survives only in copies complete or incomplete, accurate or inaccurate, ancient or modern. If we possessed the twenty-seven documents now composing the New Testament exactly in the form in which they were dictated or written by their original authors, there would be no textual criticism of the New Testament."[18] Kirsopp Lake (1872–1946), textual critic and coeditor of the original photographs of Codex Sinaiticus (01 ℵ), writes, "The

13. Benjamin B. Warfield, *An Introduction to the Textual Criticism of the New Testament* (London: Hodder & Stoughton, 1893), 4.

14. Eberhard Nestle, *Introduction to the Textual Criticism of the Greek New Testament*, trans. William Edie (London: Williams & Norgate, 1901), 156.

15. I will treat this papyrus manuscript in chapter 2.

16. Frederic G. Kenyon, *Handbook to the Textual Criticism of the New Testament*, 2nd ed. (London: Macmillan, 1912; 1st ed., 1901), 1.

17. Alexander Souter, *Novum Testamentum Graece* (Oxford: Clarendon, 1910; 2nd ed., 1947).

18. Alexander Souter, *The Text and Canon of the New Testament* (London: Duckworth, 1912), 3.

object of all textual criticism is to recover so far as possible the actual words written by the writer."[19] Leo Vaganay (1882–1969), one of the leading French textual critics, writes, "By textual criticism we mean every kind of scientific research in quest of the original, or at least, of the most nearly original text of some document."[20] J. Harold Greenlee (1918–), well-known Greek scholar and textual critic, writing in 1964, states, "Textual criticism is the study of copies of any written work of which the autograph (the original) is unknown, with the purpose of ascertaining the original text."[21] Bruce Metzger (1914–2007), one of the editors of the United Bible Societies *Greek New Testament*, also writing in 1964, notes, "The textual critic seeks to ascertain from the divergent copies which form of the text should be regarded as most nearly conforming to the original."[22] Kurt Aland (1915–1994) and Barbara Aland (1937–), subsequent editors of the Nestle Greek New Testament, write, "Only one reading can be original, however many variant readings there may be. . . . Only the reading which best satisfies the requirements of both external and internal criteria can be original."[23] J. Neville Birdsall (1928–2005), writing in 1992, states, "The objective of textual criticism in any field is to establish the original text of the work which is the object of study."[24] Finally, and not insignificantly, J. K. Elliott and Ian Moir, contemporary British textual critics, state, "Textual criticism is, primarily, the study of *any* written work, the original of which no longer survives, with the purpose of recovering that original text from those copies which have chanced to survive."[25]

19. Kirsopp Lake, *The Text of the New Testament*, 5th ed. (London: Rivingtons, 1911), 1.

20. Leo Vaganay, *An Introduction to the Textual Criticism of the New Testament*, trans. B. V. Miller (London: Sands, 1937), 9.

21. J. Harold Greenlee, *Introduction to New Testament Textual Criticism* (Grand Rapids: Eerdmans, 1964), 11 (italics removed).

22. Bruce M. Metzger, *The Text of the New Testament: Its Transmission, Corruption, and Restoration*, 2nd ed. (New York: Oxford University Press, 1968; 1st ed., 1964), v. The fourth edition (2005), done in collaboration with Bart Ehrman, retains the preface of the first edition, in which this statement appears (p. xv).

23. Aland and Aland, *Text of the New Testament*, 280.

24. J. Neville Birdsall, "The Recent History of New Testament Textual Criticism (from Westcott and Hort, 1881, to the Present)," *ANRW* II.26.1 (1992): 138.

25. Keith Elliott and Ian Moir, *Manuscripts and the Text of the New Testament: An Introduction for English Readers* (Edinburgh: T&T Clark, 1995), 1.

This whirlwind tour of textual critics is over, and the resulting catalogue of opinion, from Erasmus to the recent, seems overwhelming. The traditional task and goal of textual criticism of the Greek New Testament, within the confines of the recognition that we no longer have the autograph manuscripts, is to devise a method by which the original text, or the text that is as close as possible to the original, can be ascertained.

## Recent Proposals

Recent scholarship has not been as content as previous scholarship was with the traditional goal of textual criticism. As a result, two major developments that are worth noting have occurred with regard to the notion of an original text. One concerns appreciation of the kinds of contexts in which variations occur, and the second raises more-serious questions about finding an original text altogether. Both of these merit further consideration.

### ■ THEOLOGICAL AND OTHER CONTEXTS OF VARIATION

The first of these two major developments is the recently expressed appreciation for the cultural, social, and even theological contexts in which later textual variation occurred, as a reflection of early church developments. This is not a new concern, however. Almost since the advent of modern textual criticism and efforts to establish the Greek text of the New Testament—that is, from the mid-nineteenth century to the present—there has been recognition of the possibility of changes to manuscripts that would indicate the theological and other contexts in which these texts were being copied. Thus, although Westcott and Hort, who published the first eclectic text based on early majuscule (capital letter) manuscripts from the fourth century, especially Codex Sinaiticus (01 א),[26] asserted that "there are no signs WiH of deliberate falsification of the text for dogmatic purposes,"[27] a claim

---

26. Later in this chapter, in the section "The History of the Printed Greek Text of the New Testament," I will consider this Greek text, the basis of its development, and the types of manuscripts used.

27. Westcott and Hort, *New Testament in the Original Greek*, 2:282–83. They were followed in the main thrust of this statement by a number of scholars, including Caspar René Gregory, *Canon and Text of the New Testament*, ITL (New York:

that they subsequently attempted to defend,[28] this claim was scruti-
nized by a succession of textual scholars.

This scrutiny came from at least two quarters. Westcott and Hort's
opponents who defended the Textus Receptus, a text based on the
Greek text published first by Erasmus in the sixteenth century on
the basis of several late minuscule (lowercase writing) manuscripts,[29]
accused the transcribers of the early majuscule manuscripts, for example, of deleting the two longer endings of Mark's Gospel (e.g.,
Mark 16:9–20, the longest, but usually referred to as the long ending)
and of questioning the authenticity of the pericope of the woman
caught in adultery (John 7:53–8:11).[30] Those who defended the kind of
text advocated by Westcott and Hort also registered concern for due
recognition of later theological and other textual changes. J. Rendel
Harris, after citing a number of significant textual variants, noted,
"These instances may suffice to show how the religious movements
of any time or country affect the text of that time or country. Nor
can such changes be considered as unimportant or insignificant."[31]
Kirsopp Lake, right after making his positive statement quoted above
regarding the object of textual criticism, stated, "But in order to do

---

Scribner, 1907), 485 (but Gregory [p. 504] cites John 7:8 as an example of a change
made for "dogmatical or even apologetical" reasons); Robertson, *Introduction to the
Textual Criticism*, 158–60.

28. In a prefatory note to the second edition of *The New Testament in the Original
Greek* (1896), Westcott wrote, "No arguments have been advanced against the general
principles maintained in the Introduction and illustrated in the Notes, since the publication of the first Edition, which were not fully considered by Dr. Hort and myself
in the long course of our work and in our judgment dealt with adequately" (p. v).

29. This text edition and its development and subsequent history and influence
are discussed below in the section "The History of the Printed Greek Text of the
New Testament."

30. For example, John W. Burgon, *The Revision Revised: Three Articles Reprinted
from the "Quarterly Review"* (1883; repr., Fort Worth: Hobbs, 1983); cf. John W.
Burgon, *The Last Twelve Verses of the Gospel according to S. Mark* (1871; repr.,
Ann Arbor, MI: Sovereign Grace Book Club, 1959), 83–96 (Burgon accuses earlier
scholars, such as J. J. Griesbach, Constantin Tischendorf, Samuel Tregelles, and Henry
Alford, of something along these lines); David Otis Fuller, introduction to *Counterfeit
or Genuine: Mark 16? John 8?* ed. David Otis Fuller (Grand Rapids: Grand Rapids
International Publications, 1978), 9–10; Wilbur N. Pickering, *The Identity of the New
Testament Text* (Nashville: Nelson, 1977), 31–32.

31. J. Rendel Harris, *Side-Lights on New Testament Research* (London: Kingsgate,
James Clarke, 1909), 32. Some of the examples he cites are Marcion and the Lukan
infancy narrative, Tatian and the account of John the Baptist, and Matt. 20:4.

this properly the critic has to explain how each successive deviation from the original came to be currently adopted, and frequently he finds the clue enabling him to do this in the history of some later period, which gives some reason for a textual variation. In these researches it sometimes happens that the discoveries of the textualist are of great value to the historian; for the corrupt reading of some important document often explains otherwise inexplicable phenomena in the history of ideas or the conduct of a controversy."[32] Ernest Cadman Colwell went so far as to claim, "In the manuscripts of the New Testament most variations . . . were made deliberately," and he believed that it was for doctrinal reasons that most changes were introduced.[33]

A few individual passages are often the subject of such theologically based text-critical discussion, with the variant seeming to reflect later theological interpretation. These include John 5:3b–4, with an angel coming down and troubling the water, and the first person entering the pool receiving healing; Acts 8:37, where the Ethiopian eunuch makes a pronouncement regarding his faith; 1 Timothy 3:16, where the question is whether the two Greek letters are the relative pronoun OC (thus "who was manifested in flesh") or the *nomen sacrum* (sacred name)[34] for God, ΘC (thus "God manifested in flesh"), with reference to Jesus Christ; and 1 John 5:7–8, the so-called *comma Johanneum* or Johannine Comma, with reference to the Father, the Word, and the Holy Spirit, three in one, bearing witness. Much of the discussion of later theological changes to the text of the Greek New Testament, however, has revolved around the so-called Western text, represented by the majuscule Codex Bezae (05 D) of Acts. Rendel Harris found

32. Lake, *Text of the New Testament*, 1.

33. Ernest Cadman Colwell, *What Is the Best New Testament?* (Chicago: University of Chicago Press, 1952), 52, with discussion of correct doctrine as the motivation for changes (52–60).

34. A *nomen sacrum* (pl. *nomina sacra*) is a term for reduced forms used in ancient Greek manuscripts to stand for theologically (and other) significant words. The original *nomina sacra* were used for a small number of important words, such as "Jesus," "God," and "Christ," and later were increased in number to around fifteen. The *nomina sacra* often were written with a supralinear line (i.e., a stroke above the letters) to help distinguish the reduced form. For recent discussion, see Larry W. Hurtado, *The Earliest Christian Artifacts: Manuscripts and Christian Origins* (Grand Rapids: Eerdmans, 2006), 95–134; Philip Comfort, *Encountering the Manuscripts: An Introduction to New Testament Paleography and Textual Criticism* (Nashville: Broadman & Holman, 2005), 199–254.

Montanist and Marcionite influence on the Bezan version of Acts, while Eldon Epp found anti-Judaic tendencies.[35]

Whereas discussion of Western theologizing has waned in more-recent scholarship, the discussion of the socioreligious context in which variants have been created has been taken up in other circles, in particular in Bart Ehrman's *The Orthodox Corruption of Scripture*. Continuing discussion that he began in earlier articles, Ehrman investigates what he calls "corruption" of the text.[36] He believes that orthodoxy was a slowly developing concept in the second and third centuries as various competing beliefs contended for primacy,[37] and as a result there were differing and competing theological positions represented in the various changes made to manuscripts. Ehrman identifies four major theological disputes, devoting a chapter to each in his book: anti-adoptionist, anti-separationist, anti-docetic, and anti-patripassionist corruptions by the orthodox against their opponents.[38] Most of the examples that Ehrman treats in his later *Misquoting Jesus*, to which I will turn below, are treated in this earlier work as well. I note here some illustrative examples of potential theologizing.

35. J. Rendel Harris, *Codex Bezae: A Study of the So-Called Western Text of the New Testament*, TS, vol. 2, no. 1 (Cambridge: Cambridge University Press, 1891); Eldon J. Epp, *The Theological Tendency of Codex Bezae Cantabrigiensis in Acts*, SNTSMS 3 (Cambridge: Cambridge University Press, 1966).

36. Bart D. Ehrman, *The Orthodox Corruption of Scripture: The Effect of Early Christological Controversies on the Text of the New Testament* (New York: Oxford University Press, 1993; updated ed., 2011).

37. This notion has been most widely attributed (at least in recent times) to Walter Bauer, *Orthodoxy and Heresy in Earliest Christianity*, trans. and ed. Robert Kraft and Gerhard Krodel (Philadelphia: Fortress, 1971), originally published in 1934. The theory goes back much earlier, however, at least to the time of Ferdinand Christian Baur, and has been endorsed by many since. There have been many able responses to this notion, including most recently Stanley E. Porter and Gordon L. Heath, *The Lost Gospel of Judas: Separating Fact from Fiction* (Grand Rapids: Eerdmans, 2007), 96–114; Andreas J. Köstenberger and Michael J. Kruger, *The Heresy of Orthodoxy: How Contemporary Culture's Fascination with Diversity Has Reshaped Our Understanding of Early Christianity* (Wheaton: Crossway, 2010).

38. "Anti-adoptionism" refers to those who opposed adoptionism, the belief that Jesus was at some time adopted by God the Father to become the divine Son; "anti-separationism" refers to those who opposed tendencies to divide the human and divine natures of Jesus; "anti-docetism" refers to those who opposed those who argued that Jesus Christ only appeared (or seemed) to be human; and "anti-patripassionism" refers to those who opposed the belief that God the Father was the Christ in human form who suffered. See Ehrman, *Orthodox Corruption*.

In the chapter on anti-adoptionism, among other examples, Ehrman examines Luke 3:22, where he opts for the reading in Codex Bezae (05 D) as original—"You are my son, today I have begotten you"—over the supposedly anti-adoptionist (and orthodox) "You are my beloved son, in whom I am well pleased." Even though the latter is found in earlier manuscripts, he contends that it is a later harmonization with Mark 1:11.[39] However, Ehrman fails to note that the words in Bezae match the words of Epiphanius of Salamis quoting the *Gospel of the Ebionites* and reflect (later) gnostic thought.[40] This makes it highly unlikely that the adoptionist reading is correct, but rather suggests that the so-called anti-adoptionist reading is to be preferred. In fact, if the anti-adoptionist reading is the original, it can hardly be called "anti-adoptionist," a term that implies a reaction to something, when in reality it was not a reaction to anything. The language that Ehrman is using is potentially misleading.

In the chapter on anti-separationism, for 1 John 4:3 Ehrman prefers "does not confess" (μὴ ὁμολογεῖ, *mē homologei*) to "looses/separates" (λύει, *luei*) (so "every spirit that does not confess Jesus is not from God" rather than "every spirit that looses/separates Jesus is not from God"). The former is found in virtually all of the Greek manuscript evidence, despite the later opinion by some scholars in favor of the variant "loose."[41] Whether one attributes theological or other motives to the variant "loose," which is found in the margin of one late Greek manuscript but in a number of translations or versions (which I will discuss in chap. 3), it clearly is not the original text but is probably, as Ehrman speculates, a later variant to combat gnostic thought that wished to "loose" or "separate" Jesus from his divinity. "Loose" may or may not be "antiseparationist," but it is certainly late.

In the chapter on anti-docetism, Ehrman rightly rejects as inauthentic Luke 22:43–44, with Jesus's sweating blood in the garden as

---

39. Ehrman, *Orthodox Corruption*, 62–67 (updated ed., 73–79). *only grounds?*

40. See Hans Foerster, "The Celebration of the Baptism of Christ by the Basilideans and the Origin of Epiphany: Is the Seemingly Obvious Correct?" *JGRChJ* 5 (2008): 114–15.

41. Ehrman, *Orthodox Corruption*, 125–35 (updated ed., 146–58). Ehrman notes the attractiveness of the variant "loose" because of its difficulty in understanding, but that the reading found in the manuscripts is even more "difficult" because of the use of the indicative verb with the negative μή, which normally is used with moods other than the indicative.

an attempt to show Jesus's physicality.[42] However, the manuscript evidence for inclusion of Luke 22:43–44 is very limited, with many manuscripts themselves indicating that they realize this is a later variant.[43] Ehrman also treats examples of Westcott and Hort's "Western noninterpolations," where, especially in the final chapters of Luke's Gospel (chaps. 22–24), they believe that the Western tradition with its shorter readings preserved the original text over their Neutral text of Codex Sinaiticus (01 אֹ) and Codex Vaticanus (03 B).[44] Ehrman argues that each variant must be examined on its own merits.

In the chapter on anti-patripassionism, Ehrman briefly treats a number of texts, including John 14:9; Mark 2:7; Mark 12:26; 2 Peter 1:1; and Philippians 2:9, where the evidence of the variant is slender or the variant is clearly seen to be a later modification.[45] Ehrman attempts by these and other examples to illustrate various contexts that gave rise to later textual variants. Whether or not he provides evidence of the corruption of Scripture (and I generally think that he has not, especially by the orthodox), Ehrman's book provides an inadvertent defense of the traditional agenda of textual criticism. He assumes—and he must assume in order for his argument to work—an original text intended by the author. As Moisés Silva states, "Indeed, Ehrman's book is unimaginable unless he can identify an initial form of the text that can be differentiated from a later alteration."[46]

No doubt there is great merit in investigating the history of changes made to the text of the New Testament. Insights unquestionably can be gained into some of the theologically related controversies of the time and into the cultural milieu in which the copying of a document occurred. One need not, however, believe that these contexts

42. Ibid., 187–94 (updated ed., 220–27).

43. See Bruce M. Metzger, *A Textual Commentary on the Greek New Testament*, 2nd ed. (Stuttgart: Deutsche Bibelgesellschaft; United Bible Societies, 1994), 151.

44. Besides individual passages, Ehrman discusses the notion in *Orthodox Corruption*, 223–27 (updated ed., 254–59). The so-called Western noninterpolations in Luke 22–24 include 22:14, 16, 19–20, 35–37, 43–44, 47, 49–51, 62; 23:1–5, 17; 23:32–24:1; 24:3, 6, 12, 36, 40, 43, 51, 52.

45. Ehrman, *Orthodox Corruption*, 264–69 (updated ed., 309–15). Ehrman's reliance on English translation of the article is misleading in at least one instance (Phil 2:9, p. 268; updated ed., 314). His contrast of "the" name with "a" name, based upon English understanding of the function of the definite and indefinite article, must clearly be abandoned.

46. Moisés Silva, "Response," in *Rethinking New Testament Textual Criticism*, ed. David Alan Black (Grand Rapids: Baker Academic, 2002), 150.

"corrupted" the text to appreciate various local and even theological situations in which the manuscripts of the New Testament were copied. For example, taking an approach that focuses on location, rather than the documents themselves, Eldon Epp has recently undertaken to classify papyrus manuscripts of the Greek New Testament on the basis of their location. He notes that most of the papyri have been found in Egypt, with a few found in other regions (e.g., $\mathfrak{P}^{59}$, $\mathfrak{P}^{60}$, and $\mathfrak{P}^{61}$ were found in the Negev at 'Auja-el-Hafir [Nessana]; $\mathfrak{P}^{11}$, $\mathfrak{P}^{14}$, and $\mathfrak{P}^{68}$ at Sinai; and $\mathfrak{P}^{83}$ and $\mathfrak{P}^{84}$ at Khirbet Mird near the Dead Sea). The vast majority of those from Egypt have been discovered at the ancient site of Oxyrhynchus: roughly 40 percent of the total number of New Testament papyri, and nearly 60 percent of those that date from before the third/fourth centuries. Epp wants to explore the scribal techniques of a place such as Oxyrhynchus, as well as the possible relations of Oxyrhynchus to other nearby sites, to see whether there might be theological influence indicated in the texts.[47]

Despite potentially interesting insights from these recent efforts of Ehrman, Epp, and others, several points of further observation and reservation are to be noted. In other words, discussion of context must be put in its own proper context.

(1) The most important observation is that the number of variants being investigated by Ehrman and others with respect to their theological influences, when compared to the entirety of the New Testament, is fairly small, despite sometimes sensationalist claims to the contrary. We now have somewhere over 5,800 New Testament Greek manuscripts in part (mostly) and in whole, ranging from the second century to the fifteenth or sixteenth centuries. Within those manuscripts, if one counts every possible type of variant, there are well over one hundred thousand variants (a number I will return to below). Nevertheless, despite all of this purported textual evidence of variance, calculations have indicated that, on the basis of the editions of the Greek New Testament produced by Tischendorf, Westcott and Hort,

47. Eldon J. Epp, "Issues in New Testament Textual Criticism: Moving from the Nineteenth Century to the Twenty-First Century," in Black, *Rethinking New Testament Textual Criticism*, 17–76, esp. 64. On papyri at Oxyrhynchus, see A. K. Bowman et al., *Oxyrhynchus: A City and Its Texts*, GRM 93 (London: Egypt Exploration Society, 2007); Peter Parsons, *City of the Sharp-Nosed Fish: Greek Lives in Roman Egypt* (London: Weidenfeld & Nicolson, 2007).

Hermann von Soden, Heinrich Joseph Vogels, Augustin Merk, and José Maria Bover, 62.9 percent of the verses of the Greek New Testament show no variants.[48] The individual books range from a low of 45.1 percent of verses with no variants (in Mark) to a high of 81.4 percent of verses with no variants (in 1 Timothy).[49] According to the estimates of Aland and Aland, when one compares the two major text-types for the Greek New Testament—the Byzantine and the Alexandrian[50]—they "actually exhibit a remarkable degree of agreement, perhaps as much as 80 percent!"[51] Other scholars have estimated this degree of agreement to be as high as 90 percent.[52] Even this is perhaps not high enough, however. Most recently, Martin Heide has compared and calculated the stability of the New Testament manuscripts. Manuscripts vary in their textual stability from about 89 to 98 percent. As he states, "The stability of the New Testament text under consideration, from the early papyri to the Byzantine text, achieves an average of 92.6 percent."[53]

This means that the textual evidence confirms the existence of a stable text, with the lack of variation indicating that we probably have 80–90 percent, if not more, of the Greek text of the New Testament unquestionably established, so far as that can be determined from our existing manuscripts; and that is really all we have on which to base such a decision. The impression sometimes given in discussions of the text of the New Testament is that the text itself is entirely fluid and unstable, and that it was subject to so much variation and change through especially the first two centuries that its very stability is threatened. This simply is not true.

(2) With 90 percent of the text established in the two major text-types, one can reasonably work from the supposition that we have,

48. See below for information on the editions not yet mentioned.

49. Aland and Aland, *Text of the New Testament*, 29.

50. I will address text-types and related matters in chapter 2.

51. Aland and Aland, *Text of the New Testament*, 28.

52. Maurice A. Robinson and William G. Pierpont, *The New Testament in the Original Greek: Byzantine Textform, 2005* (Southborough, MA: Chilton, 2005), 584.

53. K. Martin Heide, "Assessing the Stability of the Transmitted Texts of the New Testament and the *Shepherd of Hermas*," in *The Reliability of the New Testament: Bart D. Ehrman and Daniel B. Wallace in Dialogue*, ed. Robert B. Stewart (Minneapolis: Fortress, 2011), 138. Heide also compares the *Shepherd of Hermas*, a very popular early Christian text, which has a stability rate of only 86 percent, lower than the lowest of any individual manuscript of the New Testament (146).

for all intents and purposes, the earliest text that we can establish, at least for those portions where there is no textual variation. There is little point in disputing that we have the original text when the vast majority of the textual evidence points in the same direction—at least for 90 percent (or more) of the text. This does not mean that it is not pertinent to try to ascertain the original text of the rest of the (less than) 10 percent that is not established, but the amount that is established should provide us with a firm foundation and guidance for how to go about establishing the rest. *?Assuming the eclectic approach is best*

(3) The belief in an achievable original text is a necessity for deciding whether there are variations from that text. The fact that Ehrman speaks of the "corruption" of the text indicates that he works from a functional perspective of a stable and original text that has been changed or altered. Virtually all of the studies that have undertaken to examine the theological tendencies of passages in the New Testament begin from the standpoint that there is an original text (or at least that one of the texts they are using preserves the original) and that changes can be evaluated in terms of their relation to that original.

(4) If the above indicators are correct, the number of passages for theological dispute is relatively and proportionately small. There are three relatively major passages that recur in the discussion: the longer ending of Mark, the pericope of the woman caught in adultery, and the relation in Acts of the Western tradition, especially as found in Codex Bezae (05 D), to the Alexandrian tradition.[54] There are also a number of smaller passages, such as the so-called Western noninterpolations in Luke 22–24. Many of the same passages are treated by those who discuss this issue. In most of the discussions the text as found in the Alexandrian tradition is endorsed. Even when all of the possible passages that have been brought forward for discussion are taken into account— notwithstanding the considerable variation in the persuasiveness of these examples—there remain many other passages that were not changed, corrupted, or otherwise altered. Rather than seeing major theological tendencies in the various textual changes to manuscripts, we should at best probably see theological fine tuning in a few noteworthy passages.

54. Codex Bezae (05 D) is a fifth-century bilingual Greek and Latin majuscule manuscript that now contains a longer version of Acts than is found in earlier majuscule manuscripts that represent the Alexandrian tradition, such as Codex Sinaiticus (01 ℵ) and Codex Vaticanus (03 B). These manuscripts are discussed in more detail below.

(5) This observation concerns the nature of changes in the first two centuries. Many textual critics, following in the line of Westcott and Hort, think that the vast majority of changes to the manuscripts are accidental or unintentional, and not theological. A subsequent group of scholars, following the comment of Colwell cited above regarding most manuscript changes being made deliberately for theological reasons, think that the vast majority of changes are theologically motivated. The above analysis, together with James Royse's recent study of scribal habits in six early papyri, indicates that a view closer to Hort's is appropriate. Royse states, "We have seen a few examples in connection with $\mathfrak{P}^{72}$ of scribal change for (as it seems) theological reasons. While the comparative rarity of such examples indicates that revision of the text for theological purposes was not very common, it is thus seen to occur."[55] It occurs, but it is comparatively rare, and it is ascertainable in comparison with the established text.

(6) The final observation concerns the supposed state of radical flux that several scholars have claimed to observe during the second and third centuries. Such severe change simply is not present. The stability of the text in 80–90 percent of the two major text-types throughout their history indicates little fluctuation, as does the reasonably small set of examples commonly cited as illustrating the kinds of changes that were occurring. Royse's recent analysis, confirmed by a number of other similar though smaller-scale studies, indicates that there are definite tendencies in such scribal changes. These changes tend toward omission from, rather than addition to, the text. The kinds of omissions, rather than being theologically motivated additions, often are accidental or involve jumping over text as the scribe looked forward. The additions tend to be assimilations to the immediate context or to parallel passages.[56] These tendencies do not indicate a wildly fluctuating text,

---

55. James R. Royse, *Scribal Habits in Early Greek New Testament Papyri*, NTTSD 36 (Leiden: Brill, 2008), 738. See also James R. Royse, "Scribal Tendencies in the Transmission of the Text of the New Testament," in *The Text of the New Testament in Contemporary Research: Essays on the Status Quaestionis*, ed. Bart D. Ehrman and Michael W. Holmes, SD 46 (Grand Rapids: Eerdmans, 1995), 239–52.

56. Royse, *Scribal Habits*, 717–18. Some of the other studies are Peter M. Head, "Observations on Early Papyri of the Synoptic Gospels, Especially on the 'Scribal Habits,'" *Bib* 71 (1990): 240–47; "The Habits of New Testament Copyists: Singular Readings in the Early Fragmentary Papyri of John," *Bib* 85 (2004): 399–408; Kyoung Shik Min, *Die früheste Überlieferung des Matthäusevangeliums (bis zum 3./4. Jh.):*

and certainly not one that is being wantonly added to for theological reasons. In fact, Royse formulates his principle regarding "transcriptional probability" of early manuscripts in terms of the longer reading generally being preferred, unless, as is often seen to be the case, the longer reading appears to be late as established through other manuscript evidence, appears to have arisen from some form of harmonization, or appears to be a grammatical improvement—a formulation similar to the earlier qualified formulation developed by Johann Jakob Griesbach in the late eighteenth century.[57] This would account both for individual verses where the longer text may be the original and more theologically loaded later additions, such as the longer text of Acts in Codex Bezae (05 D) and quite possibly the longer endings of Mark, and for the later theological additions such as characterize the Byzantine tradition.

Thus, whereas understanding of the variety of contexts in which variants are produced is worth pursuing, such discussion must be considered in its own proper context, in which there are definite scribal tendencies that are weighed against a stable text. These considerations do not constitute a sufficient reason to change the purpose of textual criticism from that of reconstructing the original text.

### ▪ QUESTIONING THE ORIGINAL TEXT

The second, and probably more telling, recent development in textual criticism concerns the issue of whether it is possible to find the original text itself. In recent years a number of scholars have raised the question of whether we should be seeking the original text, or whether we should in effect abandon such a task and instead be simply examining the contexts in which changes are made. Among the scholars who have raised this type of question are William Petersen, David Trobisch, Michael Holmes, Eldon Epp, David Parker, and Gerd Mink (using his "coherence-based genealogical method," which I will discuss below), although not all in the same way.

---

*Edition und Untersuchung*, ANTF 34 (Berlin: de Gruyter, 2005); Moisés Silva, "The Text of Galatians: Evidence from the Earliest Greek Manuscripts," in *Scribes and Scripture: New Testament Essays in Honor of J. Harold Greenlee*, ed. David Alan Black (Winona Lake, IN: Eisenbrauns, 1992), 17–25.

57. Royse, *Scribal Habits*, 735. For Griesbach's formulation, see Metzger, *Text*, 120 (4th ed., 166–67). Griesbach offers criteria for both the shorter reading and the longer reading.

William Petersen, using Mark as an example, wonders whether by "original" one means the text found in the fourth-century manuscripts or reconstructed from the "minor agreements," and how the *Secret Gospel of Mark* fits into this.[58] He further cites the difficulties caused by complicating textual considerations such as the abundance of manuscript evidence to consider, as well as problems in the determination of the oldest manuscript, the unknown reasons why the papyri have not been used in the Nestle-Aland critical edition and hence do not play a major role in establishing an earlier text, and the widespread neglect of the patristic evidence in the task of textual criticism.[59] These are important questions to raise, but they are difficulties to be addressed, not solutions to a problem. Trobisch attempts to circumvent the major crux of the issue by positing that seeking the original text is not about the individual books or their manuscripts so much as about the canonical text. As he states, "The history of the New Testament is the history of an edition, a book that has been published and edited by a specific group of editors, at a specific place, and at a specific time."[60] He places this edition in the late second century. As a result, one is seeking not the original text, but rather the original canonical edition (what he calls the *editio princeps*),[61] from which the later manuscripts can be traced as derivative. As interesting as canonical development may be, this too is not a solution to the question of the original text, as it begs the question of the prehistory of any book before it was "canonized" and instead concentrates on the ordering and features of manuscripts that indicate their later editing. Holmes raises the question of what an autograph is, when there are possibly two editions of Mark (long and short), multiple copies of Romans

58. I think (and have long thought) that the *Secret Gospel of Mark* is probably a twentieth-century document, and so it probably does not fit into this at all. See Stephen Carlson, *The Gospel Hoax: Morton Smith's Invention of Secret Mark* (Waco: Baylor University Press, 2005). I am pleased to see that others are now coming to this position as well, although this will no doubt continue to be debated.

59. William L. Petersen, "What Text Can New Testament Textual Criticism Ultimately Reach?" in *New Testament Textual Criticism, Exegesis, and Early Church History: A Discussion of Methods*, ed. Barbara Aland and Joël Delobel, CBET 7 (Kampen: Kok Pharos, 1994), 136–52, esp. 136–40. I will return to the question of the papyri below.

60. David Trobisch, *The First Edition of the New Testament* (Oxford: Oxford University Press, 2000), 6.

61. Ibid., 103.

(one with chap. 16 and one without) or Ephesians ("in Ephesus," ἐν Ἐφέσῳ, in 1:1 is missing in the earliest manuscripts), and related questions.[62] This is less of a problem than Holmes realizes, when we understand that not all of these editions existed simultaneously (see below for discussion of the example of Mark's endings), or had equal authority (e.g., Romans with and without chap. 16), or are even a real problem (e.g., if Ephesians was passed from city to city as a circular letter and was only later inscribed with a single destination). In all of these cases, one version was the authoritative edition licensed by the author, even if the author retained other copies or others were developed in the course of transmission. Epp, in logic similar to that of Holmes, claims that the bases for questioning the original text are three: the Gospels had earlier forms or used preexistent sources; Acts has been transmitted in two different textual versions (Alexandrian and Western); and the doxology in Romans (16:25–27) is located in two different places in the textual tradition (also after 14:23; or after 15:33 in 𝔓[45]), indicating two forms of the book.[63] As a result, Epp distinguishes four different uses of the term "original text": what he calls the predecessor text-form, the autographic text-form, the canonical text-form, and the interpretive text-form.[64] Epp's examples, as interesting and even sometimes difficult as they might be to explain, do not necessarily indicate that the two forms of the book (if such existed) were considered to be equally authoritative. In fact, we know that they were not, as we do not have these preexistent sources for the Gospels (the Western text of Acts is treated below).

Parker, a recent major advocate of such a position, begins his volume addressing this issue by claiming, "Textual criticism is in essence the act of understanding what another person means by the words

---

62. Michael W. Holmes, "Reasoned Eclecticism in New Testament Textual Criticism," in Ehrman and Holmes, *Text of the New Testament*, 353. Cf. Michael W. Holmes, "Text and Transmission in the Second Century," in Stewart, *Reliability of the New Testament*, 61–79, which includes his proposal (74–78) and a critical review of several of the proposals mentioned here.

63. Epp, "Issues," 73.

64. Eldon Jay Epp, "The Multivalence of the Term 'Original Text' in New Testament Textual Criticism," *HTR* 92 (1999): 245–81, esp. 276–78; repr. in Eldon Jay Epp, *Perspectives on New Testament Textual Criticism: Collected Essays, 1962–2004*, NovTSup 116 (Leiden: Brill, 2005), 551–93 (see 558–88). Epp reviews a number of the authors treated here.

that are laid before me."[65] He proceeds from this definition—one that recognizably skews the direction of the discussion from its traditional orientation toward the original text—to select and treat a small set of examples. Several of his conclusions regarding these examples are telling, in that they do not actually address the question of the original text as the text that originated with the author of the document. Instead, he ably and interestingly describes instances of the "living text"—that is, the tradition, development, or afterlife of the text.

Parker's first example is the Lord's Prayer. There are several versions of the Lord's Prayer (Matt. 6:9–13 and Luke 11:2–4, with variants), which arouses the curiosity of scholars. Concerning these several versions, Parker concedes that the Byzantine textual harmonization (found in the Textus Receptus), in which there is a fuller form for the Lukan prayer, is not original. However, he wants to affirm that all six of the forms of the prayer that he has identified "contribute to our overall understanding of the tradition: the Doxology in Matthew [6:13], because the intention to end with one is likely to be authentic even if the wording is spurious; the two longer forms in Luke, because they state strongly a belief in the unity of Jesus' teaching; and the last [with an addition to Luke's] because it deserves serious consideration as authentically Lukan, and because it is Lukan in spirit if not in fact."[66]

A second major example is the Gospel passages on marriage and divorce. In his discussion of these four passages (Matt. 5:27–32; 19:3–9; Mark 10:2–12; Luke 16:18), Parker is not seeking the original text of Matthew, Mark, or Luke; he is seeking the original saying by Jesus regarding marriage and divorce by comparing these four Gospel texts. He speaks of interpreters seeking a "single text," "definitive 'original' text," and "authoritative text" on divorce, but he means one single original statement attributable to Jesus.[67] Failing to find that, Parker concludes that the sayings on divorce had "a life of their own."[68]

---

65. D. C. Parker, *The Living Text of the Gospels* (Cambridge: Cambridge University Press, 1997), 1. Parker apparently arrives at this definition through examination of the fact that Shakespeare's plays have come down to us in Quarto and Folio editions, and that Mozart's opera *The Marriage of Figaro* has the composer's copy as well as performance copies changed for the performance. These are "red herring" arguments, as I will point out.

66. Ibid., 69–70 (cf. 53).

67. Ibid., 76, 91, 92.

68. Ibid., 94.

A third example is the classic instance of the woman caught in adultery (John 7:53–8:11). This passage does not appear in many, especially early, manuscripts, but it is found after John 7:52 in Codex Bezae (05 D) and the Byzantine text, while a number of other manuscripts have it in a variety of other places, some of them indicating that it may be a later addition. The text form—based upon a comparison of Codex Bezae (05 D) and the Byzantine tradition—indicates that this piece of oral tradition was early (perhaps the second century) but not original. Nevertheless, Parker says that all of this information contributes to our interpretation of both this account and John's Gospel.[69]

A fourth example is the longer endings of Mark's Gospel. Parker identifies five other endings in addition to the one at 16:8. He traces the earliest of these, the long ending (16:9–20) and the short ending (16:1–8), back to the second century, with the others later. He also notes how the short ending can account for the rise of the longer endings as forms of explanation, though he hesitates to see it as the original ending. In fact, he wants to show how reading the Gospel with different endings leads to different interpretive results.[70]

A fifth example is variants in the Synoptic Gospels. Parker's treatment of the minor agreements in Matthew and Luke against Mark leads him to favor the notion of conjectural emendation (i.e., emending the text on the basis of one's own speculation rather than following manuscripts) on the basis of a supposed earlier form of Mark, since, as Parker admits, there is no convincing textual evidence as we currently have it.[71] This is not much of a solution. Nevertheless, this is a solution that Parker also uses for treatment of John's Gospel, where he admits that there is no evidence of, for example, John's Gospel ever being known without chapter 21. However, he wants to assert that "written texts are only a part of the process by which the traditions about Jesus were passed on."[72] In these examples, Parker

69. Ibid., 95–102.

70. Ibid., 147. For a lengthier treatment of the long ending, see James A. Kelhoffer, *Miracle and Mission: The Authentication of Missionaries and Their Message in the Longer Ending of Mark*, WUNT, 2nd ser., vol. 112 (Tübingen: Mohr Siebeck, 2000).

71. Parker, *Living Text*, 122. For a recent treatment of this passage in more detail, but with a view to what it indicates regarding Jesus's literacy as the reason for its placement within John's Gospel, see Chris Keith, *The Pericope Adulterae, the Gospel of John, and the Literacy of Jesus*, NTTSD 38 (Leiden: Brill, 2009).

72. Parker, *Living Text*, 179.

clearly skirts the issue of the original text by instead focusing on its pre- and posthistory.

In the process of working on the Editio Critica Maior project, Gerd Mink, a researcher connected with the Institut für neutestamentliche Textforschung at Münster University in Germany (founded by Kurt Aland), developed what he calls the "coherence-based genealogical method" (CBGM).[73] This method, made possible by advances in computer technology and not the same as the Alands' local-genealogical method, allows all variants in all extant manuscripts to be recorded (without differentiation of variants) and coherence relationships established among these manuscripts. Individual variants are examined, and a local stemma (a means of tracing the relationships of textual variants back to the original text from which all of the variants originate) is established among the variants. Compiling all the data allows for the establishment of coherence relations among the texts and, ideally, a larger stemmatic relationship among the manuscripts. The method therefore attempts to overcome the limitation of evidence from the earlier centuries and makes full use of all of the variants found in all of the manuscripts, because it works from the notion that variants appear only once but are then copied. It also overcomes the limitations of traditional text-types by taking into account textual contamination, which mitigates against finding clear genealogical coherence. Mink contends that the CBGM is able to establish with reasonable certainty what he calls the "initial text." The initial text is the "reconstructed form of text from which the manuscript transmission started." This is not the place to offer a full critique of the CBGM.[74] Here, I only note the difficulty with the term "initial text."

73. See Gerd Mink, "Contamination, Coherence, and Coincidence in Textual Transmission," in *The Textual History of the Greek New Testament: Changing Views in Contemporary Research*, ed. Klaus Wachtel and Michael W. Holmes, SBLTCS 8 (Atlanta: Society of Biblical Literature, 2011), 141–216. Mink has written other articles on this method, but this one appears to be the fullest published to date. An excellent compact summary of the method is also provided by Holger Strutwolf, "Original Text and Textual History," in Wachtel and Holmes, *Textual History*, 23–41, esp. 29–41. The entire volume is dedicated to recent work in textual criticism, especially the changing views of the original or authorial text, and how to proceed methodologically in textual criticism (the CBGM figures largely).

74. There are a number of apparent problems with this method, which purports to be a "scientific" approach to textual criticism, including the following: it is still based upon a number of assumptions that emerge as Mink outlines his approach; its

Mink himself (apparently) clarifies the "initial text" as either the "authorial text, redactor's text, or the archetype of the tradition as preserved."[75] As with Epp above, however, the initial text as authorial text—the traditional goal of textual criticism—is not the same as, and is distinguishable from, a later redacted text or even a textual archetype of a given tradition.

This discussion of the issue of the original text of the New Testament leads to four provocative considerations.

The first is that there is no doubt a conceptual and even practical problem with the concept of the original text, since we have neither the original autographs nor a reasonable hope of finding them. As Robert Grant admits, "The primary goal of New Testament textual study remains the recovery of what the New Testament writers wrote." However, his opinion is that "to achieve this goal is well nigh impossible."[76] Nevertheless, "we must be content with what Reinhold Niebuhr and others have called, in other contexts, an 'impossible possibility.' Only a goal of this kind can justify the labours of textual critics and give credit to their achievements and to the distance between what they have achieved and what they have hoped to achieve."[77] What Grant said half a century ago remains true now. In fact, this is what Parker (inadvertently?) does throughout his treatment. Parker has to concede that there are what

---

treatment of variants fails to note that some are of greater significance than others; it fails to define coherence as other than a statistical result in terms of percentage of similarity; it is unclear what exactly it is attempting to ascertain in the "initial text"; it treats variants in isolation from actual manuscripts; and the results are, so far, quite minimal. As a result of the Editio Critica Maior project on the Catholic Epistles using this method, there were only two changes from the text of NA$^{27}$/UBS$^4$. See Schnabel, "Textual Criticism," 62–63, 71–72, where he quotes Bart Ehrman that we have gotten as close to the original text as we ever will (assuming reference to an eclectic text), short of uncovering the autographs themselves.

75. Mink, "Contamination," 143. Klaus Wachtel and Michael Holmes claim that Mink "distinguishes the initial text from the text of the author . . . and . . . from the archetype of the manuscript tradition" (introduction to Wachtel and Holmes, *Textual History*, 12). I read Mink otherwise, as saying that the initial text may be defined in various ways, including as the authorial text or as other texts. This is part of the ambiguity of the method. I think that Wachtel and Holmes perhaps are trying to distance the intentional text from the authorial text, when this is not necessarily the case in Mink's essay or the approach.

76. Robert M. Grant, *A Historical Introduction to the New Testament* (New York: Harper & Row, 1963), 51.

77. Ibid.

he calls the "oldest and most reliable" manuscripts.[78] He uses these as the basis for being able to make the judgments that he does regarding the variant readings that he cites. Others, even recent critics, are not as skeptical of achieving the original text. The current head of the Institut für neutestamentliche Textforschung, Holger Strutwolf, writing in the same volume as Mink in his exposition of his method, recognizes that the goal of textual criticism has always been, as we have noted above, "the recovery or reconstruction of the original text, that is, the text that the author wrote or wanted to have written down if he dictated his text to a secretary." He calls this the "unanimous consensus of the discipline from the beginning."[79] No doubt, he admits, other forms of the text—such as its pre-text, its early redactions or first editions, and even its subsequent living tradition—have been neglected. I share his concern that manuscripts themselves have been treated more as "reservoirs of readings" than the artifacts that they are.[80] Nevertheless, after treating two examples similar to those treated by others, he concludes that the "exploration of the history of the living text of the Gospel leads us back to the concept of an 'original text.'"[81] This original text is not necessarily at variance with the "initial text" of the CBGM, but in fact may be the same thing if the method is used accordingly.

The second consideration is that this purported problem really becomes an insuperable roadblock only if the goal of textual criticism is changed, from reconstructing an original autograph on the basis of the textual evidence as found in the manuscripts to a new goal of seeking either some abstract earlier concept—whether sources, the sayings of Jesus, or the like—or some later form of the tradition, the living text that was changed by others, as Ehrman and Parker are keen to discuss. Finding and determining the originality of these has never been the main or focal intention or goal of textual criticism, and they are distinguishable from the original text, at least as a theoretical goal of textual criticism. This shift probably accounts for the definition of textual criticism that Parker uses—one that changes textual criticism into a form of exegesis or hermeneutics, rather than a form of textual reconstruction.[82]

78. Parker, *Living Text*, 10.
79. Strutwolf, "Original Text," 23.
80. Ibid., 24.
81. Ibid., 39.
82. Or as a matter of canon. See Epp, "Multivalence," 270–75 (repr., 580–86).

The third consideration is that the notion of conjectural emendation, suggested by Parker as a solution to the minor agreements and John 21, while widely used in classical studies where the manuscripts are few and far removed from the time of composition, does not have a place in establishing the text of the Greek New Testament. We have sufficient manuscripts, including early ones not far removed from the date of composition, so as to preclude—apart from only the most extreme of cases—the need for appeal to conjectures that cannot be found within the textual tradition.

The fourth consideration is that textual criticism has always recognized that there is an antecedent history to the text, whether it is in terms of earlier written sources or the very words and deeds of the protagonists. Textual criticism has also recognized that even original authors may have revised their work, and these works have gone through editions. It has also recognized, of course, that texts have an afterlife that is evident in the manuscript evidence. However, the object of textual criticism has been the study of the written document as it passes out of the hands of the author in the recognizable literary form in which it is found in the Greek New Testament. On some occasions, even this may be a difficult notion, but for the most part it is at least an achievable notional goal and provides the impetus for textual criticism. As Philip Comfort states,

> When I speak of the original text, I am referring to the "published" text—that is, the text in its final edited form as released for circulation in the Christian community. For some books of the New Testament, there is little difference between the original composition and the published text. . . . As is the case for books published in modern times, so in ancient times the original writing of the author is not always the same as what is published—due to the editorial process. Nonetheless, the author is credited with the final edited text, and the published book is attributed to the author and considered the autograph. This autograph is the original published text.[83]

Thus, whether the first or a subsequent edition is the published text, the original text is the published text that goes forth as the author's, is

83. Philip W. Comfort, *The Quest for the Original Text of the New Testament* (Grand Rapids: Baker Academic, 1992), 19. For refinement of the notion of published text, see Comfort, *Encountering the Manuscripts*, 11–17.

circulated in the Christian community, and is found in the Greek New Testament.[84] We might even differentiate an intermediate set of books in the New Testament: those that were compiled from sources, went through a process of editing, and then were published (the Gospels may belong to this category). In any case, the "published" version that was then circulated and eventually collected into authoritative bodies of Scripture and then came to be recognized as authoritative constitutes the authorized "original" text of the given book. Reconstructing this text constitutes the goal of textual criticism. Thus, the goal of the study of the text of the New Testament remains to establish by the best means possible, through the available manuscript evidence, the original or "published" (i.e., authorized) text of the biblical book concerned, or as close as is possible on the basis of the manuscript evidence.

## The History of the Printed Greek Text of the New Testament[85]

Once movable-type printing was invented, around 1452–1456, the Bible—the first book published, in its Latin Vulgate form—understandably became widely published. The Greek version was not the first form of the Bible to be published, however, no doubt because of several considerable reasons: (1) in the Latin Western church the Vulgate was the "Bible" of record; (2) the development of type for a Greek Bible was a huge undertaking, as the first printed editions duplicated the complex alphabet and sets of ligatures used in late minuscule manuscripts (Metzger estimates that this required around two hundred character sets);[86] and (3) there was possible resistance by Greeks who had fled to Europe during the fall of Constantinople

---

84. In this sense, the original text may in many instances be equated with the archetype or the initial text, and in some instances the canonical text. See Klaus Wachtel, "Conclusions," in Wachtel and Holmes, *Textual History*, 217–26, esp. 218.

85. The basic story of the development of the Greek New Testament is taken from Metzger, *Text*, 95–146 (4th ed., 137–94); Aland and Aland, *Text of the New Testament*, 3–36; Eldon Jay Epp, "Decision Points in Past, Present, and Future New Testament Textual Criticism," in Eldon J. Epp and Gordon D. Fee, *Studies in the Theory and Method of New Testament Textual Criticism* (Grand Rapids: Eerdmans, 1993), 17–44, but supplemented with information from others, as indicated. There are numerous histories of the development of the Greek New Testament.

86. Metzger, *Text*, 96 (4th ed., 138).

in 1453. Nevertheless, it was only a matter of time before the Greek New Testament was to find its way into print. However, this question arose: which Greek New Testament was to be published, and why?

## Editions of the Greek New Testament

Tracing the history of the development of printed editions of the Greek New Testament provides a fascinating account of scholarly exploration and development, as well as politics and personal interest. I offer only the barest recounting of this story in order to provide the basis for my subsequent discussion. Again, as above, there are a number of players in this tale, and they may quickly enter and exit the stage.

### ■ DESIDERIUS ERASMUS AND THE COMPLUTENSIAN POLYGLOT

In 1514, some sixty years after the invention of movable-type printing, the first Greek New Testament was printed. It was produced as part of a huge joint Bible publishing project in Spain, organized by Cardinal Ximenes de Cisneros and carried out in the town of Alcalá, whose Latin name was "Complutum." There they produced a printed polyglot Bible with Hebrew, Aramaic, Greek, and Latin texts, called the Complutensian Polyglot. The fifth volume out of six (the sixth had a Hebrew lexicon and grammar), and the first of the six to be printed, contained the Greek New Testament (along with a bilingual Greek-Latin lexicon), while the first four volumes contained the Old Testament in Hebrew, the Latin Vulgate,[87] and the Septuagint.[88] Although this text was printed in 1514, it was not distributed or published until 1522 because of political delays in getting papal approval of the project. The textual basis of this Greek New Testament has never been firmly agreed upon, although it probably made use of Vatican manuscripts. These manuscripts appear to have been dated from the

87. The Latin Vulgate, the Latin version of the Bible produced by Jerome (AD 347–420), is discussed in chapter 3 as part of the Old Latin translations.
88. The Septuagint, also referred to as the Old Greek, is the translation of the Hebrew Bible, as well as a number of other sacred writings, some of them originally written in Greek, produced by Egyptian Judaism, and begun in the third century BC. On the Septuagint as a whole, see Karen Jobes and Moisés Silva, *Invitation to the Septuagint* (Grand Rapids: Baker Academic, 2000). The Septuagint is discussed in more detail in chapter 3.

thirteenth to the fifteenth centuries, and this reflected the Byzantine text—that is, the text that had come to be used throughout the eastern Roman or Byzantine Empire and was reflected in the vast majority of extant manuscripts, especially those known at the time.[89]

The distinction of being the editor first to publish, even if not to print, the Greek New Testament fell to the Dutch scholar Desiderius Erasmus. In 1514 he apparently was finally convinced by the publisher Froben to produce such a text while on a trip to Basel. In Basel, where he undertook to produce this text, he made use of a total of about a half dozen minuscule manuscripts dating from the tenth to the twelfth centuries. He relied primarily upon two twelfth-century minuscules (2 and 2ap [2815], and 1r [2814] for Revelation) with the Byzantine text-type (with the exception of one manuscript, Minuscule 1, which was not Byzantine but which he apparently did not use very much). In a few places, such as the last six verses of the book of Revelation, and some other places (e.g., Acts 8:37; 9:5–6) where his manuscripts had muddled text and commentary (not an uncommon feature of minuscule manuscripts), Erasmus retroverted from the Latin Vulgate into Greek. The end result was not only a book full of numerous typographical errors, no doubt due to haste and the difficulty of the typesetters working off of the edited manuscripts themselves, but also a book that contains numerous instances of Greek devised by Erasmus and not found in any actual ancient Greek manuscript.[90] Not only did Erasmus produce an eclectic text, but he also created one that introduced readings into the Greek New Testament that have been retained in some subsequent editions to this day.[91] Nevertheless, Erasmus published this volume in 1515, and then a further four editions (1519, 1522, 1527, 1535). The significance of this event is marked by Erasmus's own words, found in the preface:

> I totally disagree with those who are unwilling that the Holy Scriptures, translated into the common tongue, should be read by the unlearned. Christ desires His mysteries to be published abroad as widely as possible. I could wish that even all women should read the Gospel and

89. Tregelles, *Account of the Printed Text*, 8.
90. See Metzger, *Text*, 100n1 (4th ed., 145n17).
91. The editions that print the Textus Receptus (see below) still contain some of these renderings (e.g., in Rev. 22:16, 17, 18, 19, 21).

St Paul's Epistles, and I would that they were translated into all the languages of all Christian people, that they might be read and known not merely by the Scots and the Irish but even by the Turks and the Saracens. I wish that the farm worker might sing parts of them at the plough, that the weaver might hum them at the shuttle, and that the traveler might beguile the weariness of the way by reciting them.[92]

This is a noble purpose that to a great extent mitigates the failings of the actual edition itself.

One important story regarding Erasmus and the preparation of his edition bears repeating.[93] When his first edition appeared, he was accused by Stunica (Diego Lopez de Zuñiga) (c. 1531), one of the editors of the Complutensian Polyglot and the chief editor of the New Testament, of excluding the trinitarian words found in 1 John 5:7–8: "the Father, the Word, and the Holy Ghost: and these three are one. And there are three that bear witness in earth." Erasmus's response was that these words were not found in any of the manuscripts that he had consulted for his Greek New Testament or subsequently. One of the manuscripts that he apparently consulted subsequently was Codex Vaticanus (03 B), which Erasmus asked a friend to examine for him, after which he received a letter, dated June 18, 1521, copying out the text and confirming that there was no such passage.[94] Erasmus—precipitously and unwisely, we now see—said that he would include these words (the so-called Johannine Comma) if they could be found in a single Greek manuscript. Lo and behold, such a manuscript appeared, now known as Gregory 61, held in the Trinity College Dublin library. It appears to have been written in 1520 in Oxford by someone named "Froy" or "Roy." Erasmus fulfilled his obligation and put the Johannine passage in his third edition of 1522, but with a footnote that indicated his doubts regarding its authenticity.

Erasmus was right to question its authenticity. It appears that for the Complutensian Polyglot, in which most of these words appear, these verses were translated from the Latin Vulgate. As Stunica himself

92. Cited in F. F. Bruce, *History of the Bible in English: From the Earliest Versions*, 3rd ed. (Guildford: Lutterworth, 1979), 29.

93. Metzger, *Text*, 101–2 (4th ed., 146–47).

94. Tregelles, *Account of the Printed Text*, 22. This incident is apparently the first time there is record of Codex Vaticanus (03 B) being used in textual criticism.

admitted when asked by Erasmus regarding his manuscript support, "You must know that the copies of the Greeks are corrupted; that OURs [i.e., the Latin], however, contain the very truth."[95] The Greek manuscript that Erasmus was shown (Gregory 61), reflecting Latin, which has no article, did not have articles before "father," "word," and "spirit," which Erasmus corrected in subsequent editions.[96] Metzger notes that this passage has been found only in three other manuscripts: Gregory 88 (twelfth century), in which it is written marginally in a seventeenth-century hand; Tischendorf ω 110 (sixteenth-century copy of the Greek text of the Complutensian Polyglot); and Gregory 629 (fourteenth century or later). The so-called Johannine Comma does appear in the Latin treatise *Liber apologeticus* (fourth century), attributed to Priscillian or Instantius. The Johannine Comma appears for the first time in Latin Vulgate manuscripts around AD 800. According to Metzger, "The *Comma* probably originated as a piece of allegorical exegesis of the three witnesses and may have been written as a marginal gloss in a Latin manuscript of I John, when it was taken into the text of the Old Latin Bible during the fifth century."[97]

- ■ TEXTUS RECEPTUS

Other publishers soon published versions of Erasmus's Greek text of the New Testament. Several of these to note include the four editions published by Robert Estienne (Stephanus) (1503–1559). The third edition (1550) followed Erasmus's later editions and included a critical apparatus that referred to other manuscripts, including Codex Bezae (05 D) when it was apparently located in Italy. This edition was widely used in England, and it formed the basis for the English theologian Brian Walton's (1600–1661) Polyglot Bible, with the fifth volume including the Greek New Testament (1657). The fifth volume includes variant readings from Codex Alexandrinus (02 A), and the

95. Tregelles, *Account of the Printed Text*, 9–10. The Complutensian Polyglot also leaves out 1 John 5:8b, "and the three are one," following the Lateran council and Thomas Aquinas, and Latin manuscripts after 1215 (ibid., 10).

96. Ibid., 26n.

97. Metzger, *Text*, 102 (4th ed., 148). He also notes that it was included in the Latin Vulgate edition of 1592, and hence Pope Leo XIII in 1897 approved a pronouncement regarding its authority. However, Roman Catholic scholars do not treat it as authentic in the Greek New Testament.

sixth volume, an appendix, contains a critical apparatus with variants from Stephanus's edition and fifteen other manuscripts. Stephanus's fourth edition (1551) was the first edition that included the enumeration of verses. Théodore Beza (1519–1605), the early Reformer, published nine editions of the Greek New Testament. However, even though he owned a number of manuscripts, such as Codex Bezae (05 D) and Codex Claromontanus (06 Dp), these were not used in any significant way in preparing his editions, which tended to follow that of Stephanus. The Authorized Version (1611) probably made use of Beza's editions.[98] The famous Elzevir publishing house published an edition of the Greek New Testament that followed Beza. In the preface to the second edition (1633) they referred to "the text which is now received by all, in which we give nothing changed or corrupted" (*textum ergo habes, nunc ab omnibus receptum: in quo nihil immutatum aut corruptum damus*) (trans. Metzger). From this statement, we get the term "Textus Receptus." Due to the strength of this statement, and the fact that this and related editions had established themselves as the Greek text of the New Testament, the Textus Receptus became the basis for all of the major Protestant translations until 1881, while Roman Catholics continued to use the Latin Vulgate. John Fell (1625–1686), the English theologian during the Civil War (1642–1651), used the second Elzevir edition for an edition that included a critical apparatus with variants from over one hundred manuscripts and versions, including Codex Vaticanus (03 B), although a number of these manuscripts, Vaticanus included, are cited en masse rather than individually.[99]

### ▪ JOHN MILL (1645–1707)

Several other early editions are also worth noting. The English theologian John Mill in 1707 published Stephanus's third edition of 1550, along with a critical apparatus of all the manuscripts and versions to which he could gain access and a prolegomena on critical issues. The result was reference in his critical discussion to over three

98. Some think that an edition of the text of Stephanus was used. See Stanley E. Porter, "Language and Translation of the New Testament," in *The Oxford Handbook of Biblical Studies*, ed. John W. Rogerson and Judith M. Lieu (Oxford: Oxford University Press, 2006), 197.

99. Metzger, *Text*, 103–6 (4th ed., 148–52): 107 (153) on Walton; 107 (4th ed., 153–54) on Fell.

thousand verses in the New Testament, and the noting of thirty thousand variant readings. Reaction to Mill's work was divided. Daniel Whitby (1633–1726), also an English theologian, was horrified to find that there were so many variants, while Edward Wells (1667–1727), a polymath and theologian, used Mill's results and edited a new critical text that used earlier manuscripts instead of the Textus Receptus. This is apparently the first published Greek New Testament edited along these lines. Daniel Mace (d. 1753), a Presbyterian minister and textual critic, in 1729 published a similar edition that disputed readings in the Textus Receptus and used common sense and earlier manuscript evidence to develop his own text.

### ■ JOHANN ALBRECHT BENGEL (1687–1752)

Apparently disturbed by the thirty thousand variants that Mill had indicated, Johann Albrecht Bengel, a Lutheran cleric and author of the deservedly famous commentary entitled *Gnomon Novi Testamenti*,[100] undertook a wide-ranging examination of the manuscripts of the Greek New Testament. He differentiated between two types of manuscripts: the Asiatic, or those originating from Constantinople and surrounding areas, and that were more recent in origin; and the African, which included two groups, those following Codex Alexandrinus (02 A) and those following the Old Latin. He further noted that manuscripts should be weighed according to their type rather than simply counted. Bengel arrived at a principle of textual criticism on the basis of study of these manuscripts in which he posited that the difficult reading is to be preferred over the easy one (*proclivi scriptioni praestat ardua*). In his published Greek New Testament (1734) he printed a corrected text based on the Textus Receptus, in which only readings for which there was earlier printed textual support were incorporated. He also derived a rating system for variant readings, according to whether they were original, better, just as good, less good, or clearly inferior in relation to the printed text.

Bengel's assistant, Jacob Wettstein (1693–1754), built upon Bengel's work by including more manuscripts, and he published a Greek New

---

100. John Albert Bengel, *Gnomon Novi Testamenti*, ed. M. Ernest Bengel and John Steudel, 3rd ed. (Stuttgart: J. F. Steinkopf, 1864 [1742]); ET, *Gnomon of the New Testament*, ed. M. Ernest Bengel and J. C. F. Steudel, 5 vols. (Edinburgh: T&T Clark, 1857–1858).

Testament (1751–1752) in which he rated variants. Wettstein was the first to include the majuscule manuscripts designated by capital letters and minuscule manuscripts by Arabic numbers. In 1763 William Bowyer Jr. (1699–1777) published a critical edition of the Greek New Testament in which he marked in square brackets passages that he thought lacked manuscript support. Some of the passages that he marked would recur in textual criticism, including Matthew 6:13, the doxology of the Lord's Prayer; John 7:53–8:11, the woman caught in adultery; 1 John 5:7–8, the Johannine Comma; and a number of individual verses (e.g., Acts 8:37; 15:34).

- JOHANN SALOMO SEMLER (1725–1791) AND JOHANN JAKOB GRIESBACH (1745–1812)

The wide-ranging theologian and church historian Johann Salomo Semler, again building upon Bengel's work, attributed the Asian (or Eastern, as he called it) group of manuscripts to Lucian's early fourth-century recension, and the African (or Western or Egypto-Palestinian) group to Origen. He arrived at what he differentiated as three major manuscript recensions: Alexandrian, attributed to Origen and found in the Syriac, Bohairic, and Ethiopic versions; Eastern, found in the Antiochian and Constantinopolitan churches; and Western, found in the Latin versions (1767).[101] Semler was followed by his student Johann Jakob Griesbach. Griesbach studied numerous manuscripts and eventually refined Semler's classification system into three: Alexandrian, Western, and Byzantine. The Alexandrian text he attributed to Origen, the Western contained Codex Bezae (05 D) and Codex Claromontanus (06 Dp), and the Byzantine was a later amalgamation of the other two. Griesbach also developed fifteen principles of textual criticism. For example, his principle regarding the shorter and longer readings was vindicated on the basis of his analysis of the Lord's Prayer as found in Luke 11:3–4, where Codex Vaticanus (03 B) confirmed his supposition of the shorter reading being earlier. A number of scholars continued to add to the numbers of manuscripts available for collation. Johannes Scholz (1794–1852), a professor at Bonn University, provided the first comprehensive list of New Testament Greek manuscripts, along with their geographical provenance.

---

101. The versions are discussed in chapter 3.

■ KARL LACHMANN (1793–1851)

Marking a significant shift in New Testament textual criticism, Karl Lachmann, the well-known German classical philologist, represented a total break with the Textus Receptus when he published his edition (1831) of what he thought the Greek New Testament text in the East was like in the late fourth century. For this edition he used only earlier manuscripts, such as majuscules, Old Latin and church fathers, but no minuscules. Although his approach was progressive, he did not have a significant textual basis for his new edition, and so it did not fulfill its promise.

■ CONSTANTIN TISCHENDORF (1815–1874) AND SAMUEL PRIDEAUX TREGELLES (1813–1875)

Constantin Tischendorf, the Leipzig New Testament scholar, is to this day probably the single most significant figure in New Testament textual criticism. In part because of his theological beliefs in the integrity of the Bible, he devoted his life to discovering and publishing more biblical manuscripts than any other scholar, as a means of demonstrating the reliability of the text. He also published numerous critical editions and editions of the Greek New Testament (as well as the Greek Old Testament). However, Tischendorf's eighth edition of the Greek New Testament (1869–1872) contains a comprehensive critical apparatus of all the (then) available manuscripts, versions, and ancient authorities, and it is still unparalleled in its scope and accuracy. Tischendorf also developed a comprehensive set of criteria for doing textual criticism.[102] He is most famous for his discovery, over the course of three trips to St. Catherine's Monastery on Mount Sinai, of the Codex Sinaiticus (01 ℵ), which was published in beautiful facsimile in 1862 to commemorate the millennial anniversary of the Russian Empire.[103] There has been persistent criticism of Tischendorf, with accusations being made and

---

102. These are found in Eldon Jay Epp, "The Eclectic Method in New Testament Textual Criticism: Solution or Symptom?" in Epp and Fee, *Theory and Method*, 155–56.

103. Constantin Tischendorf, *Bibliorum Codex Sinaiticus Petropolitanus: Auspiciis augustissimis imperatoris Alexandri II; Ex tenebris protraxit in Europam transtulit ad iuvandas atque illustrandas sacras litteras*, 4 vols. (St. Petersburg, 1862). These volumes are a phenomenal tribute to primarily one man's industry. Tischendorf not only edited the manuscript but also arranged for the printing, designing unique fonts and securing special paper for the publication.

repeated that he essentially stole the manuscript from Sinai.[104] However, recent research in the archives of the Russian state have discovered two interesting sets of correspondence. One involves Tischendorf himself pushing the Russian authorities to ensure an equitable and timely settlement of the issue of the manuscript with the monks at St. Catherine's, and the other is the actual receipt and surrounding documents, where the monks acknowledge payment for the manuscript.[105] Tischendorf's accomplishments and reputation remain intact.

Although his text is not widely used or cited, despite his high standing in textual criticism, the edition of Samuel Tregelles reflects the painstaking work of a life devoted to textual criticism in the belief that establishing the text of the New Testament would serve God and his church. Even though Tregelles did not have the benefit of an academic position to support his work (he was an ironworker), he was deeply involved in textual criticism, including developing principles of textual criticism (found in his *Account of the Printed Text*, cited above), editing of manuscripts, and correcting the work of others. His major effort, however, was to undertake over the course of fifteen years to publish a critical edition of the Greek New Testament based upon the earliest manuscripts.[106] Despite having a stroke near the end of the project, he accomplished the task (with the help of B. W. Newton [1807–1899], the well-known evangelist and member of the Plymouth Brethren church), which resulted in an edition in six parts, completed by publication of a volume of prolegomena and corrections by F. J. A. Hort and A. W. Steane in 1879.

- B. F. WESTCOTT (1825–1901) AND F. J. A. HORT (1828–1892)

In 1881, a year that was to be significant for the change brought about in textual criticism and Bible translation (as we will see),

---

104. This topic is discussed again in chapter 2.

105. See Christoph Böttrich, "Constantin von Tischendorf und der Transfer des Codex Sinaiticus nach St. Petersburg," in *Die Theologische Fakultät der Universität Leipzig: Personen, Profile und Perspektiven aus sechs Jahrhunderten Fakultätsgeschichte*, ed. Andreas Gössner, BLUW 2A (Leipzig: Evangelische Verlagsanstalt, 2005), 253–75; A. V. Zaharova, "The Acquisition of the Codex Sinaiticus by Russia in the Light of New Documents from Russian Archives," in *Montfaucon: Études de paléographie, de codicologie et de diplomatique* [in Russian] (Moscow and St. Petersburg: Allianse-Archéo, 2007), 209–66.

106. Samuel Prideaux Tregelles, *The Greek New Testament, Edited from Ancient Authorities, with Their Various Readings in Full, and the Latin Version of Jerome*, 2 vols. (London: Bagster, 1875–1897).

Brooke Foss Westcott and Fenton John Anthony Hort, both New Testament scholars and theologians, published their edition of the Greek New Testament, along with a volume that contained discussion of their critical principles and selected passages. They did not collate any manuscripts themselves but instead used the published results of others, along with advancing the critical principles of previous scholars such as Griesbach and Lachman. It is to Hort's discussion of critical principles that we owe the principles of internal evidence used by most scholars in current textual criticism. As a result, Westcott and Hort also developed the genealogical relationship among manuscripts. They differentiated four major textual types: Neutral, Alexandrian, Western, and Syrian. Westcott and Hort believed that the Neutral text was the one nearest to the original. It is represented by Codex Vaticanus (03 B) and Codex Sinaiticus (01 ℵ), and the readings of these manuscripts should be considered the original unless there is strong contrary internal evidence. The Alexandrian text reflects Alexandrian philological scholarship and is found in Codex Ephraemi Rescriptus (04 C) and Codex Regius (019 L) and in many early church fathers. The Western text, reflected in Codex Bezae (05 D) for the Gospels and Acts and in Codex Claromontanus (06 Dp) for the Epistles, originated in the early-to-middle second century. The Syrian text, which reflects fourth-century revision by Lucian, is a mixed text that is the furthest from the originals. Westcott and Hort were able to show that the Syrian text often combined readings from earlier texts, and no church father from before AD 320 has a distinctly Syrian reading. This text was the one used in the Byzantine Empire; it is found in the Gospels portion of Codex Alexandrinus (02 A), later majuscules, and most minuscules, and it is the textual basis of the Textus Receptus. Westcott and Hort's edition of the Greek New Testament became the edition used by the translators of the Revised Version of the Authorized Version (1881). The results of Westcott and Hort's work were confirmed through a very different means by the German New Testament scholar Bernhard Weiss (1827–1918), who, in preparing his edition of the Greek New Testament (see below), classified readings on the basis of intrinsic probability and then classified the types of variants that he encountered.

## ■ HERMANN VON SODEN (1852–1914)

Hermann von Soden, a German New Testament scholar, developed a complex (and many would say confusing) system of manuscript classification, along with describing three main manuscript families: Koine (K), with numerous subclassifications, produced by Lucian and used by the Byzantine church; Hesychian (H), with the oldest majuscules, some early versions and fathers; and Jerusalem (I), not preserved in any major manuscripts but reconstructed from mixed manuscripts and found in Codex D (05).[107] Von Soden's family K corresponds to the Syrian text of Westcott and Hort, and H to the Neutral and Alexandrian. Von Soden believed that there was a common archetype for these three texts, but that it was corrupted by Marcion for the Pauline Epistles and by Tatian for the Gospels and Acts, but later used by Origen.

## ■ TRADITIONAL TEXTS

At the same time that various scholars have been developing their understanding of the Greek manuscript tradition, including publishing new editions usually based on the Alexandrian text-type, there have been several different efforts to promote what are often referred to as traditional texts. Several editions continued to promulgate forms of the Textus Receptus. These editions include those by Alexander Souter (1910), whose text was reconstructed from the Revised Version of 1881,[108] using the Textus Receptus as its base text (hence its closeness to the Textus Receptus); Heinrich Joseph Vogels (1920);[109] and Augustin Merk (1933),[110] these last two editions being diglots with the Vulgate. The Textus Receptus continues to be published by the Trinitarian Bible Society.[111] More effort has been expended recently,

107. Hermann von Soden, *Die Schriften des Neuen Testaments in ihrer ältesten erreichbaren Textgestalt, hergestellt auf Grund ihrer Textgeschichte*, 2 parts in 4 vols. (Göttingen: Vandenhoeck & Ruprecht, 1911–1913).

108. Alexander Souter, *Novum Testamentum Graece* (Oxford: Clarendon, 1910; 2nd ed., 1947) (already mentioned above).

109. Heinrich Joseph Vogels, *Novum Testamentum Graece et Latine*, 2 vols. (Düsseldorf: L. Schwann, 1922; 4th ed., Freiburg: Herder, 1955).

110. Augustin Merk, *Novum Testamentum Graece et Latine* (Rome: Pontifical Biblical Institute, 1933; 10th ed., 1984).

111. *H KAINH ΔIAΘHKH, The New Testament: The Greek Text Underlying the English Authorised Version of 1611* (London: Trinitarian Bible Society, n.d.), following Beza's 1598 edition.

however, on the Majority text and the Byzantine text. In 1980 Zane Hodges and Arthur Farstad published their Majority text Greek New Testament.[112] This text tries to account for the origins of variant readings based upon the belief that the majority of texts have the correct reading. In 1991, and then again in 2005, the New Testament scholar Maurice Robinson and his colleague William Pierpont published the Greek New Testament according to the Byzantine text.[113] This edition simply follows the texts that have the greatest number. Finally, some others have gone their own way, including José Maria Bover (1943) with his Western and Caesarean text.[114]

- EBERHARD NESTLE (1851–1913) AND THE UNITED BIBLE SOCIETIES GREEK NEW TESTAMENT

In 1898 the German scholar Eberhard Nestle developed what has become the most widely used text of the Greek New Testament. He did not make any examination of manuscripts but instead used the editions of Tischendorf (eighth edition); Westcott and Hort; and, originally, the Baptist scholar Richard Weymouth, later replaced by that of the German New Testament scholar Bernhard Weiss (1827–1918) for Nestle's third edition of 1901.[115] Weymouth's edition itself was a composite text based upon the printed editions since 1550 (he lists seventeen sources in his preface).[116] Where two of the three editions agreed, Nestle selected that reading, but when all three disagreed he used what he called a "mean reading." Although some agreed-upon readings have since been incorporated, these editions are the basis of what has become the standard Greek New Testament, edited after Eberhard Nestle's death by his son Erwin Nestle (1883–1972), from the twenty-first edition of 1952 with Kurt Aland (1915–1994), and

112. Zane C. Hodges and Arthur L. Farstad, *The Greek New Testament according to the Majority Text*, 2nd ed. (Nashville: Nelson, 1985).

113. Maurice A. Robinson and William G. Pierpont, *The New Testament in the Original Greek: Byzantine Textform, 2005* (Southborough, MA: Chilton, 2005) (already mentioned above).

114. José Maria Bover, *Novi Testamenti Biblia Graeca et Latina* (Madrid: Consejo Superior de Investigaciones Científicas, 1943).

115. Bernhard Weiss, *Das Neue Testament*, 3 vols. (Leipzig: Hinrichs, 1894–1900; 2nd ed., 1902).

116. Richard F. Weymouth, *The Resultant Greek Testament* (London: James Clarke, n.d.), ix–xv.

then Barbara Aland and a committee from the United Bible Societies edition (see below).[117] This edition was adopted in 1904 as the Greek New Testament for the British and Foreign Bible Society, although a second edition under the influence of the British textual critic G. D. Kilpatrick (1910–1989) departed in a few places from this text to reflect his approach to textual criticism.[118] The Nestle edition was also the basis for the eclectic text produced by the British New Testament scholar R. V. G. Tasker in 1964 as the text that reflected the translational decisions of the New English Bible Committee.[119] In 1966 the United Bible Societies, at the instigation of Eugene Nida (1914–2011), the dean of modern Bible translation and the creative force behind many such projects,[120] and who selected the editorial team for the project, began publishing their own edition of the Greek New Testament for the use of Bible translators.[121] This text was first based upon Westcott and Hort's edition, but with comparison of a number of other recent editions, including Nestle, Bover, Merk and Vogels, as well as Tischendorf and von Soden. This edition has gone

117. *Novum Testamentum Graece* [edited by (E. Nestle and E. Nestle), Barbara Aland, Kurt Aland, Johannes Karavidopoulos, Carlo M. Martini, and Bruce M. Metzger, 27th rev. ed. (Stuttgart: Deutsche Bibelgesellschaft, 1993)], still known and styled on the title page as "Nestle-Aland." The twenty-eighth edition of the Nestle-Aland was published in 2012, after this manuscript was completed. A preliminary examination indicates that the twenty-eighth edition is an uneven edition in that the text of the Catholic Epistles now follows the Editio Critica Maior (discussed elsewhere), and the apparatus includes the latest manuscripts—although not all of them figure into actual textual decisions.

118. Η Καινη Διαθηκη: *Text with Critical Apparatus* (London: British and Foreign Bible Society, 1904; 2nd ed., 1958). Kilpatrick believed in an approach to textual criticism referred to as thoroughgoing eclecticism, as opposed to the reasoned eclecticism of most who use an eclectic text (such as the Nestle text, which is a composite from all of the manuscripts and their readings, even if certain manuscripts are relied upon more heavily than others). In Ehrman and Holmes, *Text of the New Testament*, see J. Keith Elliott, "Thoroughgoing Eclecticism in New Testament Textual Criticism," 321–35; Michael W. Holmes, "Reasoned Eclecticism in New Testament Textual Criticism," 336–60.

119. R. V. G. Tasker, *The Greek New Testament* (Oxford: Oxford University Press; Cambridge: Cambridge University Press, 1964), ix.

120. Eugene Nida's important contribution to Bible translation is discussed in chapter 3.

121. The United Bible Societies *Greek New Testament* has gone through five editions: first (1966), second (1968), third (1975), third corrected (1983), and fourth revised (1993). See Kurt Aland et al., eds., *The Greek New Testament* (New York: United Bible Societies).

through four editions, and since the third edition has agreed with the twenty-sixth edition of Nestle-Aland. Thus today the major critical edition for widespread scholarly use is NA²⁷/UBS⁴, which are virtually identical texts (though punctuation and apparatus vary, and there are reportedly other occasional inconsistencies).

■ RECENT DEVELOPMENTS

There continue to be many important developments in New Testament textual criticism, including attempts to reconstruct the Greek New Testament. In the first half of the twentieth century there were efforts at international cooperation between Britain and Germany in producing a new, major critical edition of the New Testament. This project fell apart, although the British team led by S. C. E. Legg continued to publish critical apparatuses to editions of Mark and Matthew. These were not deemed satisfactory. After World War II the project was revived in 1948 in a new form with the International Greek New Testament Project (IGNTP), using both English and American scholars, which has had a slowly developing history. So far it has published Luke's Gospel[122] and has been working on John's Gospel,[123] with a view (according to its website) to completing the Pauline Epistles by 2031. In the meantime, the project has joined with the Institut für neutestamentliche Textforschung on their Editio Critica Maior (ECM) project. This project, announced originally in 1969 by Kurt Aland,[124] so far has published the Catholic Epistles[125] and is now partnering with the

122. American and British Committees of the International Greek New Testament Project, *The Gospel according to St. Luke*, 2 vols. (Oxford: Oxford University Press, 1984–1987).

123. W. J. Elliott and D. C. Parker, eds., *The Gospel according to St. John*, vol. 1, *The Papyri*, NTTS 20 (Leiden: Brill, 1995); U. B. Schmid, with W. J. Elliott and D. C. Parker, eds., *The Gospel according to St. John*, vol. 2, *The Majuscules*, NTTSD 37 (Leiden: Brill, 2007). These are not to be considered new editions, in that they have not actually examined all of the manuscripts that they publish. There are places where these editions probably can be corrected on the basis of firsthand observation of the manuscripts themselves.

124. Kurt Aland, "*Novi Testamenti Graeci Editio Maior Critica: Der gegenwärtige Stand der Arbeit an einer neuen grossen kritischen Ausgabe des Neuen Testamentes,*" *NTS* 16 (1969): 163–77.

125. Barbara Aland et al., eds., *Novum Testamentum Graecum: Editio Critica Maior*, vol. 4, *Die katholischen Briefe* [= *Catholic Letters*], 4 vols. (Stuttgart: Deutsche Bibelgesellschaft, 1997–2005).

IGNTP on the rest of the New Testament. More recently, text-critical scholar Michael Holmes has published the Society of Biblical Literature Greek New Testament edition (SBLGNT).[126] In many ways similar to the Nestle project, Holmes's edition uses Westcott and Hort's edition as the base and then compares it with those of Tregelles, the NIV,[127] and the Byzantine text of Robinson and Pierpont. His procedure is generally to accept their reading when they all agree (although this is not always the case) and then to determine the correct reading where they do not all agree. In a few cases he adopts a reading not found in any of the editions. It appears that Holmes has simply used these four editions to ensure the secure 90 percent or more of the established text, and then he has gone on to make his own decision for the remaining portion—except, apparently, where he thinks he knows better, even than the undisputed tradition. This may not be the best way forward in textual criticism of the Greek New Testament.

## The Manuscript Basis of the Greek New Testament

The brief outline above of the major printed editions of the Greek New Testament leads to further questions regarding the basis of the Greek New Testament. There are two major considerations to pursue: the traditional texts and the various manuscript types.

### ■ WHAT SHOULD WE THINK OF THE TRADITIONAL TEXT?

This brief history of major published editions of the Greek New Testament clearly raises the question of which edition should be used in study of the Greek New Testament today. This is not such an easy question to answer. A reader who wants the text that represents a particular translation wants the Greek text that was used to make that translation. Up to 1881, that would invariably, at least in English, have been a form of the Textus Receptus, except in Catholic circles, where the translation was of an edition of Jerome's Vulgate (which I will discuss in chap. 3). After 1881, the vast majority of translations

---

126. Michael W. Holmes, ed., *The Greek New Testament: SBL Edition* (Atlanta: Society of Biblical Literature; Bellingham, WA: Logos Bible Software, 2010).

127. The Greek text of the NIV was reconstructed by Edward Goodrick and John Kohlenberger III and is published in Richard J. Goodrich and Albert L. Lukaszewski, *A Reader's Greek New Testament* (Grand Rapids: Zondervan, 2003).

use a Greek text similar to that developed by Westcott and Hort. A reader who wants a text that reflects the earliest manuscripts wants a text based on the Alexandrian majuscules, such as Codex Sinaiticus (01 א) and Codex Vaticanus (03 B). A reader who wants the text that represents the text of the Byzantine church and continues to be used in the Greek Orthodox tradition wants a form of the Byzantine text. A reader who wants the text that represents the text of the overwhelming majority of manuscripts, when all of the 5,813 or so manuscripts are taken into account, wants the Majority text.

The distinction between the Textus Receptus, on the one hand, and the Majority text or the Byzantine texts, on the other hand,[128] is one worth making here, if only briefly. All of these Greek texts are often referred to as forms of the "traditional text." The Textus Receptus is any form of the Greek text that goes back to the edition of Erasmus and the several late manuscripts that he used. The Textus Receptus is a more restricted and limited form of Byzantine text, but it is not the Byzantine text as found in the edition of Robinson and Pierpont, or the Majority text found in the edition of Hodges and Farstad. Daniel Wallace notes that Hodges and Farstad's edition of the Majority text differs from the Textus Receptus in 1,838 places.[129] Aland and Aland list fifteen verses that they indicate are in the Textus Receptus but not in the Nestle-Aland critical edition.[130] Four of those—Luke 23:17; Acts 8:37; 15:34; 24:6b–8a—are not found in the Majority text (Farstad and Hodges) or the Byzantine text (Pierpont and Robinson) either.[131] I note also that the portions where Erasmus or others translated from Latin back into Greek, such as the final six verses of Revelation and 1 John 5:7–8 (the Johannine Comma), are also not part of the Byzantine text or the Majority text.

128. There is a distinction between the Byzantine text and the Majority text, but it is not important to make such a distinction here. Unless otherwise stated, they will be treated as similar. See Daniel B. Wallace, "The Majority Text Theory: History, Methods, and Critique," in Ehrman and Holmes, *Text of the New Testament*, 297–320.

129. Wallace, "Majority Text Theory," 302n28.

130. Aland and Aland, *Text of the New Testament*, 298–300. The passages are Matt. 17:21; 18:11; 23:14; Mark 7:16; 9:44, 46; 11:26; 15:28; Luke 17:36; 23:17; John 5:3b–4; Acts 8:37; 15:34; 24:6b–8a; 28:29; Rom. 16:24.

131. Note that after Rom. 16:24 in the Textus Receptus Rom. 16:25–27 is included. These verses are included after Rom 14:33 in the Majority text and the Byzantine text.

While use of the Textus Receptus has greatly declined,[132] the Majority or Byzantine text continues to have some who support its use—besides use by Orthodox church communities. Robinson has recently argued at length on behalf of the Byzantine text. He rejects modern eclectic texts, such as those of Westcott and Hort or Nestle-Aland, as "simply hav[ing] no proven existence within transmissional history," as the modern eclectic text does not conform to any extant manuscript or other versional or patristic data.[133] Instead of arguing for eclecticism (when manuscripts are compared to arrive at the reconstructed earliest form of the text), Robinson argues for what he calls "reasoned transmissionalism" that evaluates all of the internal and external evidence. He proposes a number of criteria. I will state them at some length because most are probably not as familiar to readers as are some of the criteria used in eclectic textual criticism.[134]

The internal criteria that Robinson proposes include (1) accepting the reading that gives rise to the others, the more difficult reading, the reading that conforms with authorial style, and the reading with "transcriptional probability"; (2) rejecting readings that harmonize or assimilate to other passages, reflect "scribal piety" or theologically based changes, and reflect transcriptional error; and (3) showing no preference for either shorter or longer readings.

Robinson's external criteria include (1) rejection of conjectural emendation due to the quantity of evidence; (2) suspicion of "sporadically" occurring readings, especially when only in a single or small group of manuscripts or other ancient sources; (3) consideration of a variety of evidence, including various versions or church fathers, or differing text-types; (4) reduction of the raw numbers of manuscripts where possible (such as Family 1); (5) weighing rather than counting manuscripts; (6) seeking readings with "demonstrable antiquity"; (7) rejection of the notion of one or a small group of preferred manuscripts and rejection of the "exclusive" following of

---

132. The exception is that the Textus Receptus is still favored as the basis of some translations. See chapter 3 on translations.

133. Maurice A. Robinson, "Appendix: The Case for Byzantine Priority," in Robinson and Pierpont, *New Testament in the Original Greek*, 534.

134. Criteria used in eclectic textual criticism can be found in a variety of places, including Metzger, *Text*, 209–11 (4th ed., 302–4).

the oldest evidence; and (8) "transmissional considerations," which "coupled with internal principles point to the Byzantine Textform as a leading force in the history of transmission."[135]

A closer look at these criteria exposes particular difficulties in their formulation. One obvious problem is that several of the internal and external criteria are qualified in ways that aid the Byzantine text or dismiss the Alexandrian text-type. For example, the internal criterion regarding the more difficult reading is qualified to exclude difficult readings "created by individual scribes" not in keeping with the transmissional history, which transmissional history is based on the Byzantine text; or the external criterion regarding "demonstrable antiquity" makes sure that the lack of early attestation for a reading found in the Byzantine tradition does not exclude a reading from being posited as early; or the endorsing of the idea that once minuscules (of which the vast majority are Byzantine) were copied, their preceding majuscule text was usually destroyed leads to inevitable arguments from silence regarding readings found in the Byzantine tradition;[136] or the external criterion concerning "exclusive" following of the oldest evidence dismisses following the oldest manuscripts. A second difficulty is that a number of the external criteria (the second, third, and seventh), essentially, are ways of restating the numerical superiority of Byzantine manuscripts. The number of manuscripts is a single factor, not a determining one, and must be kept in perspective. A third problem is that Robinson, in effect, accepts simply a numerical argument when he discusses the "essence of a Byzantine-priority method."[137] A fourth difficulty is the obvious bias of the last external criterion regarding the Byzantine text-type, especially when there is no independent manuscript, versional, or patristic evidence for the Byzantine text-type before the fourth century that is not found in other text-types, such as the Western text.[138] Harry Sturz has argued that

135. Robinson, "Appendix," 545–66.

136. Robinson (ibid., 562n88) rightly rejects the argument that early Byzantine manuscripts were worn out from their use, and hence their disappearance, but he accepts this argument regarding minuscules. See D. A. Carson, *The King James Version Debate: A Plea for Realism* (Grand Rapids: Baker Academic, 1979), 47–48n5.

137. Robinson, "Appendix," 538–40.

138. Wallace, "Majority Text Theory," 303, 311; Carson, *King James Version Debate*, 44–46. Robinson ("Appendix," 556n73) rejects this argument by considering patristic sources that match the Alexandrian text, as reflecting the Byzantine text. He

there are Byzantine readings in early papyri;[139] however, this argument
does not prove a Byzantine text-type, but only that there are readings
in the papyri that are found in Byzantine texts—they are virtually
always found in other text-types as well.

Let us look more closely at the arguments used in defense of the
various forms of the traditional text. Defenders of the Textus Receptus, and by extension of the Majority and the Byzantine texts, often
do so on three grounds.[140]

(1) The first is a doctrine of verbal inspiration that includes provi-
dential preservation of the text until today. For defenders of the
Textus Receptus, this view includes the preservation of that text,
and often extends to the Authorized (King James) Version as well.
This viewpoint goes far beyond any traditional view of inspiration,
especially when it extends inspiration to translation—even apparently
translation by Erasmus from Latin back into Greek. Sometimes verses
are cited in defense of this position—such as Psalm 119:89; Isaiah
40:8; Matthew 5:17–18; John 10:35; 1 Peter 1:23–25[141]—but at other
times this viewpoint is defended simply as a theological presupposi-
tion.[142] In either case, the notion is problematic, as it seems to require
more than the doctrine of inspiration can provide. Furthermore, it
requires more than the prooftexts exegetically indicate, especially
in light of historical evidence of the manuscripts themselves, which
have variants in them—even the Byzantine ones, and even the ones
used by Erasmus (to say nothing of the other textual difficulties mentioned above). In fact, this position regarding textual preservation
is self-contradictory, as it does not endorse the preservation of the
non-Byzantine manuscripts, when many of these are even older and

---

bases this on an analysis of Origen by Darrell D. Hannah (*The Text of I Corinthians
in the Writings of Origen*, NTGF 4 [Atlanta: Scholars Press, 1997], 269, 271–72).
This does not address the fact that the Alexandrian tradition is still predominant
in comparison, or as Carson (*King James Version Debate*, 110–11) points out, that
Byzantine readings, whether found in other sources or not, do not necessarily establish
a Byzantine text-type, which is lacking in the manuscript evidence.

139. Harry Sturz, *The Byzantine Text-Type and New Testament Textual Criticism*
(Nashville: Nelson, 1984), 55–69.

140. Wallace, "Majority Text Theory," 307–15.

141. Donald L. Brake, "The Preservation of the Scriptures," in Fuller, *Counterfeit
or Genuine*, 181–84.

142. Pickering, *Identity*, appendix A, 143–44.

have been preserved longer than the Byzantine ones;[143] or, if one is a Textus Receptus advocate, this position does not endorse preservation of most of the Byzantine tradition itself (which has manuscripts that differ), or vice versa if one is a Byzantine advocate (note the differences between the Textus Receptus and other forms of the "traditional text" noted above).[144]

(2) The second ground of defense is a numerical argument that posits that the text of the New Testament should be the one found in the "majority" of manuscripts. It is true that the vast majority of the 5,813 today extant Greek New Testament manuscripts follow the Byzantine text—in fact, it may be as many as 95 percent.[145] However, as Wallace indicates, the Byzantine text has not always been in the majority. It is only in the majority cumulatively. There was no Byzantine text for the first four centuries, and it did not become the majority text until the ninth century.[146] Further, Wallace contends that the Byzantine text as found in the editions of Hodges and Farstad and of Pierpont and Robinson follows a Byzantine form not found in the majority of manuscripts until the fifteenth century.[147] Besides all of this, there is no inherently logical reason to believe that the majority of manuscripts contain the original or earlier reading, especially when that text-type does not appear until the fourth century.

(3) The third line of defense is that advocates for the traditional text often discount internal evidence—hence their appeal to external evidence, and its numerical value—arguing that the internal reasons are subjective compared to the objective evidence of countable manuscripts. Despite necessarily arguing that the other text-types are corrupt and thus should have their readings dismissed, advocates of the Majority or Byzantine text are still confronted with the problem of needing to use internal criteria to adjudicate between readings in their own manuscripts. For example, for Romans 5:1 Byzantine

143. Carson, *King James Version Debate*, 56.

144. For further discussion, see Carson, *King James Version Debate*, 68–74; Wallace, "Majority Text Theory," 308–10.

145. Carson, *King James Version Debate*, 50. Wallace ("Majority Text Theory," 311) thinks 80 percent. In any case, it is the vast majority.

146. Wallace, "Majority Text Theory," 311.

147. Ibid., 312n78. Wallace cites statistics from Hermann von Soden showing that the particular form of Byzantine text that he contends is the basis of these editions was in the minority until the fifteenth century.

manuscripts can be found for the *omicron* in ἔχομεν or the *omega* in ἔχωμεν.[148] The pericope of the woman caught in adultery—one of the hallmark passages for advocates of the traditional text—has sufficiently diverse witnesses to require special treatment in most discussions, including the printed editions.[149]

There have been essentially no new arguments advanced since Westcott and Hort for the traditional-text hypothesis, and the reasons advanced clearly remain unconvincing.[150]

■ THE THREE TEXT-TYPES

In the previous discussion I have often referred to various text-types. Throughout the development of modern textual criticism there have been different ways of examining and categorizing manuscripts, as well as there being different ways in which they are used in textual criticism. In fact, the field of textual criticism today is in somewhat of a state of flux, as the methods of categorizing and using manuscripts are undergoing serious reevaluation. This is not the place to recount the history of this discussion, or necessarily to adjudicate the current state of play. For the sake of this volume, I will merely recount quickly some of the major theories regarding manuscripts and their relationships, before outlining the theory of text-types that I am following here. Parker provides a brief and succinct, though not always altogether clear, exposition of the major theories.[151]

148. Robinson and Pierpont print the form with the *omega* in the margin, with angle brackets around the form in the text with the *omicron*. As they explain, "Where the manuscripts comprising the Byzantine Textform are significantly divided, superior angle brackets . . . mark the affected word or words in the main text. The alternate Byzantine readings are displayed in the side margin" (*New Testament in the Original Greek*, xviii).

149. Robinson and Pierpont (*New Testament in the Original Greek*, xi) say that von Soden detected seven distinct lines of transmission in this section—and that he may have "underestimated the complexity of its transmissional lines."

150. J. H. Petzer, "The History of the New Testament—Its Reconstruction, Significance and Use in New Testament Textual Criticism," in Aland and Delobel, *New Testament Textual Criticism*, 17.

151. D. C. Parker, *An Introduction to the New Testament Manuscripts and Their Texts* (Cambridge: Cambridge University Press, 2008), 159–79. I use Parker as the basis of the summary that follows, supplemented with Comfort, *Encountering the Manuscripts*, 289–320; Metzger, *Text*, 156–85 (4th ed., 205–49), updated by Ehrman to include developments up to the time of writing, including the International Greek New Testament Project and the Editio Critica Maior of the Institut für neutestamentliche

Besides the Majority text theory, which I have already discussed above, there are at least four other major theories of manuscript categorization worth discussing. First, some have used theories of local origin. B. H. Streeter (1874–1937), the English biblical scholar and philosopher, is known for his work on developing the theory of local origins of manuscripts, based upon his study of the Gospels.[152] Most scholars today, while perhaps recognizing general geographical origins or relationships among manuscripts, are skeptical that these can be used to identify textual types. This is because there are inconsistencies among manuscripts, even those that are from the same purported geographical location, to say nothing of the difficulty, if not sometimes impossibility, of establishing geographical origins. The result is often a circular argument by which the place is assumed on the basis of a manuscript's text-critical character.

Second, others have identified archetypal or genealogical relationships among manuscripts, sometimes called a "stemmatic" approach. In stemmatics, attributed to Lachmann, the origin of a variant is described on the basis of a stemmatic relationship among the extant manuscripts, while also accounting for missing manuscripts. Kurt Aland combined these two approaches in his local-genealogical approach, which is also a form of reasoned eclecticism (as are all of the approaches discussed here).[153] However, whereas this kind of genealogical relationship is still used in other types of textual criticism, such as classical studies,[154] and is to a large extent being revived in the coherence-based genealogical method (CBGM) that originated at the Alands' Institut für neutestamentliche Textforschung, the huge number of New Testament manuscripts (and the reliance upon being able to process all of this information), as well as the missing stages in the tradition at key places (hence reliance on Byzantine manuscripts), make this impractical for the time being.

---

Textforschung in Münster (but not, apparently, mentioning the coherence-based genealogical method).

152. Burnett Hillman Streeter, *The Four Gospels: A Study of Origins, Treating of the Manuscript Tradition, Sources, Authorship, and Dates* (London: Macmillan, 1924), 26–148.

153. Aland and Aland, *Text of the New Testament*, 34–35. See Holmes, "Reasoned Eclecticism," 337.

154. See Martin L. West, *Textual Criticism and Editorial Technique Applicable to Greek and Latin Texts* (Stuttgart: Teubner, 1973).

Third, a number of quantitative methods have been developed. The
New Testament scholar and textual critic Colwell developed what has
come to be known as the Claremont Profile Method.[155] Manuscripts
are compared in terms of their variants and then categorized on the
basis of the percentage of agreement that they have among themselves.
With increased technological resources, this method may prove more
effective in the future, although it does a better job of profiling manuscripts than it does of adjudicating individual variants.

Fourth, the newest development in text-critical analysis is the CBGM.
According to this method, the textual critic attempts what are called
"substemmata" on the basis of individual variants, and from the results of these individual variants a description of the relations among
the manuscripts becomes possible. This approach is being used in the
production of the latest major text-critical project of the Institut für
neutestamentliche Textforschung, the Editio Critica Maior. There are
some limitations to this approach, not least of which is the difficulty of
utilizing it on an individual basis without the kinds of resources available to the Institut when wanting to evaluate a particular variant—not
to mention that it has produced minimal results so far in application
to the Catholic Epistles in the Editio Critica Maior. There is also the
difficulty with what is meant by "coherence." Parker contends that "it
is not wedded to a preconceived method" of analysis, whether the use
of manuscripts (external criteria) or possible scribal issues (internal
criteria).[156] However, there are the questions of how one uses these criteria, what is meant by "coherence" (is it merely statistical?), whether all
variants should be treated as equal, whether variants should be treated
in isolation from their manuscripts, and what role the individual textual
critic plays in the process. As a result of these recent developments,
some textual critics, of whom Parker is one of several, have called for
the abandonment of the traditional text-types.[157] They see problems
regarding the length of time over which they were created, the different
criteria by which they are grouped together and identified as a text-type,
and the lack of cohesion among the individual manuscripts.[158]

---

155. For bibliography, see Parker, *New Testament Manuscripts*, 164.
156. Ibid., 169.
157. See Mink, "Contamination," 148–49n16.
158. Parker, *New Testament Manuscripts*, 171. Parker uses the term "coherence"
to describe the lack among Western manuscripts. I prefer the term "cohesion." I think

Although many would now dispute the use of text-types as a means of classifying manuscripts, the fact that they still appear to form the underlying basis for much of the previous discussion of textual criticism, I believe, makes them relevant, especially for my discussion here. Nevertheless, I can only offer a brief synopsis of the origin and development of the Greek New Testament textual tradition. Many, if not most, scholars today would still recognize three text-types: the Alexandrian, the Western, and the Byzantine.[159] I will treat them in reverse order, along with the Caesarean.

- ■ *BYZANTINE*

The Byzantine text-type has already been discussed in relation to the traditional text. The Byzantine text-type emerges as a distinct text-type only in the fourth century. After the fall of Rome in AD 380, the center of gravity of the Roman Empire shifted to the east, where Greek remained the language of communication and there was a need for manuscripts in Greek, a situation that continued until the fall of Constantinople to the Turks in AD 1453.[160] Westcott and Hort proposed that Lucian of Antioch (d. AD 312) was responsible for the recension that we now know as the Byzantine text by combining readings from earlier text-types.[161] Although few have held to this theory, it has recently been revived as a means of accounting for earlier readings in the Byzantine text-type that do not require the existence

---

that this perhaps reveals one of the problems with the CBGM. The issue is perhaps not coherence, which indicates the cognitive process of appropriation, so much as cohesion, the textual indices that create a text and hold it together.

159. See esp. Metzger, *Text*, 211–19 (4th ed., 305–15). See also Eldon Jay Epp, "The Significance of the Papyri for Determining the Nature of the New Testament Text in the Second Century: A Dynamic View of Textual Transmission," in *Gospel Traditions in the Second Century: Origins, Recensions, Text, and Transmission*, ed. William L. Petersen (Notre Dame, IN: University of Notre Dame Press, 1989), 71–103 (repr. in Epp and Fee, *Theory and Method*, 274–97); "The Papyrus Manuscripts of the New Testament," in Ehrman and Holmes, *Text of the New Testament*, 3–21. Both of these articles are reprinted in Epp, *Perspectives* (345–82, 411–36), with his proposal on four major textual clusters, where Epp (381) reaffirms his list, even if the contents are provisional. I think that Comfort's documentary approach supports this position, including his endorsement of not simply text-types but early and diverse types in support of a variant. See Comfort, *Encountering the Manuscripts*, 302–6, 309–20.

160. Carson, *King James Version Debate*, 50.

161. Westcott and Hort, *New Testament in the Original Greek*, 2:138.

of an independent text-type.[162] The great preacher and writer John Chrysostom arrived in Constantinople from Antioch in AD 398 and brought with him the form of the New Testament text used in Antioch that we would now identify as the Byzantine text-type. Largely through his influence, the Byzantine text-type began to gain widespread currency in the Byzantine Empire. Increased institutionalization of religion in the empire, including the copying and preservation of manuscripts, led to less freedom and more rigidity in the Byzantine textual tradition.[163] Rather than there being more diffuse readings with increased copying, as we find in the Alexandrian tradition, the Byzantine text-type tends toward homogenization.[164]

▪ CAESAREAN

The fortunes of the Caesarean text have been mixed, just as it is posited as a mixed text combining Western and Alexandrian textual readings. Streeter was the first to identify the Caesarean text as one that Origen had used at Caesarea. Streeter's theory of local texts, noted above, identified five different text-types, each in a physical location, of which this was one.[165] The manuscripts often put in this type include Mark's Gospel in 𝔓[45] and Codex Washington (032 W), Codex Koridethi (038 Θ), and Families 1 and 13.[166] Others have modified this theory by, for example, finding its origins in Egypt. Larry Hurtado, however, has shown that the Caesarean text at best is a secondary (or derived) and not a primary text-type,[167] and so most textual critics no longer recognize it and do not treat it as one of the three major or distinct text-types.

162. Petzer, "History," 17.

163. Gordon D. Fee, "Modern Textual Criticism and the Revival of the *Textus Receptus*," *JETS* 21 (1978): 19–33, summarized in Carson, *King James Version Debate*, 51.

164. T. J. Ralston, "The 'Majority Text' and Byzantine Origins," *NTS* 38 (1992): 133–34.

165. Streeter, *Four Gospels*, 26–148. The text-types are located in Alexandria, Caesarea, Antioch, Italy-Gaul, and Africa. See his chart on 26.

166. These families include a number of similar manuscripts in each group. They are minuscule texts. Minuscule texts, which are not referred to as often in this volume, date from about the ninth century and later. Erasmus used minuscule manuscripts in preparing his Greek New Testament, as noted above. See also chapter 2.

167. Larry W. Hurtado, *Text-Critical Methodology and the Pre-Caesarean Text: Codex W in the Gospel of Mark*, SD 43 (Grand Rapids: Eerdmans, 1981), 85–89.

■ *ALEXANDRIAN AND WESTERN*

Many, if not most, textual critics today (see the discussion above) believe that there were two major early text-types that can be ascertained, the Alexandrian and the Western. A number of scholars see the Alexandrian and Western text-types as being equally early, with both having their origins in the second century.[168] What we now call the Alexandrian text-type is Westcott and Hort's Neutral text, consisting of Codex Vaticanus (03 B) and Codex Sinaiticus (01 א), plus their Alexandrian text. This text-type is also represented by a number of early papyri, such as 𝔓[66] and 𝔓[75]. The Western text has some early papyri, most of them fragmentary, and Codex Bezae (05 D), as well as the Old Latin and Old Syriac versions, which date possibly to the end of the second century.

Those who have argued since the time of Westcott and Hort that the Western text-type is at least as ancient as the Alexandrian base this position primarily on evidence related to the book of Acts, where we have two versions of Acts to compare. Some scholars, such as the classical philologist Friedrich Blass (1843–1907) and others since his time, argue that the Western text of Acts was written before the Alexandrian text, as it is supposedly more Lukan in style.[169] In response, questions have been raised about such a stylistic method of analysis. Instead, many textual critics see the Western text as derived from the Alexandrian, which accounts for the diffuseness of the evidence of the Western text in a number of different and inconsistent manuscripts. There are also a number of other features of the Western text that appear to be late, including theological additions,[170] harmonization, and paraphrase.[171] I have examined the early Greek papyri and parchments that are claimed to attest to the Western text of Acts. I studied nine

168. See Epp, "Issues," 38, 41.

169. Friedrich Blass, *Acta apostolorum sive Lucae ad Theophilum liber alter* (Göttingen: Vandenhoeck & Ruprecht, 1895), 24–32; *Philology of the Gospels* (London: Macmillan, 1898), 96–137; M.-E. Boismard and A. Lamouille, *Le texte occidental des Actes des Apôtres: Reconstitution et réhabilitation*, Synthèse 17 (Paris: Recherche sur les Civilisations, 1984), 1:ix.

170. Peter M. Head, "Acts and the Problem of Its Texts," in *The Book of Acts in Its First Century Setting*, vol. 1, *Ancient Literary Setting*, ed. Bruce W. Winter and Andrew D. Clarke (Grand Rapids: Eerdmans, 1993), 415–44, esp. 428–44. Head notes the tendency to expand christological titles.

171. Petzer, "History," 18–25.

such manuscripts for what have been identified as distinctly Western readings. I found that in the nine manuscripts there are textual variants, as one might expect. However, where a given manuscript does not agree with both Codex Sinaiticus (01 ℵ) and Codex Vaticanus (03 B), it is not unusual to find the manuscript agreeing with one of them. There are variants in these manuscripts that appear in Codex Bezae (05 D), but in some instances in Sinaiticus (01 ℵ) and/or Vaticanus (03 B) as well. An even smaller number of variants can be characterized as distinctly Western, and these are confined to only two of the nine manuscripts, $\mathfrak{P}^{38}$ (AD 300) and $\mathfrak{P}^{48}$ (late third century), the latter of which appears to be mixed. I conclude from this that the so-called Western text-type was a definably later development when compared to the Alexandrian text-type, and it tends to draw upon a number of variants out of a wider number that came to be identified with this tradition.[172]

The Alexandrian text-type was identified by Westcott and Hort as the earliest, on the basis of both external evidence of age and internal evidence regarding readings.[173] Previous scholarship has suggested a number of different possible recensions of the Alexandrian tradition. They range from a gradual process of recension in the second and third centuries, or a recension by Origen in the early third century, to a recension by Hesychius in the early fourth century.[174] However,

---

172. Stanley E. Porter, "Developments in the Text of Acts before the Major Codices," in *The Book of Acts as Church History: Text, Textual Traditions and Ancient Interpretations* [= *Apostelgeschichte als Kirchengeschichte: Text, Texttraditionen und antike Auslegungen*], ed. Tobias Nicklas and Michael Tilly, BZNW 120 (Berlin: de Gruyter, 2003), 65–66. For similar conclusions, see Joël Delobel, "The Nature of 'Western' Readings in Acts: Test-Cases," in *Recent Developments in Textual Criticism: New Testament, Other Early Christian and Jewish Literature; Papers Read at a Noster Conference in Münster, January 4–6, 2001*, ed. Wim Weren and Dietrich-Alex Koch, STR 8 (Assen: Van Gorcum, 2003), 69–94; Christopher Tuckett, "The Early Text of Acts," in *The Early Text of the New Testament*, ed. Charles E. Hill and Michael J. Kruger (Oxford: Oxford University Press, 2012), 157–74, though with some (unnecessary?) trepidation.

173. Bart D. Ehrman, "The Cup, the Bread, and the Salvific Effect of Jesus' Death in Luke-Acts," in *Society of Biblical Literature 1991 Seminar Papers*, ed. Eugene H. Lovering Jr. (Atlanta: Scholars Press, 1991), 578n6; Silva, "Response," 144.

174. See Gordon D. Fee, "$\mathfrak{P}^{66}$, $\mathfrak{P}^{75}$ and Origen: The Myth of Early Textual Recension in Alexandria," in *New Dimensions in New Testament Study*, ed. Richard N. Longenecker and Merrill C. Tenney (Grand Rapids: Zondervan, 1974), 19–45, esp. 20–23; repr. in Epp and Fee, *Theory and Method*, 247–73, esp. 248–51.

with the discovery of the Greek papyri, especially the publication of $\mathfrak{P}^{75}$ in 1961 and the contrastive $\mathfrak{P}^{66}$ in 1958,[175] theories regarding the recensional nature of the Alexandrian text-type as a whole have been discounted.[176] $\mathfrak{P}^{75}$, although dated by the original editors from around AD 175 to 225,[177] is a carefully copied manuscript that is homogenous with Codex Vaticanus (03 B) and thus shows that the text found in Vaticanus was already in existence in the second century. $\mathfrak{P}^{66}$, dated originally to no later than the beginning of the third century AD (i.e., c. AD 200), but possibly to the mid-second century and probably AD 200 at the latest (the same for $\mathfrak{P}^{75}$),[178] however, shows sloppy recensional activity that changes and then corrects the text.[179] This points to the fact that, with $\mathfrak{P}^{66}$ as a recensional contrast, the text of $\mathfrak{P}^{75}$ and Codex Vaticanus (03 B) does not reflect recensional activity but reflects a stable tradition. Thus, the manuscript evidence, as found in the major majuscule codexes, and then confirmed by early papyri, points to the Alexandrian text-type as the earliest (and a very stable) textual witness. It is the Alexandrian text that has been the basis of virtually all major critical texts of the New Testament from Westcott and Hort to the present.

175. These papyri manuscripts, $\mathfrak{P}^{66}$ and $\mathfrak{P}^{75}$, were originally published in Victor Martin and Rodolphe Kasser, *Papyrus Bodmer XIV: Évangile de Luc, chap. 3–24* (Cologny-Geneva: Bibliotheca Bodmeriana, 1961); *Papyrus Bodmer XV: Évangile de Jean, chap. 1–15* (Cologny-Geneva: Bibliotheca Bodmeriana, 1961); Victor Martin, *Papyrus Bodmer II: Évangile de Jean, chap. 1–14* (Cologny-Geneva: Bibliotheca Bodmeriana, 1956); *Papyrus Bodmer II, supplément: Évangile de Jean, chap. 14–21* (Cologny-Geneva: Bibliotheca Bodmeriana, 1958); Victor Martin and J. W. B. Barns, *Papyrus Bodmer II, supplément: Évangile de Jean, chap. 14–21*, corrected ed. (Cologny-Geneva: Bibliotheca Bodmeriana, 1962).

176. Fee, "$\mathfrak{P}^{66}$, $\mathfrak{P}^{75}$ and Origen," 44.

177. Martin and Kasser, *Papyrus Bodmer XIV*, 13. For discussion of the range of dates of New Testament manuscripts, see Joseph van Haelst, *Catalogue des papyrus littéraires juifs et chrétiens*, SPap 1 (Paris: Sorbonne, 1976); Philip W. Comfort and David P. Barrett, *The Text of the Earliest New Testament Greek Manuscripts*, corrected ed. (Wheaton: Tyndale, 2001).

178. Martin, *Papyrus Bodmer II: Evangile de Jean, chap. 1–14*, 18. The use of ευαγγελιον κατα (*euangelion kata*, "Gospel according to") in both manuscripts points to second-century dates for these manuscripts, at least for the tradition if not the actual dating. On ascriptions, see Martin Hengel, *Studies in the Gospel of Mark*, trans. John Bowden (Philadelphia: Fortress, 1985), 65–72, where he cites not only the papyri mentioned above, but also $\mathfrak{P}^4$, $\mathfrak{P}^{64}$, $\mathfrak{P}^{67}$ (see chap. 2), the Old Latin (last quarter of the second century AD), and Coptic versions.

179. Fee, "$\mathfrak{P}^{66}$, $\mathfrak{P}^{75}$ and Origen," 31.

## Bart Ehrman and *Misquoting Jesus*

In light of the preceding discussion and the evidence presented, especially regarding the Byzantine text and its relationship to the Textus Receptus, I am surprised to read on the dust cover of Bart Ehrman's book *Misquoting Jesus* that he "reveals" the following: "The King James Bible was based on inferior manuscripts that in many cases do not accurately represent the meaning of the original text"; and "The favorite story of Jesus forgiving the woman caught in adultery (John 8:3–11 [*sic*]) does not belong in the Bible." I am surprised because, first of all, Ehrman "reveals" nothing that has not already been thoroughly discussed by scholars before him. Further, although the language is hyperbolic and could be construed as potentially inflammatory and misleading, all that the dust cover says that is true is already commonly known to most biblical scholars and those informed in textual criticism, especially those who accept the Alexandrian text as the oldest and arguably closest to the original. The Authorized Version was based upon inferior later manuscripts, and the story of the woman caught in adultery does not belong to the earliest form of the text. However, the statement is clearly misleading in that it neglects to note that perhaps more than 90 percent of the Greek text that lies behind the Authorized Version and our current Greek text is firmly established, and only by taking an extreme position can one say that it misrepresents the meaning of the original. Those who hold to the Byzantine text would, I believe, object to even more of what is said here, although they might admit that the Authorized Version was based upon inferior manuscripts when compared to the best manuscripts of the Byzantine tradition. This is not the only surprise, or serious disappointment, to be found on the cover of or, indeed, within this book.

Ehrman notes, as I already mentioned above, that John Mill examined around one hundred manuscripts and found thirty thousand variants. Now, Ehrman notes, with over 5,700 manuscripts, we have somewhere between two hundred thousand and four hundred thousand variants. Or, as Ehrman likes to say, we have more variants than words in the New Testament.[180] This sounds rather shocking; in fact,

---

180. Bart D. Ehrman, *Misquoting Jesus: The Story behind Who Changed the Bible and Why* (San Francisco: HarperSanFrancisco, 2005), 88–90. There are about 138,000 words in the Greek New Testament.

it is sensationally so. Mill had on average three hundred variants per manuscript. Is that a lot? Given that some of these are minor variants, others changes in word order, and others obvious slips of the pen, I think not. However, with roughly 5,800 manuscripts and, for the sake of argument, four hundred thousand variants (the largest number selected), this means only seventy variants per manuscript. With 5,800 manuscripts and two hundred thousand variants, that reflects only thirty-five variants per manuscript. So, in fact, the situation with variants is getting better with the discovery of new manuscripts, not worse. Ehrman should be applauding, rather than declaiming. Another way to look at these statistics is to recognize that, on a conservative estimate, 80 percent of the text is established (some say 90 percent or more), regardless of the textual variants present in the manuscripts. If textual variants are distributed equally throughout manuscripts—they may or may not be, but there is no other way to examine this, and some of them, such as spelling, transpositions, and accidental scribal errors, almost certainly will be—this means that, if there are four hundred thousand total variants, there are only eighty thousand in the part of the New Testament that is not established, or an average of only fourteen variants per manuscript in the disputed portion; or if there are only two hundred thousand total variants, only seven variants per manuscript in the disputed portion. This is manuscript production—remember, the copying of ancient manuscripts was done by hand—that nearly rivals that sometimes found today in modern print![181] Ehrman's comments, then, are a clear instance of unwarranted sensationalism. Of course, the way to treat variants is not simply to average them, but there is no need to sensationalize and exaggerate the situation so as to engage in fearmongering. After all, besides those mentioned above, many if not most of these variants will be unique variants, probably (on the basis of the distribution of dates of manuscripts, in which the vast majority are late) in later manuscripts, with little impact on the text; others will simply be the repeating of similar types of errors, again with little impact. This no

181. As an example, I have examined a scholarly book published by a well-known academic publisher. This volume has 745 "textual variants" (typographical and related mistakes) in 173 pages of print text, an average of 4.3 per page. Yet, I think that not one person has found even this extreme number of "variants" so many as to affect understanding of the text.

doubt accounts for why in his treatment of the subject Ehrman returns to the same relatively limited number of examples of textual variants. In *Misquoting Jesus* Ehrman's sensationalism, besides a few incidental examples, begins with the story of the woman caught in adultery (John 7:53–8:11) and the ending of Mark's Gospel (Mark 16:9–20), two of the best-known and most widely discussed passages where the Textus Receptus and the Majority or Byzantine text differ from the Alexandrian text from Westcott and Hort to the present.[182] The "traditional text" includes these two passages, whereas the Alexandrian text in its earliest attested forms, including Codex Sinaiticus (01 ℵ) and Codex Vaticanus (03 B), omits them (and for the woman caught in adultery $\mathfrak{P}^{66}$ and $\mathfrak{P}^{75}$). There is no surprise here to anyone who has any knowledge of textual matters, although Ehrman does not treat the development of the text of Erasmus (the so-called Textus Receptus) until a subsequent chapter. What is surprising is Ehrman's conclusion: "The passages discussed above represent just two out of thousands of places in which the manuscripts of the New Testament came to be changed by scribes."[183] Ehrman is misleading on at least two fronts. First, he makes it seem as if many, if not most, of the textual variants are ten to fourteen verses in length, as these two passages are, when he knows better. In fact, most of the others that he discusses in the book are a word or a phrase in length. This latter length is by far more representative. Second, Ehrman gives the possible impression that the scribes, in changing the text, deleted two valuable early passages, when quite the contrary is true. Later scribes, for whatever motives, added later material, but material that on the best textual grounds was never originally there in the first place.

182. See Craig A. Evans, "Textual Criticism and Textual Confidence: How Reliable Is Scripture?" in Stewart, *Reliability of the New Testament*, 161–72, citing these two common examples (162–63). I must disagree, however, with his conclusions regarding Rom. 5:1 (the subjunctive should be read, not the indicative) and 1 Cor. 14:33b–36 (the verses should be retained) (164–66), where I think that he accepts a traditional reading of the passages and does not follow the clear manuscript evidence. See Stanley E. Porter, "The Argument of Romans 5: Can a Rhetorical Question Make a Difference?" *JBL* 110 (1991): 655–77, esp. 661–65; repr. and revised in Stanley E. Porter, *Studies in the Greek New Testament: Theory and Practice*, SBG 6 (New York: Peter Lang, 1996), 213–38; "Reframing Social Justice in the Pauline Letters," in *The Bible and Social Justice*, ed. Cynthia Long Westfall and Bryan Dyer (Eugene, OR: Wipf & Stock, forthcoming).
183. Ehrman, *Misquoting Jesus*, 68.

An examination of several of these other shorter examples, however, shows that Ehrman is on thin ice to claim that there is radical and gratuitous change of the text of the New Testament. I will not treat accidental errors, because to know that it is an accident assumes that we know what it is not to have the accident. In other words, where such occurs, the original is easily discernible. I will also not treat intentional changes where it is clear why the change was made—for historical, theological, or factual reasons—but where the original or unchanged text is easily restored, or where the Byzantine tradition is the only one that supports it.[184] I am more concerned with claims of radical changes that have been incorporated into the text, with the idea that they undermine our confidence in the text that we have. I am not claiming that we have the original text of the Greek New Testament; I am claiming that there is far less evidence of later changes that have been integrated into our text so as to shatter our confidence in the text.

The first example is Mark 1:41, where there is a variant between a word translated "having compassion" (σπλαγχνισθείς, *splanchnistheis*) and one translated "becoming angry" (ὀργισθείς, *orgistheis*). Mark says that Jesus was either "having compassion" or "becoming angry" with the man who had leprosy. Ehrman contends that the reading "becoming angry," found in both Greek and Latin manuscripts, goes back to the second century.[185] The reading "becoming angry" is found in Codex Bezae (05 D), which dates to the fifth century; the Old Latin manuscript designated "a," which dates to the fourth century; the Latin manuscript "ff2," which dates to the fifth century; and the seventh-century Latin manuscript "r1." First, I do not see any more than one Greek manuscript listed, and it is bilingual with Latin (Codex Bezae [05 D]). Second, I see nothing earlier than the fourth century. I think that Ehrman is saying that the Western tradition, which these manuscripts represent, has been thought by some scholars to go back to the second century. However, that position is questionable, as

---

184. For example, Luke 22:43–44, treated in Ehrman, *Misquoting Jesus*, 139–44. Ehrman first treated this passage in Bart D. Ehrman and Mark A. Plunkett, "The Angel and the Agony: The Textual Problem of Luke 22:43–44," *CBQ* 45 (1983): 401–16; then in *Orthodox Corruption*, 187–94 (updated ed., 220–27). See also 1 Tim. 3:16, discussed below, where there may be anti-adoptionist readings introduced much later by especially correcting hands, treated in Ehrman, *Orthodox Corruption*, 77–78 (updated ed., 91–92); *Misquoting Jesus*, 157–58.

185. Ehrman, *Misquoting Jesus*, 134.

we have seen above, with the textual evidence itself for the Western tradition going back only to the fourth century. The evidence for the reading "having compassion" is found in the Alexandrian tradition (including Codexes Sinaiticus [01 א] and Vaticanus [03 B]) and the Byzantine tradition, along with the Syriac versions (which probably go back to the fourth century at the earliest). So the external evidence indicates "having compassion." In regard to the internal evidence of what likely occurred, logically it makes more sense for a scribe to change from "becoming angry" to "having compassion" than the other way around, as that softens Jesus's response. This, however, does not explain why in Mark 1:43, when it says that Jesus was stern with the man and threw him out, there are no textual variants. In this case, even if we were to concede that either reading is possible (compassion or anger), neither one would introduce a problematic idea, since Mark uses similar strong language in the rest of the account. This is hardly a knock-down-drag-'em-out argument by Ehrman.

Another attempt by Ehrman is made at Hebrews 2:9, with the variants of "by the grace of God" and "apart from God." The verse says, "We do see Jesus, who was made lower than the angels for a little while, now crowned with glory and honor because he suffered death, so that by the grace of God he might taste death for everyone" (TNIV). Ehrman acknowledges that the manuscript evidence for "apart from God" is late, being confined to two tenth-century manuscripts (0243 and 1739); however, the reading is known by the church fathers Origen, Ambrose, and Jerome, as well as Latin Vulgate manuscripts.[186] Ehrman acknowledges that virtually all the other manuscripts have "by the grace of God," but he fails to mention that this includes not only the early codexes, but also $\mathfrak{P}^{46}$, a papyrus dated to around AD 200.[187] Minuscule 1739, Ehrman notes, was produced from a copy that he says was as early as any of our earliest texts. What he does not note is this: "The prescript to the Pauline Epistles [of 1739] shows that its archetype was copied (probably c. 400 at Caesarea) from a very ancient MS, but the marginal notes indicate that the writer of the archetype also had access to Origen's commentaries on Romans

---

186. Ibid., 145; cf. Ehrman, *Orthodox Corruption*, 146–50 (updated ed., 171–76).
187. If not earlier (I will discuss this in the next chapter). Some have dated it to the late first century, although this is not widely accepted by scholars. See Comfort and Barrett, *Text*, 204–7.

and other Epistles. . . . Zuntz finds close links between the archetype of 1739 and $\mathfrak{P}^{46}$ and B."[188] Thus, 1739 is at least two transcriptional generations removed from the earliest manuscripts. Instead of 1739 having the original reading, it appears that when 1739 was copied or its direct archetype was copied, a variant reading from Origen was introduced rather than including the Alexandrian reading.[189] Again, however, one must raise the question of whether either reading actually introduces an insuperable difficulty into the text, in light of passages such as Mark 15:34 and parallels.

Ehrman cites John 1:18 as an example of an anti-adoptionist change, where the later (and orthodox) "unique God" was inserted for the original "unique son" ("one and only Son" below). The verse says, "No one has ever seen God, but the one and only Son, who is himself God and is in closest relationship with the Father, has made him known" (TNIV). Ehrman notes that the Alexandrian witnesses almost exclusively have "unique God," but he questions what this means and believes that "unique son," found in most of the other manuscripts, is probably authentic.[190] Ehrman may be correct, although "unique God" is found in $\mathfrak{P}^{66}$, $\mathfrak{P}^{75}$, Codex Sinaiticus (01 $\aleph$), Codex Vaticanus (03 B), the original hand of Codex Ephraemi Rescriptus (04 C), some church fathers (e.g., Clement and Origen, but they have other readings as well), and the Coptic and Syriac versions.[191]

188. F. G. Kenyon, *The Text of the Greek Bible*, rev. A. W. Adams, 3rd ed., ST (London: Duckworth, 1975), 109. See Günther Zuntz, *The Text of the Epistles: A Disquisition upon the Corpus Paulinum* (London: Oxford University Press, for the British Academy, 1953), 68–84.

189. That this position is probable is confirmed by examination of the variant reading of "God" (ΘC) for "who" (OC) in 1 Tim. 3:16, where various correcting hands of Codexes Sinaiticus (01 $\aleph$), Alexandrinus (02 A), Ephraemi Rescriptus (04 C), and Bezae (05 D) are followed by 1739 with "God," whereas the original hands of these codexes have "who." The word for "God" was often written in this form, called a *nomen sacrum* (sacred name), discussed earlier in this chapter. The only difference between this and the relative pronoun "who" is the first of two letters, both of which are formed very similarly, the difference being the horizontal crossbar in the Greek letter *theta*.

190. Ehrman, *Misquoting Jesus*, 161–62; cf. Ehrman, *Orthodox Corruption*, 78–82 (updated ed., 92–96).

191. See Metzger, *Text*, 169–70 (4th ed., 214–15). NA[27] cites Codex Sinaiticus (01 $\aleph$) as reading "God" in the first correcting hand. Tischendorf (*Novum Testamentum Graece*, ad loc.) gives no indication of this in his justly famous eighth edition, and there is none in his facsimile edition, the photographs by Helen Lake and Kirsopp Lake, or the recent photographic reproduction (see chap. 2).

There is also the possibility that the scribe mistook the *nomen sacrum* YC ("son"), used earlier, for ΘC ("God").[192] Nevertheless, even if Ehrman has accounted for the change, the variant should not cause great theological consternation. The reading "unique son" is found in the Byzantine tradition, including the Textus Receptus, and up to and including Tischendorf's eighth edition. Westcott and Hort read "unique God," and texts seem to have followed that since.

In treating Luke 22:17–20, Ehrman notes that "in one of our oldest Greek manuscripts, as well as in several Latin witnesses,"[193] the text reads only Luke 22:17–19a. He contends that there is the addition of the words normally found in this passage in most of the other witnesses (i.e., vv. 19b–20). The "one" manuscript that Ehrman cites is Codex Bezae (05 D), from the fifth century, and the Latin witnesses are some of the same ones cited above, including Latin manuscripts "a" from the fourth century, "d" from the fifth century, "ff2" from the fifth century, "I" from the fifth century, and "l" from the eighth century. The longer reading of vv. 17–20 is found in virtually all other Greek manuscripts, including 𝔓[75], most of the ancient versions, and the church fathers.[194] (There are also some variants in the ordering of the elements of the shorter and longer readings.) There are a number of internal arguments that are used for either of the readings. In defense of the shorter reading as authentic, Ehrman sees no reason why the words, if original, would have been omitted, plus they introduce theological ideas not to be found in Luke elsewhere regarding Jesus's death being a salvation from sin for those partaking.[195] Ehrman also finds reasons for questioning the words on the basis of the ordering of the cup (v. 17), the bread (v. 19), and then the cup again (v. 20) to be theologically confusing.[196] However, appeal to the shorter reading as the preferred one is unconvincing in the light of recent studies of textual tendencies;[197] and the observa-

---

192. See Tischendorf, *Novum Testamentum Graece*, ad loc.; see also the comment by Allen Wikgren in Metzger, *Textual Commentary*, 170. The difference in the *nomen sacrum* is the first letter only.

193. Ehrman, *Misquoting Jesus*, 165; cf. Ehrman, *Orthodox Corruption*, 197–209 (updated ed., 231–45).

194. Metzger, *Textual Commentary*, 148.

195. Ehrman, *Misquoting Jesus*, 166.

196. Compare Metzger, *Textual Commentary*, 149. There are also less compelling reasons given.

197. See discussion of the work of Royse and others on pp. 26–27.

tion that Luke's longer version follows Paul's words in 1 Corinthians 11:24b–25, rather than being an argument against inclusion, may be a compelling reason for vv. 19–20 being authentic, as it leaves intact the apparently more difficult reading (even if this longer passage does not follow Luke's theology). In any case, it is not certain that the longer version represents a later addition in the light of this evidence.

Ehrman, despite the bravado that accompanies his text, provides less-than-compelling arguments that the New Testament in fact misquotes Jesus, or any other text, in a way that presents destabilizing textual difficulties.

### Eclectic or Single Manuscript?

In light of the use of the Alexandrian text-type as the basis of our modern printed Greek New Testaments, some scholars have come to argue that we now have, if not quite the original Greek text, at least one that is very close to it.[198] For example, Aland and Aland refer in their introduction to several categories of texts. One is "the ancient text, presumably the original text. As a working hypothesis this is the text of Nestle-Aland[26]."[199] A statement such as this requires further examination.

The text of NA[25], by the Alands' own estimate, is different only in 700 places from the original edition of Nestle's text of 1898, and different from Westcott and Hort's edition only in 558 places.[200] The supposedly more radical NA[26] (the twenty-seventh edition is the same textual edition) has been changed only in 176 places, but it rejects 980 possible places where the earliest papyri have another reading, including rejecting readings from $\mathfrak{P}^{45}$, $\mathfrak{P}^{46}$, and $\mathfrak{P}^{66}$.[201] As a result, Robinson has estimated that the current Nestle-Aland edition is 99.5 percent the same as Westcott and Hort's edition.[202]

---

198. Kurt Aland, "Der neue 'Standard-Text' in seinem Verhältnis zu den frühen Papyri und Majuskeln," in *New Testament Textual Criticism: Its Significance for Exegesis; Essays in Honour of Bruce M. Metzger*, ed. Eldon J. Epp and Gordon D. Fee (Oxford: Clarendon, 1981), 257–75, esp. 274–75.

199. Aland and Aland, *Text of the New Testament*, 333; cf. 24, 335.

200. Ibid., 20, 26.

201. Comfort, *Quest for the Original Text*, 123, 125.

202. Robinson, "Appendix," 551.

There are three major considerations to weigh here. The first is the minimal role that the papyri have played in the development of the modern critical Greek New Testament. At the time that Tischendorf published his eighth edition in 1869–1872, and Westcott and Hort published their New Testament in 1881, there was only one Greek New Testament papyrus known and published, and it only in part.[203] Nestle used Tischendorf, Westcott and Hort, along with Weymouth, and then Weiss. Weymouth was also a compilation text of previous editions. By the time Weiss published his edition in 1900, only about seven papyri had been published. To date, 127 papyri numbers have been assigned, but 41 of these after NA[26]; however, at least 20 of these 127 numbers probably should be excluded because the papyrus is not a continuous text of the New Testament (and instead is a lectionary, talisman, commentary, or the like) or duplicates another number. Of those 107 or so remaining, as many as 63 were inscribed before the copying of the major codexes (although as many as seven of these may not qualify as continuous text manuscripts). However, even if all of the possible papyri had been taken into account, there is some question of how that would have influenced the resulting text, as the papyri tend to be highly fragmentary (there are only a few relatively complete New Testament books) and do not so much represent a text as support readings and push back in time readings found in the major codexes.[204] As a result, according to Petersen, there is no single place indicated in the critical apparatus for the Gospels in the NA[27]/UBS[4] text where a textual reading is supported on the basis of papyri or papyri and patristic evidence alone.[205]

203. This was published by Tischendorf in 1862 (*Verhandlungen der 25. Versammlung der deutschen Philologen und Schulmänner in Halle* [Leipzig, 1868]). It consisted of five fragments of 1 Corinthians with 1:17–20; 6:13–15, 16–18; 7:3–4, 10–11, 12–14 (see Gregory, *Prolegomena*, 434–35). It was completed by Kurt Aland ("Neue Neutestamentliche Papyri," *NTS* 3 [1956–1957]: 261–86, esp. 269–78, 286) with seventeen fragments. See Kurt Aland, "The Significance of the Papyri for Progress in New Testament Research," in *The Bible in Modern Scholarship: Papers Read at the 100th Meeting of the Society of Biblical Literature, December 28–30, 1964*, ed. James Philip Hyatt (London: Carey Kingsgate, 1966), 326.
204. Petersen, "What Text," 138–39.
205. Ibid., 138. Petersen notes five instances where the text is established on the basis of papyri and one majuscule codex. All others have more than one majuscule or minuscule.

The second consideration is that the major codexes are the basis of our eclectic critical texts, both in their origins as critical texts and so far as their further development indicates. As noted above, the basis of the Westcott and Hort critical text was their so-called Neutral text of Codex Vaticanus (03 B) and Codex Sinaiticus (01 ℵ). Nestle used Westcott and Hort's text along with Tischendorf's eighth edition, which was heavily influenced by his discovery and the publication of Codex Sinaiticus (01 ℵ) in 1862, an event that had occurred since his publication of his seventh edition in 1859. Thus, when Nestle made decisions by comparing editions, the two primary sources of information and the basis of his edition were the major codexes, in particular Codex Vaticanus (03 B) and Codex Sinaiticus (01 ℵ). The influence of the papyri since then has been negligible.

The third consideration is to reinforce that the major critical editions are eclectic texts, and therefore they do not conform to any extant ancient manuscript. Ever since Tischendorf, including Westcott and Hort, Nestle, and the rest, the resulting critical text is one formulated on the principles of reasoned or rational eclecticism.[206] This means that a range of both external and internal evidence is weighed, and text-critical decisions are made, with the result that no single early manuscript conforms to the reconstructed eclectic text. In that sense, the critical text of the New Testament today is only as old as nineteenth-century scholarship.

In light of this, I recommend that those seeking the original text of the New Testament consider seeking it through individual manuscripts. As I stated in an earlier publication, "I would suggest that we recognize what tacitly is the case and move away from an idealized eclectic text that never existed in any Christian community back to the codexes that still form the basis of our modern textual tradition. . . . These codexes represent the Bible of a given Christian community, and while they may not represent the text as it came penned from the author, this is probably as early as we can get while still preserving the integrity of the New Testament."[207] For the entire New Testa-

---

206. For the origins of the term, see Holmes, "Reasoned Eclecticism," 336–38.
207. Stanley E. Porter, "Why So Many Holes in the Papyrological Evidence for the Greek New Testament?" in *The Bible as Book: The Transmission of the Greek Text,*

ment in Greek, the earliest complete Greek New Testament is that of Codex Sinaiticus (01 א), since Codex Vaticanus (03 B) is lacking part of the book of Hebrews and beyond (which presumably included the Pastoral Epistles, Philemon, and Revelation). For individual books within the New Testament, one could use the individual books in Codex Sinaiticus (01 א), and those in Codex Vaticanus (03 B) for everything up to Hebrews. A few papyri manuscripts might possibly qualify.[208] These papyri perhaps would include 1 Corinthians, 2 Corinthians, Galatians, Ephesians, and Hebrews, except for up to six verses in each, missing at the bottoms of pages, in 𝔓[46] (Philippians, Colossians, and 1 Thessalonians are more fragmentary); and possibly 1 Peter, 2 Peter, and Jude in 𝔓[72].[209]

This proposal makes sense in several ways. If Westcott and Hort's edition is clearly based on the two major codexes, and the current text is 99.5 percent the same—that is, with all of the other evidence that has been brought to bear, including papyri and all else, only 0.5 percent different—it seems as if we are already in essence using the text of the two major codexes. If our goal is to seek the earliest text that we legitimately can find, without abandoning the claim to be seeking the original even if we know that we can only get back so far, then it makes sense to use the earliest actual texts that we can find. These manuscripts preserve texts that were actually used in the early church and, though not the originals, in some cases get back to actual texts that date to the early fourth century, if not earlier, such as AD 200 or earlier for 𝔓[46] and AD 300 for 𝔓[72]. These actual texts were written and used in the early church, and in reality they get closer to the original autographs in terms of quantifiable evidence than a text edited in the nineteenth, twentieth, and now twenty-first centuries.[210]

---

ed. Scot McKendrick and Orlaith A. O'Sullivan (London: British Library Publications and Oak Knoll Press, 2003), 176–77.

208. I am not necessarily endorsing their use, even in terms of the perspective I am advocating, but am noting that we come close to entire books in a few other manuscripts.

209. These papyri manuscripts are discussed in more detail in chapter 2.

210. A similar philosophy is behind the Brill Septuagint Commentary Series. Published by E. J. Brill of Leiden and edited by me, along with Richard Hess and John Jarick, this series uses an early codex manuscript for each book. Nine volumes have appeared so far, and more are in process.

## Conclusion

The goal of textual criticism—rightly, I believe—has traditionally focused upon establishing the original text as it came from the hand of the author. Some scholars have recently challenged this notion of an original text, either on the basis of the available evidence or on the basis of the methods used to recover such a text. Nevertheless, despite such challenges, the notion of an original text has withstood the variety of attacks of such scholars as Bart Ehrman and David Parker. Their objections and attempts to call the text of the New Testament into question have failed to provide substantive arguments of any kind of widespread, sustained, or early effort to detrimentally change or distort the text. In fact, their arguments often are based upon little substantive textual evidence at all. The best evidence of the early text of the New Testament comes from the Alexandrian text-type, although the Western tradition developed early as well. There are those who continue to advocate for the traditional text, whether the Textus Receptus or the Byzantine or Majority text. Despite the overwhelming similarity between the Byzantine or Majority text-type and the Alexandrian text-type, it appears that the Alexandrian is the earliest text-type and gets closer to the original autograph as published by the author. Nevertheless, there are limits to textual reconstruction, and perhaps it is time to reconsider the use of an eclectic text and restore the use of the earliest manuscripts that we have at our disposal.

# 2

# The Transmission of the New Testament

## Introduction

Imagine with me what the scene must have looked like the first time one of our books of the New Testament was committed to paper—by which I mean papyrus, the paper of the ancient world, which was made by pressing together the sliced stems of the papyrus reed.[1]

Perhaps this scene took place in a small room in Rome. Some people think that the apostle Peter, having made it to Rome on his lesser-known missionary endeavors, and nearing the end of his life, decided to leave a written record of his remembrances of being with Jesus the Christ. Tradition says that he recounted his remembrances to John Mark, who wrote them down and formed them into a Gospel, quite possibly our first Gospel (Eusebius, *Hist. eccl.* 2.15.1; 3.39.14–15). In this room is Peter, perhaps with some other Christians, and Mark is positioned at a bench with a papyrus scroll spread before him, or he is sitting, Egyptian style, crossed-legged with a scroll on his lap. He

---

1. On the writing materials and physical means of writing, see Bruce M. Metzger, *The Text of the New Testament: Its Transmission, Corruption, and Restoration*, 2nd ed. (New York: Oxford University Press, 1968; 4th ed., with Bart D. Ehrman, 2005), 3–19 and plate 1 (4th ed., 3–11); D. C. Parker, *Codex Sinaiticus: The Story of the World's Oldest Bible* (London: British Library; Peabody, MA: Hendrickson, 2010), 54–55.

sharpens a stick into a nib, dips it into a container of ink made from charcoal and other ingredients, and presses the nib to the papyrus. The fibers of the papyrus scroll, made up of a number of sheets, run lengthwise along the papyrus, and Mark begins to write carefully as Peter speaks.

Or perhaps another scene took place, not in a small room in Rome, but in a prison cell in Ephesus or Caesarea or Rome. The apostle Paul is determined to write another letter. A Christian with connections to the city in which the church is located has reported to Paul that there have been some recent problems. Some teachers from outside the community have come in, and a number of the Christians there are being lured away from the local gathering of believers. Paul's secretary, perhaps Tertius, is sitting on the floor in the Egyptian style, cross-legged with the open papyrus scroll on his lap. He takes the stick and dips it in ink as Paul begins to dictate. Or perhaps, knowing the importance of this letter and wanting to make sure that he can read it through and make some corrections before sending it, Tertius is writing the first draft of the letter onto a set of wax tablets. These stone or wooden tablets covered in wax allow Paul to go back and make changes before the letter is copied onto papyrus for actual sending or retaining as a record of the correspondence.

In another scene in another place, one of Paul's letters has arrived in a city, such as Colossae, and its carrier is eager to gather the local Christians together for a reading of the letter. They need to hurry because the Laodiceans have also received a letter, and Paul wants them to exchange the letters so that they can both benefit from these epistles. In order to be sure that they retain a copy after they have exchanged letters, one of the elders hastily enlists a literate member of the local group of Christians to grab some papyrus and write down the letter as it is read aloud. He finds sheets of papyrus that have already been gathered, folded, and bound into a codex or small book. As the letter carrier reads Paul's correspondence to them, the scribe furiously transcribes the letter, using a number of different standardized abbreviations so that he can keep up with the pace of the reading.[2]

---

2. He may have even used a form of shorthand, which had developed in scribal circles. On ancient shorthand, see H. J. M. Milne, *Greek Shorthand Manuals: Syllabary and Commentary* (London: Egypt Exploration Society, 1934). See also Carl Wessely, *Ein System altgriechischer Tachygraphie* (Vienna: Tempsky, 1895).

Moving forward a number of years, we enter what looks to be a scriptorium. This is a room where manuscripts are regularly copied, usually located in a monastery. There are two monks in a small room, and one is about to start reading from the biblical book that the scribes are working on. As they are ready, the reader begins to read slowly, giving the other scribe time to write out each word as he goes. In another place in the monastery is another monk. He is not writing down words that are being read out by another monk. Instead, he has his own papyrus book beside him on his desk, and he is copying this text into his own parchment book made of prepared dry skins. He carefully keeps one hand on the complete manuscript and then attempts to copy what he sees into the blank one. He is careful not to skip a line, or even a letter, as he moves his eyes back and forth between the two. When the monk taking dictation is done, the monk who did the reading comes down to check the work that the scribe has been doing. Similarly, the scribe who is working on his own manuscript carefully counts the number of rows, and letters in a row, so that he can check the work that he has been doing to ensure fidelity to the original.

All of these stages are very important in the transmission of the text of the New Testament. We cannot reconstruct the exact circumstances under which the original books of the New Testament were produced, but we do know something about how scribes copied and what they copied, giving us some idea of the process. Rather than go into detail about the physical characteristics of manuscripts, here I first will briefly discuss the types of materials on which manuscripts were copied. Next I will trace in reverse chronology the transmission of the texts of the New Testament, so far as that can be reconstructed from the evidence at hand, going back to the earliest evidence that we can recover. Then I will turn to the major types of manuscripts through which the text of the New Testament has been transmitted and conclude with a proposal regarding how such transmissional evidence should be used in establishing the text of the New Testament.

## The Manuscripts of the Greek New Testament

The various types of manuscripts that we have are often referred to in four basic categories, besides reference to the numerous early

versions or translations (which I will discuss in chap. 3). The four
types of manuscripts are referred to as papyri, majuscules (or uncials),
minuscules, and lectionaries.[3]

As widely used as these terms are, they are also highly problematic.
The first, "papyri" (singular, "papyrus"), refers to a material on which
manuscripts were written; the second, "majuscule" or "uncial," to
a type of handwriting consisting of large or capital-like letters; the
third, "minuscule," to a type of smaller cursive handwriting using
ligatures or linked letters; and the fourth, "lectionary," to a certain
usage for a manuscript whereby it was read, for example, in the church.
Needless to say, these categories are unsatisfactory. Virtually all of
the majuscules or uncials, minuscules, and most of the lectionaries
are written on parchment, with perhaps a few of the later ones on
other materials. So, by this reckoning, we have essentially two classes
of manuscripts: papyri and parchments. This is especially valuable to
note, as the handwriting of the vast majority of the papyri follows a
type of majuscule hand, in many cases very similar to that found in the
majuscules or uncials. Most, but not all, of the lectionaries, however,
are written in the minuscule cursive hand. With these categories, it
is difficult to differentiate the types of materials and means by which
the New Testament manuscripts were transmitted. In light of this
confusion, I will offer what I think is a clearer way to think of these
manuscripts in terms of writing material, handwriting, and usage.

The earliest New Testament manuscripts were written on papyrus,
a relatively cheap and abundant writing material.[4] Papyrus was made

3. These are discussed in all of the standard books on textual criticism. For
significant and fairly recent treatments, see Metzger, *Text*, 36–66 (4th ed., 52–94);
Kurt Aland and Barbara Aland, *The Text of the New Testament: An Introduction to
the Critical Editions and to the Theory and Practice of Modern Textual Criticism*,
trans. Erroll F. Rhodes, 2nd ed. (Grand Rapids: Eerdmans, 1989), 75–158; D. C. Parker,
*An Introduction to the New Testament Manuscripts and Their Texts* (Cambridge:
Cambridge University Press, 2008), 35–38.

4. New Testament studies distinguishes papyrus from other writing materials,
but the term "papyrus" in classical and papyrological studies is used of any ephemeral
writing surface (as opposed to inscriptions written on stone and other permanent
materials), such as papyrus, parchment, ostraca, wood, and the like. See Roger S.
Bagnall, *Reading Papyri, Writing Ancient History* (London: Routledge, 1995), 9–10.
François Bovon ("*Fragment Oxyrhynchus 840*, Fragment of a Lost Gospel, Witness
of an Early Christian Controversy over Purity," *JBL* 119 [2000]: 705–28, esp. 706) is
confused on this point when he questions P.Oxy. 840 being called "papyrus" (and given

from the plentiful papyrus reed that grew in the Mediterranean, especially in Egypt. It was prepared by slicing the reed and laying down adjacent strips of the stem, placing a corresponding set of sliced stems perpendicular atop the first set, and then pressing them together. The juices of the papyrus plant hold the strips together to form a surprisingly durable writing material. At first, papyrus sheets were bound together end to end into scrolls, and writing occurred on one side of the papyrus only. However, early on and for any number of possible reasons, Christians widely adopted the practice of writing on both sides of folded sheets of papyrus bound together. Sometimes the sheets were written on before being bound and other times afterwards. This process of gathering sheets was the basis of the codex or book.[5] The codex had many advantages over the scroll, including economies of space and cost due to writing on both sides of the papyrus sheet, and ease of handling and reference. We have several early Greek New Testament papyrus fragments that may have been parts of scrolls,[6] but the vast majority are written on both sides and were parts of codexes (or codices). This papyrus evidence indicates that the book form was adopted very early by Christians. A few scholars think that Paul wrote, or had his scribe write, his letters onto individual sheets to be bound into codexes. Most scholars, however, think that, at least at first, individual works were written on papyrus scrolls and then recopied onto sheets gathered into codexes, before several books—such as Paul's letters—were gathered together into one codex, when it became obvious that the codex form allowed greater content to be included in one document. The papyri were written in a form of capital letters early on, but they underwent changes as writing styles developed. As the Christian Scriptures were repeatedly copied and then became part of established Christianity

---

a papyrus number in the Oxyrhynchus collection) though it is written on parchment. The use of the terminology is entirely appropriate.

5. See C. H. Roberts, "Books in the Graeco-Roman World and in the New Testament," in *The Cambridge History of the Bible*, vol. 1, *From the Beginnings to Jerome*, ed. P. R. Ackroyd and C. F. Evans (Cambridge: Cambridge University Press, 1970), 48–66; Colin H. Roberts and T. C. Skeat, *The Birth of the Codex* (London: Oxford University Press, for the British Academy, 1983).

6. There are questions about four ($\mathfrak{P}^{12}$, $\mathfrak{P}^{13}$, $\mathfrak{P}^{18}$, $\mathfrak{P}^{43}$) of these five ($\mathfrak{P}^{2}$) papyri, however, as they have other texts on the reverse, though either not of the same New Testament book or not in the same hand. A manuscript containing a different text or written in a different hand on the back is called an "opisthograph."

during the time of Constantine and beyond, a more formalized or book hand began to be used, sometimes influenced by the Egyptian bilingual Greek and Coptic environment, often referred to as the Alexandrian hand. Papyrus continued to be used as a writing surface for Greek New Testament manuscripts at least up to the eighth century, when Arabic capture of Egypt made papyrus difficult to find. Thus far, 127 papyrus numbers have been assigned, although not all of these are separate manuscripts or manuscripts of continuously written New Testament text—a topic to which I will return below.

The next stage in the use of materials was the use of parchment.[7] Although parchment was invented much earlier, in the third century BC,[8] its widespread use for the writing of New Testament manuscripts seems to have begun to take place in the late second century.[9] We have several parchment manuscripts that date to the late third century, but the vast majority of the parchment manuscripts date to the fourth century and after. The parchment manuscripts were written in capital letters, probably better called "majuscules" than "uncials,"[10] and were produced from the late third century to the tenth or eleventh century. The great codex manuscripts were produced in forms of this capital hand on parchment. There are some who promote the importance of the papyrus manuscripts over the parchment manuscripts (often referred to as the papyri versus the codexes or majuscules).[11] However, contrary to the view of some, the difference in materials does not indicate superiority of the manuscript. What is important is the characteristics of the individual manuscript (text-type) and the age of

7. "Parchment" is a term used of any number of different types of animal skins used as a writing surface, including those from sheep, goats, cattle, and other animals (e.g., squirrel).

8. Legend says that parchment was invented at ancient Pergamum, whose name was given to the writing material, when the kingdom there was denied access to papyrus. See John McRay, *Archaeology and the New Testament* (Grand Rapids: Baker Academic, 1991), 352.

9. The Dead Sea Scrolls are written on tanned leather and were written earlier than the manuscripts of the Greek New Testament.

10. See D. C. Parker, "The Majuscule Manuscripts of the New Testament," in *The Text of the New Testament in Contemporary Research: Essays on the Status Quaestionis*, ed. Bart D. Ehrman and Michael W. Holmes, SD 46 (Grand Rapids: Eerdmans, 1995), 22–42, esp. 22.

11. See Philip W. Comfort, *The Quest for the Original Text of the New Testament* (Grand Rapids: Baker Academic, 1992).

the manuscript. There are many early parchment manuscripts that, due to their age and text-type, such as the major codexes and some earlier parchment manuscripts, are far more valuable for textual criticism than many later papyri. In fact, in many instances the parchment manuscripts are more valuable simply because the papyri tend to be fragmentary, with only a few entire books of the New Testament having been found on papyrus, whereas there are a number of complete books in various parchment manuscripts. We now have around 322 majuscule manuscripts on parchment, only a few of which have the complete New Testament.

The third stage of material transmission does not actually change the writing surface, but rather the handwriting on the surface. The minuscule hand, developed around the eighth or ninth century, is essentially a cursive form of handwriting that allows the connection of letters and creation of signs that represent several letters (ligatures) so as to aid in speed of writing and space allocation. There has been a resurgence of interest in minuscule manuscripts lately, as a number of these have been recently discovered. The vast majority of the minuscules, most of them written on parchment (though some very late ones on paper), reflect the Byzantine text-type and contain a subcorpus of the New Testament, such as the Pauline Epistles or the Gospels. There are nearly three thousand minuscule manuscripts (2911 at last count).

I must briefly mention lectionaries, even though these do not figure into the subsequent discussion as much as they probably should. All of the manuscripts identified above are, or at least are supposed to be, continuous-writing texts of at least one book of the New Testament. Lectionaries are texts that are not continuous writing of the New Testament but instead include excerpts or portions used for a variety of liturgical purposes, ranging from private use to public worship. The dates for lectionaries range from the fourth or the fifth century to the late Byzantine period (and even beyond the fifteenth century), with the vast majority being late. Some scholars (including me) think that some of the so-called papyri are actually lectionaries, or at least manuscripts used in ecclesial settings or for other personal devotional purposes. In any case, they are not continuous text, but excerpts extracted for various reasons. The range of dates means that lectionaries possibly were written on papyrus in the early period, certainly written on parchment or even the later ones on paper, and in majuscule and minuscule hands. There are nearly 2,500 manuscripts currently identified as lectionaries (2,453 or so).

With these categories and distinctions in mind, we can proceed to an analysis of the transmission of the text of the New Testament, noting major manuscripts and their physical characteristics.

## A Reconstructed History of the Transmission of the Greek New Testament before the Major Codexes

At some point in the first century the books of the New Testament were written. This statement is controverted by some scholars who want to place particular New Testament books in the second century. I do not believe that this is accurate, and I believe that there is substantial evidence that points in the opposite direction. However, my purpose here is not to discuss the original date of composition of the books of the New Testament, but to discuss their textual transmission and how that fits within a reconstruction of the formation of the New Testament.

The New Testament is conveniently divided into three major subcorpora. For the sake of discussion, I will begin with the Gospels and Acts, then go to the Pauline Epistles, and then make a few comments on the rest of the New Testament. For each subcorpus of the New Testament I will offer my reconstruction of the transmissional history of this body of books, so far as it is possible from the available manuscript and related evidence.[12]

### The Gospels and Acts

Tradition regarding Jesus circulated orally for a short period of time. The first and only sustained evidence that we have of the words and tradition of Jesus, however, is in Greek or embedded in Greek documents.[13] Whatever languages Jesus spoke, and the proportions in

12. I note a somewhat similar approach, though in abbreviated form, in Michael J. Kruger, *Canon Revisited: Establishing the Origins and Authority of the New Testament Books* (Wheaton: Crossway, 2012), 239–47.

13. See Hans Dieter Betz, "Wellhausen's Dictum 'Jesus was not a Christian, but a Jew' in Light of Present Scholarship," *Studia Theologica* 45 (1991): 83–110; repr.

which he spoke them,[14] very early these words were put into Greek. In fact, on the basis of the extant evidence, it is difficult to imagine that Jesus's words were ever widely recorded or transmitted in any language other than Greek, as there is no extant evidence of anything but early Greek New Testament documents. If there was a document called "Q,"[15] and if it was in written form, then it appears that it would have been written in Greek.[16] Regarding Synoptic origins, the Markan priority and two/four-source hypothesis still commands the most assent.[17] This hypothesis seems to work on the basis of Mark being written in Greek and used in Greek by Matthew and Luke. Even if another hypothesis is adopted, the documents seem already to have been in Greek.[18]

The estimated dates for the composition of the Gospels vary considerably, but all agree that they were written in the first century. Acts was almost certainly written in the first century as well. I think that Acts was written around AD 64/65, while Paul was in prison and before he was either released or killed. If this is so—and I think that it is the most plausible explanation of the ending of Acts and the traditional view

in his *Antike und Christentum: Gesammelte Aufsätze IV* (Tübingen: Mohr Siebeck, 1998), 1–31. By embedded, I mean the instances of Jesus's use of Aramaic (e.g., Mark 5:41) as found within the Greek Gospels.

14. Most scholars (rightly) believe that Jesus spoke Aramaic. A significant and growing number think (rightly, I believe) that he also spoke Greek. He probably also knew Hebrew. See Stanley E. Porter, *Criteria for Authenticity in Historical Jesus Research: Previous Discussion and New Proposals*, JSNTSup 191 (Sheffield: Sheffield Academic Press, 2000), esp. 89–99, 126–80. See now also Stanley E. Porter, "The Language(s) Jesus Spoke," in *Handbook for the Study of the Historical Jesus*, ed. Tom Holmén and Stanley E. Porter (Leiden: Brill, 2011), 3:2455–71; and Steven E. Fassberg, "Which Semitic Language Did Jesus and Other Contemporary Jews Speak?" *CBQ* 74 (2012): 263–80 (but who overlooks important studies that place Hebrew language discussion in context). Cf. Porter, "The Role of Greek Language Criteria in Historical Jesus Research," in Holmén and Porter, *Handbook*, 1:361–402. I have yet to see a convincing refutation of my proposal.

15. Q is the name given to the material that Matthew and Luke have in common that is not found in Mark's Gospel.

16. The statement by Papias regarding Matthew gathering logia in the "Hebrew dialect" does not necessarily refer to a Gospel, as it says that each interpreted or translated as able, perhaps using these logia for their own writings (Eusebius, *Hist. eccl.* 3.39.16). For options, see Lee Martin McDonald and Stanley E. Porter, *Early Christianity and Its Sacred Literature* (Peabody, MA: Hendrickson, 2000), 297–98.

17. For a traditional treatment of Markan priority, see Craig A. Evans, *Mark 8:27–16:20*, WBC 34B (Nashville: Nelson, 2001), xliii–lviii.

18. For an alternative involving Matthean priority, see William R. Farmer, *The Synoptic Problem: A Critical Analysis* (New York: Macmillan, 1964).

regarding authorship and Paulinism[19]—and if Acts was written after the Gospel of Luke, then Luke's Gospel was written before AD 64/65.[20] If that is so, then Mark was written before this date as well.[21] Matthew may have been written later, but since Matthew's apocalyptic account (chap. 24) gives little specific historical information that correlates with the fall of Jerusalem[22] and seems to have made use of the same body of common tradition as Luke's Gospel, it seems to me to have been written around the same time as Luke's Gospel. Virtually all scholars agree that John's Gospel was the last written and that this would have occurred, at the latest, around AD 90. It may have been written earlier.[23] However, even if I am wrong on this reconstruction, the evidence seems to indicate that John's Gospel was the last of the Gospels and was written somewhere around AD 90, on the basis of $\mathfrak{P}^{52}$, the small fragment of John's Gospel (18:31–33, 35–38) found in Egypt,[24] and that the other Gospels and Acts were written sometime before this.

19. See Stanley E. Porter, "Was Paulinism a Thing When Luke-Acts Was Written?" in *Reception of Paulinism in Acts* [= *Réception du paulinisme dans les Actes des Apôtres*], ed. Daniel Marguerat, BETL 229 (Leuven: Peeters, 2009), 1–13.

20. Some are too quick to dismiss this date for Acts, even though it has been held by a number of serious scholars, such as Adolf von Harnack. I think that the standard date of around AD 80/85 is simply a compromise based upon taking a mid-point between AD 65 and approximately AD 120, the date held by the Baur school.

21. There are many theories regarding proto-Luke and even proto-Mark, but they have not caught on, because they seem too much like an admission of the early date while trying to retain critical legitimacy. These theories resemble Ptolemaic explanations of the orbits of the planets, with various epicycles proposed to account for data made aberrant by working from an erroneous hypothesis.

22. On Matthew's Gospel, see D. A. Carson, "Matthew," in *The Expositor's Bible Commentary*, ed. Frank E. Gaebelein (Grand Rapids: Zondervan, 1984), 8:489.

23. This has been occasionally proposed but usually too quickly dismissed. I think that there are some good reasons to at least consider a much earlier date for John's Gospel. This is not the place to discuss these proposals.

24. See C. H. Roberts, ed., *An Unpublished Fragment of the Fourth Gospel in the John Rylands Library* (Manchester: Manchester University Press, 1935), 11–35. Some, such as Brent Nongbri ("The Use and Abuse of $\mathfrak{P}^{52}$: Papyrological Pitfalls in the Dating of the Fourth Gospel," *HTR* 98 [2005]: 23–48), have tried to call such an early dating into question, linking it with the date of P.Egerton 2 (see below), but I find the arguments unconvincing. See Stanley E. Porter, "Recent Efforts to Reconstruct Early Christianity on the Basis of Its Papyrological Evidence," in *Christian Origins and Greco-Roman Culture: Social and Literary Contexts for the New Testament*, ed. Stanley E. Porter and Andrew W. Pitts, TENTS 9 (Leiden: Brill, 2013), 71–84. I think that the revisionist thinking is too easily accepted by Paul Foster, "Bold Claims, Wishful Thinking, and Lessons about Dating Manuscripts from Papyrus Egerton 2," in *The World of Jesus*

The second century is usually viewed as a tunnel period in which we think we know very little about the development of early Christianity, and especially of the documents connected with it. However, there is surprisingly strong manuscript evidence worth considering that indicates that sometime in the second century the fixed corpus of four Gospels and Acts was firmly established. Here I will examine some of the evidence that points in this direction. If this evidence is convincing, it establishes a strong, even if not absolutely continuous, line of transmissional continuity from the original documents to the abundance of later manuscript evidence.

■ 𝔓⁴⁵

This is one of the most important early papyri of the Gospels and Acts. We know that by the time 𝔓⁴⁵ was written, the four Gospels and Acts appear to have been treated as a fixed corpus of material. 𝔓⁴⁵, one of the Chester Beatty papyri (P.Chester Beatty I), was purchased in 1930–1931 and published by Frederic Kenyon in 1933–1934.[25] The manuscript appears to have been part of a papyrus codex of an estimated 224 pages. The manuscript has been dated to the first half of the third century (c. AD 200–250) by Kenyon and a number of other papyrologists.[26] The manuscript contains portions of Matthew, Mark, Luke, John, and Acts, and apparently nothing more. On the basis of wear of

and the Early Church: Identity and Interpretation in Early Communities of Faith, ed. Craig A. Evans (Peabody, MA: Hendrickson, 2011), 193–211. The date ranges for several papyri, including 𝔓⁵², have been extended especially at the back end by Don Baker ("The Dating of New Testament Papyri," NTS 57 [2011]: 571–82 [see 573–75]), who appeals to their "graphic stream." This article more chronicles the debate than decides any issues.

25. Frederic G. Kenyon, ed., The Chester Beatty Biblical Papyri: Descriptions and Texts of Twelve Manuscripts on Papyrus of the Greek Bible, fasc. 1, General Introduction; fasc. 2.1, Gospels and Acts, Text; fasc. 2.2, Gospels and Acts, Plates (London: Emery Walker, 1933–1934). There is one leaf of 𝔓⁴⁵ in the Vienna Papyrussammlung. For the latest edition, see Stanley E. Porter and Wendy J. Porter, New Testament Greek Papyri and Parchments: New Editions, MPÖN n.s. 29 (Berlin: de Gruyter, 2008), no. 2, 1:3–10. On the significance of the Chester Beatty collection, see Barbara Aland, "The Significance of the Chester Beatty Papyri in Early Church History," in The Earliest Gospels: The Origins and Transmission of the Earliest Christian Gospels—The Contribution of the Chester Beatty Gospel Codex P⁴⁵, ed. Charles Horton, JSNTSup 258 (London: T&T Clark International, 2004), 108–21.

26. Kenyon, Chester Beatty Biblical Papyri, fasc. 2.1, x. See also Philip W. Comfort and David P. Barrett, The Text of the Earliest New Testament Greek Manuscripts, corrected ed. (Wheaton: Tyndale, 2001), 155–57; Joseph van Haelst, Catalogue des

the individual pages, and the ordering found in earlier manuscripts, it is possible that the manuscript was arranged in the order Matthew, Luke, John, Mark, Acts. This is not surprising. Although most manuscripts follow our now usual canonical order, the Western or Latin church apparently had a different order, as evidenced by the fifth-century Codex Bezae (05 D), which follows the order Matthew, John, Luke, Mark. $\mathfrak{P}^{45}$ seems to have an order that reflects the period before a fixed order within the subcorpus was determined. The character of the individual books varies. Mark has characteristics of the late fourth- or early fifth-century Freer Gospel (032 W), Codex Bezae (05 D), and some Old Latin manuscripts, as well as what some used to call the Caesarean text. Matthew, Luke, and John are a mix of Codex Vaticanus (03 B) and Codex Bezae (05 D), while Acts reflects the Alexandrian text-type.[27] Thus, by the early years of the third century, we have the four Gospels and Acts in a single codex of some size. Acts is not always linked to the Gospels in later manuscripts, however. It is found after the Gospels in Codex Vaticanus (03 B) and the fifth-century Codex Alexandrinus (02 A), and in lists from the Council of Laodicea (AD 363), Cyril of Jerusalem (fourth century), the Council of Carthage (AD 397), Amphilochius of Iconium (fourth century), Philastrius (fourth century), Rufinus (fourth/ fifth century), John Chrysostom (fourth/fifth century), the Syriac Canon (fifth century), Peshitta (Syriac) (fifth century), and John of Damascus (seventh/eighth century). However, Acts is found separate from the Gospels in Codex Sinaiticus (01 ℵ) and the sixth-century Latin Codex Fuldensis (09 F), and in the lists of Epiphanius (fourth century), Jerome (fourth/fifth century), and Eucherius (fifth century).

■ TATIAN'S *DIATESSARON*

There are other bodies of evidence to consider, however, that push our knowledge of the transmission of the Gospels even earlier. One of these is the *Diatessaron*.[28] The *Diatessaron* was created by

---

papyrus littéraires juifs et chrétiens, SPap 1 (Paris: Sorbonne, 1976), 136–37. The latter two volumes have summaries of scholarly opinion regarding the dates of manuscripts.

27. F. G. Kenyon, *The Text of the Greek Bible*, rev. A. W. Adams, 3rd ed., ST (London: Duckworth, 1975), 70.

28. For a full study, see William L. Petersen, *Tatian's Diatessaron: Its Creation, Dissemination, Significance, and History in Scholarship*, VCSup 25 (Leiden: Brill, 1994); compacted in William L. Peterson [*sic*], "Tatian's Diatessaron," in Helmut Koester,

Tatian (c. AD 120–180), a disciple of Justin Martyr (AD 100–165) in Rome.[29] Tatian took the four Gospels—the same four found in the later $\mathfrak{P}^{45}$—and harmonized them apparently around the Johannine narrative[30] into a form that was widely used in the church, possibly sometime around AD 150–172, before his expulsion from Rome (although many if not most scholars now opt for it being compiled after the expulsion, AD 173–185). It appears that the Gospels in the Latin church were early on known in the form of Tatian's *Diatessaron*.[31] There has been dispute over the original language of the *Diatessaron*, whether Latin, Greek, or Syriac, as knowledge of it is significantly later and only in indirect form. There are a number of sources or witnesses to the *Diatessaron*:[32] a commentary on it

*Ancient Christian Gospels: Their History and Development* (London: SCM, 1990), 403–30; Tjitze Baarda, "Tatian's Diatessaron and the Greek Text of the Gospels," in *The Early Text of the New Testament*, ed. Charles E. Hill and Michael J. Kruger (Oxford: Oxford University Press, 2012), 336–49; also, the still-excellent work by Bruce M. Metzger, *The Early Versions of the New Testament: Their Origin, Transmission, and Limitations* (Oxford: Clarendon, 1977), 10–36.

29. Justin himself, however, appears to have used his own harmony of the Synoptic Gospels, possibly including some, though admittedly minimal, material from noncanonical sources. This possible, though relatively minor, use of noncanonical sources has been recognized for some time. See William Sanday, *The Gospels in the Second Century: An Examination of the Critical Part of a Work Entitled "Supernatural Religion"* (London: Macmillan, 1876), 88–137, which includes a reconstruction of Justin's harmony and treatment of his Gospel quotations; and for more recent treatments, Koester, *Ancient Christian Gospels*, 402; Craig D. Allert, *A High View of Scripture? The Authority of the Bible and the Formation of the New Testament Canon* (Grand Rapids: Baker Academic, 2007), 112–15. Allert seems to be working too hard to make his point by creating a disjunctive argument, opposing Justin's harmony to canonical status for the Gospels, on the basis that the Gospels were not "arranged in a fixed collection" or "arranged in a known and fixed collection" (115). Allert says that the Synoptic Gospels (and possibly one reference to John) are the "majority source" (115) for Justin. But they are much more than that; they provide the entire framework and the overwhelming basis of the harmonization, to the point that one might well wish to argue that the Synoptic Gospels, if not the only known Gospels, are certainly the authoritative ones, at least for Justin if not for this period in church history. This kind of "exclusive definition of canon" (including a firm distinction between Scripture and canon) used by Allert is critiqued in Michael J. Kruger, "The Definition of the Term 'Canon': Exclusive or Multi-Dimensional?" *TynBul* 63 (2012): 1–20, esp. 3–8; and now in his *Canon Revisited*, 27–122.

30. See F. F. Bruce, *The Canon of Scripture* (Glasgow: Chapter House, 1988), 127.

31. Kenyon, *Text*, 114.

32. Peterson [*sic*], "Tatian's Diatessaron," 408–19; cf. Metzger, *Early Versions*, 10–25. I exclude the Dura Fragment (Peterson [*sic*], "Tatian's Diatessaron," 412–13; Metzger, *Early Versions*, 11–12), which is discussed below.

in Armenian by Ephraem of Syria in the fourth century, an Arabic translation surviving in six manuscripts from the twelfth to the nineteenth centuries, a single manuscript of a Persian harmony, Syriac versions, Gospel quotations in later writers, Old Armenian and Old Georgian versions of the Gospels, Manichaean documents, Kontakia of Romanos Melodus, Arabic and Karsuni Gospel manuscripts, the sixth-century Codex Fuldensis (actual date, AD 541–546) in Latin that uses the *Diatessaron* in the Vulgate text for its Gospel (there was probably an earlier Old Latin version),[33] the Liège harmony and its medieval Dutch and Middle High German, medieval Italian harmonies, Middle English harmony, and western poetic sources (obviously, not all of these are of equal value). The evidence seems to indicate that the *Diatessaron* was originally written possibly in Greek or more probably in Syriac,[34] but that is not crucial to what it tells us.

This document, or at least its reconstruction, tells us two probable things and possibly a third. The first is that the number of authoritative Gospel texts was established by the time Tatian created his harmony. Some note that there may have been other texts, even extracanonical Gospels, included in Tatian's harmony (the so-called fifth source). Victor of Capua (sixth century), in his preface to the Codex Fuldensis, refers to Tatian's work with the title *Diapente* ("through five"), a reference that has proved perplexing to scholars. Some have, as a result, wished to identify this "fifth source." However, Victor also says that Tatian, according to Eusebius, "combined one gospel out of the four, for which he composed the title 'Diapente.'"[35] Many possible explanations of this title have been suggested, including Victor's making an error (see below on Eusebius), but that it refers to noncanonical Gospels is unlikely (was it only one noncanonical Gospel [*Gospel of the Hebrews*, *Protevangelium of James*, and the *Gospel of Thomas*,[36]

---

33. William L. Petersen, "The Diatessaron of Tatian," in Ehrman and Holmes, *Text of the New Testament*, 78–79.

34. Kenyon, *Text*, 113–14; cf. Petersen, "Diatessaron of Tatian," 90; Peterson [*sic*], "Tatian's Diatessaron," 428–29.

35. See Petersen, *Tatian's Diatessaron*, 47 (translation), 48–49 (possible explanations).

36. John Halsey Wood Jr. ("The New Testament Gospels and the Gospel of Thomas: A New Direction," *NTS* 51 [2005]: 579–95, esp. 594) argues that it is easier to believe that the author had access to a collection of the four Gospels than to individual Gospels.

among others, have been suggested],[37] or does he lump all the possible sources together?). It is more likely that the title refers to a fifth Gospel that has been created out of the four. Tatian's was not the only *Diatessaron* known. Eusebius refers to one by a virtually unknown Ammonius of Alexandria (late second to early third century) based upon Matthew with the other three Gospels alongside.[38] Theophilus of Antioch (late second century), according to Jerome, also "put together into one work the words of the four gospels."[39] Eusebius himself is the one who names Tatian as the author of the *Diatessaron*. He states that Tatian "brought together a certain combination and collection—I do not know how—of the gospels, he called this the Diatessaron."[40] Eusebius claims that Tatian called it a *Diatessaron*, and this Greek name was used of the work even in its Syriac forms. Tatian's work, like that of the other harmonizers, was perceived to be a harmony based upon the four Gospels. It may be true that there was some influence of extracanonical sources, but this is, if anything, relatively minor. Many of the possible other sources are better explained as theologically based or possibly even later additions, so that the actual number of possible instances of extracanonical influence is relatively slight, certainly nothing that calls into question that the attribution of the work as a compilation of the four Gospels accurately describes what readers perceived.[41] Or, one might ask, if the reference is to four, what

37. See Petersen, *Tatian's Diatessaron*, 272–81. Nicholas Perrin (*Thomas and Tatian: The Relationship between the Gospel of Thomas and the Diatessaron*, SBLAB 5 [Atlanta: Society of Biblical Literature, 2002]) argues that the *Gospel of Thomas* is dependent upon the *Diatessaron*, and Simon Gathercole (*The Composition of the Gospel of Thomas: Original Language and Influences*, SNTSMS 151 [Cambridge: Cambridge University Press, 2012]) argues that the *Gospel of Thomas* is Greek literature that draws upon the Synoptic Gospels.

38. Petersen, *Tatian's Diatessaron*, 33, citing Eusebius, *Epistula ad Carpianum* 1 (NA[27] p. 84*).

39. Ibid., 32, citing Jerome, *Epistula ad Algasiam* (121) 6 (PL 22.1020).

40. Ibid., 36, citing Eusebius, *Hist. eccl.* 4.29.6. Allert (*High View*, 116–17) says, "There is no reason to think that Diatessaron was Tatian's own appellation for his work." He apparently dismisses (without argument) Eusebius's statement that Tatian named it *Diatessaron*. See also Allert, "The State of the New Testament Canon in the Second Century: Putting Tatian's *Diatessaron* in Perspective," *BBR* 9 (1999): 1–18 (incorrectly identifying William Petersen as "Peterson").

41. For examples of suggested instances of noncanonical sources used in the *Diatessaron*, see Petersen, *Tatian's Diatessaron*, 257–59, citing C. A. Phillips, "Diatessaron—Diapente," *BBC* 9 (February 1931): 6–8 (Mark 3:1; Matt. 4:5; Luke 17:3–4;

four Gospels were meant other than the four now canonical Gospels?[42] As Metzger states, "The amount of extra-canonical material that seems to have been present in Tatian's Diatessaron hardly justifies the opinion of some scholars that Tatian made extensive use of a fifth, apocryphal gospel when he compiled his Harmony."[43] More to the point regarding all of the early harmonies mentioned, of which the *Diatessaron* is the only one for which we have substantive evidence, "The *Diatessaron* supplies proof that all four Gospels were regarded as authoritative, otherwise it is unlikely that Tatian would have dared to combine them into one gospel account. At a time when many gospels were competing for attention, it is certainly significant that Tatian selected just these four—nor does the presence of an occasional extra-canonical phrase or clause in the fabric of the *Diatessaron* neutralize this consideration."[44]

---

Matt. 23:35; Matt. 27:51; and parable of the rich fool and story of the young ruler), with five of these supposed noncanonical sources also found in other early Christian authors and most explainable along other lines; Petersen, *Tatian's Diatessaron*, 252–53, citing Curt Peters, "Nachhall ausserkanonischer Evangelienüberlieferung in Tatians Diatessaron," *AcOr* 16 (1937): 258–94 (Matt. 3:15–16; Matt. 3:16; Luke 23:48; Luke 24:39; Matt. 4:5; Matt. 5:14), one of which Phillips already lists, and one of which is in the *Gospel of Thomas*. See also Petersen, "The Diatessaron and the Fourfold Gospel," in Horton, *Earliest Gospels*, 50–68, citing Luke 23:43; Matt. 3:16–17; Luke 4:28–31, all explainable as embellishments (Luke 23:43), explanations (Matt. 3:16–17), or theological clarifications (Luke 4:28–31). Petersen assumes that any extra material requires an extracanonical source. That does not follow. Allert (*High View*, 117–18) cites what he says "are really the only concrete examples of Tatian relying on extracanonical sources." These are three: Matt. 3:15–16, where a light or fire occurs at Jesus's baptism; Matt. 8:4, where the *Diatessaron* has "fulfill the law" rather than "offer the gift which Moses commanded"; and nativity readings in the Persian *Diatessaron*. The first, mentioned above, is explanatory of the situation or consonant with Matthew's use of spectacular events (or perhaps simply embellishment). The second does not require an extracanonical source; it appears to be simply a clarification of what is being said for a non-Jewish audience. The third is dismissed by Petersen (*Tatian's Diatessaron*, 260) as simply a peculiarity of the Persian *Diatessaron*, as it is unattested elsewhere. In other words, Allert's case for resisting the force of seeing the four Gospels as not merely authoritative but what one might call canonical amounts to next to nothing (at best three examples, and at least none)—that is, no single example. This hardly requires a theory of extra-canonical interference.

42. See Brooke Foss Westcott, *A General Survey of the History of the Canon of the New Testament*, 7th ed. (London: Macmillan, 1896), 328. Westcott attributes Tatian's *Diatessaron* with being the "first recognition of a fourfold Gospel."

43. Metzger, *Early Versions*, 36.

44. Bruce M. Metzger, *The Canon of the New Testament: Its Origin, Development, and Significance* (Oxford: Clarendon, 1987), 115–16. Metzger notes that it is

If the *Diatessaron* was originally written in Greek, then these four Gospels were already established as the four Gospels to use. If it was written in Syriac, then the four had almost assuredly already been established so as to be translated from Greek into Syriac for Tatian to harmonize. In either case, it shows the firm establishment of the four Gospels as a corpus by the mid-second century, if not earlier.[45]

The second probable conclusion is that the *Diatessaron* was most likely created by Tatian before he was branded a heretic in AD 172 for adopting views that led him to join the Encratites (i.e., the Continent or Self-Controlled).[46] The basis for this conclusion is that even though Tatian was branded a heretic, his *Diatessaron* continued to find widespread use in a variety of churches, and the Gospels were transmitted in this form to many of them. That his *Diatessaron* continued to be used despite his heretical views indicates that these were the four recognized Gospels at least by the time he undertook this task.

The third possible conclusion is that, especially if the *Diatessaron* was written in Syriac, it may not have been the first harmony of this type. What little evidence we have of previous harmonies (e.g., by Justin Martyr or even a source that he used) pushes recognition of the four Gospels even earlier.

- 0212

Parchment 0212 was first identified as a part of Tatian's *Diatessaron*.[47] However, 0212 has recently been reexamined by a team of text-critical scholars. The conclusion of that examination is that this Greek fragment, with parts of the four Gospels (Matt. 27:56–57; Mark 15:40, 42; Luke 23:49–51, 54; John 19:38), is not a part of the

---

"not known whether [the noncanonical additions] were present in the *Diatessaron* from the beginning, or whether some were incorporated after Tatian had published his harmony of the four Gospels" (116n5). This latter situation indicates that recognition of canonical texts does not necessarily preclude later additions, so that defining canon solely in terms of a high level of textual rigidity is probably unwarranted.

45. It is possibile that Tatian harmonized as he translated, but I find this unlikely, as his text seems more stable. However, even if he did, the date of a fixed subcorpus is still early, no later than AD 172.

46. J. Hamilyn Hill, *The Earliest Life of Christ Ever Compiled from the Four Gospels, Being the Diatessaron of Tatian (Circ. A.D. 160)* (Edinburgh: T&T Clark, 1894), 9–11.

47. Carl H. Kraeling, *A Greek Fragment of Tatian's Diatessaron from Dura*, SD 3 (London: Christophers, 1935).

*Diatessaron* but is still a Greek harmony of the Gospels from the "latter part of the second century."[48] This fragment was found at Dura Europos, in Syria, where Tatian's *Diatessaron* gained widespread currency. Even though this is perhaps not evidence of the *Diatessaron*, it indicates instead another strong piece of evidence for the four Gospels in a single harmonized form from the second century, and found in a place where at least one other harmony of the exact same Gospels became popular.

### ▪ MARCION (C. AD 85–160)

The next piece of evidence is from Marcion. We know very little about Marcion, the heretic who was excommunicated in AD 144 in Rome. All of Marcion's writings have disappeared (I will return to Marcion below), but from the words of his many adversaries in the late second century we can reconstruct something of what he thought about the Gospels. Irenaeus (AD 130–200) writes that Marcion "mutilates the Gospel which is according to Luke, removing all that is written respecting the generation of the Lord" (*Haer.* 28.2 [*ANF* 1.352]). We know that Marcion accepted only Luke's Gospel but "persuaded his disciples that he himself was more worthy of credit than are those apostles who have handed down the Gospel to us, furnishing them not with the Gospel, but merely a fragment of it" (*Haer.* 28.2 [*ANF* 1.352]). Irenaeus's use of the plural "apostles" indicates that he knew of more than one Gospel that Marcion chose from. Tertullian (AD 160–220) distinguishes between Matthew and John being written by apostles and Mark and Luke being written by apostolic men, and notes that Marcion chose Luke's Gospel for his purposes (*Marc.* 4.2, 5 [*ANF* 3.347, 350]). These all may have been referred to as "apostles" by Irenaeus. Thus, if these church fathers are to be believed, Marcion had Gospels to choose from, and they seem to be the four Gospels in our New Testament (the ones I have been discussing). This implies that these four Gospels were already recognized before Marcion did his selection, and it pushes the four recognized Gospels back to the first half of the second century.

48. D. C. Parker, D. G. K. Taylor, and M. S. Goodacre, "The Dura-Europos Gospel Harmony," in *Studies in the Early Text of the Gospels and Acts: The Papers of the First Birmingham Colloquium on the Textual Criticism of the New Testament*, ed. D. G. K. Taylor, SBLTCS 1 (Atlanta: Society of Biblical Literature, 1999), 228.

■ $\mathfrak{P}^4$, $\mathfrak{P}^{64}$, $\mathfrak{P}^{67}$

The next body of evidence concerns these three widely discussed papyri. $\mathfrak{P}^4$ was one of the earliest papyrus fragments published. It was found in 1889 and partially published in 1892 by the French scholar Vincent Scheil.[49] At first dated to the sixth century, this date was moved back to the fourth and the third centuries, and later to the late second century, perhaps even to AD 150–175.[50] This fragmentary manuscript was found in the binding of a codex of Philo discovered in Coptos, Egypt, along with a fragment in a different hand with the words ευαγγελιον κατα ματταθαιον, *euangelion kata mattathaion* ("gospel according to Matthew"). $\mathfrak{P}^4$ contains Luke 1:58–59; 1:62–2:1, 6–7; 3:8–4:2, 29–32, 34–35; 5:3–8; 5:30–6:16. The text is Alexandrian and is in well over 90 percent agreement with $\mathfrak{P}^{75}$ and Codex Vaticanus (03 B). $\mathfrak{P}^{64}$ was bought in Luxor, Egypt, by Charles Huleatt and donated to the Magdalen College library in Oxford. The manuscript was first given a third- and then a fourth-century date until it was published in 1953 by Colin Roberts, who dated it to the end of the second century.[51] This manuscript contains Matthew 26:7–8, 10, 14–15, 22–23, 31–33. The text is Alexandrian with strong agreement with Codex Sinaiticus (01 ℵ). The third papyrus, $\mathfrak{P}^{67}$, with Matthew 3:9, 25, was published in 1956 with unknown provenance,[52] and there is no record of its origins. However, Roberts was able to show in 1961 that $\mathfrak{P}^{64}$ and $\mathfrak{P}^{67}$ were from the same codex.[53] Roberts speculated that

49. Vincent Scheil, "Fragments de l'Évangile selon saint Luc, recueillis en Égypte," *RB* 1 (1892): 113–15. Caspar René Gregory at first categorized this as a lectionary text (see *Die Griechischen Handschriften des Neuen Testaments* [Leipzig: Hinrichs, 1908], 150), presumably because of it not being continuous text.

50. See Comfort and Barrett, *Text*, 52–53.

51. Colin Roberts, "An Early Papyrus of the First Gospel," *HTR* 46 (1953): 233–37. Carsten Peter Thiede ("Papyrus Magdalen Greek 17 [Gregory-Aland $\mathfrak{P}^{64}$]: A Reappraisal," *TynBul* 46 [1995]: 29–42, esp. 40; repr. from *ZPE* 105 [1995]: 13–20) has suggested a date as early as the late first century for this papyrus and for $\mathfrak{P}^{67}$. This has been widely dismissed. See Philip W. Comfort, "Exploring the Common Identification of Three New Testament Manuscripts: $\mathfrak{P}^4$, $\mathfrak{P}^{64}$ and $\mathfrak{P}^{67}$," *TynBul* 46 (1995): 43–54; Peter M. Head, "The Date of the Magdalen Papyrus of Matthew (*P. Magd. Gr.* 17 = $\mathfrak{P}^{64}$): A Response to C. P. Thiede," *TynBul* 46 (1995): 251–85.

52. Ramón Roca-Puig, *Un papiro griego del Evangelio de San Mateo* (Barcelona: Grafos, 1956). This papyrus is P.Barcelona 1.

53. Ramón Roca-Puig, "Nueva publicación del papiro número uno de Barcelona," *Helmantica* 37 (1961): 5–20; C. H. Roberts, "Complementary Note to the Article of Prof. Roca-Puig," *Helmantica* 37 (1961): 21–22. Both were published together

𝔓⁶⁷ was one manuscript among many that Huleatt had purchased that were not given to Magdalen College.[54]

Although Kurt Aland suggested in 1965 that 𝔓⁴, 𝔓⁶⁴, and 𝔓⁶⁷ belonged together as part of a single manuscript,[55] they are not listed that way in lists that he compiled. It was Roberts who claimed in 1977 that the three belonged together, an opinion that he repeated ten years later.[56] On the basis of these findings, T. C. Skeat argued not only that these three papyri were part of the same codex but also that the three of them constituted the first single-quire (or gathering) codex that contained the four Gospels.[57] A number of scholars have followed Skeat in this opinion.[58] If this is the case, then we have evidence of the four Gospels gathered in a single codex by the time of the late second century. Assuming that this is not the first time this happened, this codex would point to an earlier definitive gathering, sometime in the early to mid-second century. However, there have been some recent significant objections to Skeat's hypothesis that links the three papyri together.

There are a number of places where it appears that recent scholarship agrees regarding these three papyri: they are to be dated to the late second century, and they were written by the same scribe in a similar and compatible codicological format.[59] Nevertheless, objections have been raised to their being from the same codex, and certainly the same quire.

One objection concerns the fibers of the papyri. The argument is that, upon examination, the fibers of 𝔓⁶⁴ and 𝔓⁶⁷ indicate that they could not have come from a single quire, as Skeat suggested, but that

in R. Roca-Puig, *Un papiro griego del Evangelio de San Mateo*, 2nd ed. (Barcelona: Grafos, 1962).

54. Comfort and Barrett, *Text*, 43, 45, 47.

55. Kurt Aland, "Neue neutestamentliche Papyri II," *NTS* 12 (1965–1966): 193–95.

56. Colin H. Roberts, *Manuscript, Society, and Belief in Early Christian Egypt* (London: Oxford University Press, for the British Academy, 1979), 13; Colin H. Roberts and T. C. Skeat, *The Birth of the Codex* (London: Oxford University Press, for the British Academy, 1983), 40–41, 65. See Comfort and Barrett, *Text*, 45–46.

57. T. C. Skeat, "The Oldest Manuscript of the Four Gospels?" *NTS* 43 (1997): 1–34.

58. For example, Graham N. Stanton, "The Fourfold Gospel," *NTS* 43 (1997): 317–46.

59. Scott D. Charlesworth, "T. C. Skeat, 𝔓⁶⁴⁺⁶⁷ and 𝔓⁴, and the Problem of Fibre Orientation in Codicological Reconstruction," *NTS* 53 (2007): 582–604, esp. 600; revised in "T. C. Skeat and the Problem of Fiber Orientation in Codicological Reconstruction," in *Proceedings of the 25th International Congress of Papyrology, Ann Arbor, July 29–August 4, 2007*, ed. Traianos Gagos, ASP (Ann Arbor: Scholarly Publishing Office, University of Michigan Library, 2010), 131–40.

they came from two different quires of a multiquire codex. 𝔓⁴ also comes from a multiquire codex. A second objection is that production of the codex followed at least two different principles. The thought is that 𝔓⁶⁴ and 𝔓⁶⁷ were written on separate unbound sheets, while 𝔓⁴ was written on sheets that had already been gathered.[60] A third argument for 𝔓⁴ being separate from 𝔓⁶⁴ and 𝔓⁶⁷ is that they do not have the same provenance; there is no indication that 𝔓⁶⁴ and 𝔓⁶⁷ were ever in the binding of the Philo codex.[61] A fourth argument is that the color of the papyrus is radically different between the two sets of fragments.[62] A fifth and final argument is that the use of ekthesis varies,[63] with 𝔓⁴ having anywhere from one to two letters protruding into the margin to indicate a paragraph or equivalent unit, while 𝔓⁶⁴ and 𝔓⁶⁷ have only a one-letter-width protrusion.[64]

These are significant objections, and if they are proven, Skeat's case disintegrates. However, one must be cautious with all of these objections. The first two objections prove simply that there was not a single-quire codex, not that these could not have been written separately, even according to differing principles, and then gathered into a single codex. Hans Förster tells an interesting tale that admonishes caution:

Peter Sanz had one half of a piece of papyrus measuring 12 cm by 14.5 cm which he published in his doctoral dissertation. In six lines, more than 130 letters can be read without any doubt; thus we have an average of more than 20 letters per line, while only a few letters are unclear. There are no lacunae which would be a problem for the identification of single words, thus there is no dispute about the words which were read by this gifted papyrologist. Sanz gave a very thorough commentary on this piece and convincingly reconstructed the text. In addition, the famous Professor Gerstinger was supervising his work. However, this text had one problem. The second half of the papyrus was later found, making this piece larger than Sanz had estimated.

60. Charlesworth, "T. C. Skeat, 𝔓⁶⁴⁺⁶⁷ and 𝔓⁴," 602–3.
61. Peter M. Head, "Is 𝔓⁴, 𝔓⁶⁴ and 𝔓⁶⁷ the Oldest Manuscript of the Four Gospels? A Response to T. C. Skeat," *NTS* 51 (2005): 450–57, esp. 451–52.
62. Charlesworth, "T. C. Skeat, 𝔓⁶⁴⁺⁶⁷ and 𝔓⁴," 597–98, citing Thiede.
63. Ekthesis, or outdent, occurs when the scribe writes letters to the left of the normal line of text and protruding into the margin. Ekthesis is used for a variety of purposes, such as marking a paragraph break.
64. Ibid., 597, citing Thiede.

Thus, his entire identification and analysis are wrong, even though he read the existing passages correctly.[65]

The example is not an exact parallel, but the point can be made nonetheless. There is much speculation regarding codicology and reconstructing such manuscripts. Caution is required on all sides. The third argument, regarding provenance, is not particularly telling, as 𝔓⁴ and 𝔓⁶⁴ seem to have been found in the same area. Scholars who have no trouble linking 𝔓⁶⁴ and 𝔓⁶⁷ do not mind that 𝔓⁶⁷ has no direct provenance. The major problem is that the Matthean papyri (𝔓⁶⁴, 𝔓⁶⁷) were not found in the binding of Philo, as was 𝔓⁴. However, according to Jean Merrell's account,[66] the fragment with ευαγγελιον κατα ματταθαιαν, *euangelion kata mattathaian* ("gospel according to Matthew") was found with the Lukan text in the binding of Philo, indicating that at least at one point a Matthean text had been attached. The ascription is written in a different hand, and the form of the ascription with the word ευαγγελιον, *euangelion* ("gospel") is most likely second century (see 𝔓⁶⁶, possibly mid-second century and probably no later than AD 200, and 𝔓⁷⁵, AD 175 to possibly 225, though possibly second century for both).[67] The fourth objection, regarding the coloring of the papyri, is not significant, as I have examined other papyri from the same manuscript that vary widely in coloring and discoloration. The fifth objection, concerning ekthesis, is based upon limited evidence because of the size of the fragments. There are thirteen instances of ekthesis in 𝔓⁴, but only one each in 𝔓⁶⁴ and 𝔓⁶⁷, hardly enough for definitive comparison.

65. Hans Förster, "7Q5 = Mark 6.52–53: A Challenge for Textual Criticism?" *JGRChJ* 2 (2001–2005): 32. See also Eric G. Turner, *Greek Papyri: An Introduction* (Oxford: Clarendon, 1968), 68–70.

66. Comfort and Barrett, *Text*, 47. Jean Merrell, "Nouveaux fragments du papyrus IV," *RB* 47 (1938): 5–22. Merrell published a revised complete edition of 𝔓⁴.

67. See Comfort and Barrett, *Text*, 53–54. By the fourth century the ascription simply had the preposition and name of the author, as the word "gospel" was used of the fourfold Gospel rather than of individual books. Comfort and Barrett date the ascription connected to 𝔓⁴ later on the basis of the apostrophe in ματ'ταθαιον. This apparently stems from misunderstanding a comment by Eric G. Turner (*Greek Manuscripts of the Ancient World*, ed. Peter J. Parsons [London: Institute for Classical Studies, 1987], 11n50) regarding the frequency of this feature in the early third century. Turner cites three examples from the second century. It may be infrequent, but it can be used, as probably here.

If these objections cannot be sustained (and they are not telling), we are still left with the possibility of 𝔓⁴, 𝔓⁶⁴, and 𝔓⁶⁷ being the first testimony of a multiquire codex of the Gospels. The format for production of the two sets of fragments is similar and compatible, as one would expect from a single scribe. The format for each indicates that there could have been other material before or after in the codex. It is true that we have direct evidence for only two of the Gospels. As Peter Head has pointed out, there are a number of different collections, such as 𝔓⁵³ with Matthew and Acts (mid-third century AD), 𝔓⁷⁵ with Luke and John, and 0171 with Matthew and Luke (c. AD 300).[68] However, what Head has indicated is that there are possibilities of these also having been at one time four-Gospel (plus) collections; at least there is nothing in these combinations that precludes their having been like 𝔓⁴⁵ with all four Gospels and even Acts, and nothing that says they were limited to two books or Gospels.

I believe that the ascription with 𝔓⁴, 𝔓⁶⁴, and 𝔓⁶⁷ may be an indication that the collection of manuscripts that we call 𝔓⁴, 𝔓⁶⁴, and 𝔓⁶⁷ contained at least two Gospels if not more. This supposition may get some support from the title found in 𝔓⁷⁵, where two ascriptions are found back to back: ευαγγελιον κατα λουκαν, *euangelion kata loukan* ("gospel according to Luke") at the end of Luke's Gospel, and then ευαγγελιον κατα ιοανην, *euangelion kata ioanēn* ("gospel according to John") before the start of John's Gospel. In other words, these titles were found at the start and finish of each book for ease of reference, implying that there were more than simply two books included. John's inclusion may very well indicate that all four Gospels were originally included in either the order Matthew, Luke, John, Mark or the order Matthew, Mark, Luke, John.

■ LONGER ENDING OF MARK

The sixth and final piece of direct New Testament evidence concerns the so-called longer ending of Mark. David Parker has discussed the endings of Mark. He indicates that the short ending is early (if not original) on the basis of several key arguments, including direct and indirect manuscript evidence. Codexes Vaticanus (03 B) and Sinaiticus (01 ℵ) provide the earliest direct manuscript evidence for the short

68. Head, "𝔓⁴, 𝔓⁶⁴ and 𝔓⁶⁷," 455.

ending (Mark 16:1–8), but we know from a manuscript such as 𝔓⁷⁵ that
the Alexandrian text found in these major codexes reflects a tradition
that dates to the second century, and thus a short ending is very early.
Furthermore, and perhaps even more importantly, the fact that there
are both the intermediate and long endings indicates that there was
a short ending that was prior to the intermediate long endings, even
if the short ending was considered unsatisfactory.[69]

Concerning the long ending, however, Parker's findings are equally
significant. The earliest possible reference to a verse in the long ending
of Mark (16:20) may be in Justin Martyr (writing around AD 155),
who refers to Jesus, "whom his apostles going out from Jerusalem
proclaimed everywhere" (1 Apol. 45). The wording here shares
three words—"going out" (ἐξελθόντες, exelthontes), "proclaimed"
(ἐκήρυξαν, ekēryxan), and "everywhere" (πανταχοῦ, pantachou)—
with Mark 16:20, the only verse in the New Testament where these
three words are found together. The long ending is also reportedly
in Tatian's Diatessaron, on the basis of the Persian Gospel Harmony
(Mark 16:14, 16, 19). Irenaeus cites Mark 16:10: "At the end of the
Gospel Mark says, And so the Lord Jesus after he had spoken to
them, was taken into heaven, and sat down at the right hand of God"
(Haer. 3.10.6). There are other later references as well.[70] This evidence
indicates that, at least by AD 155, there appears to have been a long
ending to Mark, which was designed to supplement the shorter, quite
possibly original, and earlier ending of Mark.

Also important to note is that the long ending of Mark appears to
be a pastiche of passages from the other Gospels and Acts. Following
is a list of some of these:[71]

> Mark 16:9: Jesus rises on the first day of the week (Matthew 28:1;
> Luke 24:1; John 20:1; cf. Mark 16:2)
>
> Mark 16:9: Jesus appears to Mary Magdalene (John 20:11–18; cf.
> Matthew 28:1, 9–10)

---

69. D. C. Parker, The Living Text of the Gospels (Cambridge: Cambridge University Press, 1997), 137. Stylistic evidence may also play an important confirmatory role in this analysis. See Travis B. Williams, "Bringing Method to the Madness: Examining the Style of the Longer Ending of Mark," BBR 20 (2010): 397–418.

70. Parker, Living Text, 132–33.

71. For similar lists, see Evans, Mark 8:27–16:20, 546–47; Parker, Living Text, 138–40.

Mark 16:10: women's report to the others (Luke 24:10; John 20:18)

Mark 16:11: unbelief at the women's report (Luke 24:11)

Mark 16:12: Jesus appears to two on a journey (Luke 24:13–35)

Mark 16:13: report to the others (Luke 24:33–35)

Mark 16:14: Jesus appears to the eleven (Luke 24:36; John 20:19, 26)

Mark 16:14: reproach for unbelief (Luke 24:36–43)

Mark 16:15: mandate to go into all the world (Matthew 28:19a)

Mark 16:16: belief, baptism, condemnation (Matthew 28:19b; John 3:18, 36)

Mark 16:17: things done in Jesus's name (Matthew 28:19b)

Mark 16:17: casting out demons and speaking in tongues (Luke 10:17–18; Acts 2:4; 10:46; 19:6)

Mark 16:18: handling snakes (Acts 28:3–5)

Mark 16:18: laying hands on the sick (Acts 9:17; 28:8)

Mark 16:19: Jesus's ascension (Luke 24:51; Acts 1:2, 9)

Mark 16:19: the right hand of God (Mark 10:32–40; Matthew 20:20–23)

Mark 16:20: disciples sent out (Luke 9:1–2; 10:1, 17)[72]

Craig Evans sees Mark 16:12–13 as especially derived from Luke 24:13–35, and Mark 16:15–17 from the Great Commission in Matthew 28:18–20. Although a few of the passages in Mark's long ending may come from other places in the New Testament,[73] all the most convincing ones come from the four Gospels and Acts. If the reconstruction above is correct, the implication is that the long ending of Mark was created at least by the mid-second century. It was created, however, by drawing upon material at least as important and accessible as Mark's Gospel: the three other Gospels and Acts. In other words, the four Gospels and Acts were already apparently considered a collected body of authoritative writings

72. Evans (*Mark 8:27–16:20*, 546) sees Mark 16:20 as a "general summary of Acts."
73. For example, Parker (*Living Text*, 140) sees Heb. 2:4 behind Mark 16:17 and an analogy between Heb. 2:3–4 and Mark 16:20. I do not find these as convincing, but if Parker is right, the implication is that the author knew the book of Hebrews as well.

of the church by the early part of the second century, so that when later writers wished to "complete" Mark's Gospel, they drew upon these Gospels.

## ▪ EXTRACANONICAL WRITINGS

This status for the four Gospels is confirmed by examination of important extracanonical works. These texts, though never so widely neglected as some have lately erroneously contended,[74] have again been at the forefront of discussion. I select for mention several that probably were composed fairly early.

### ▪ TWO SMALL FRAGMENTS

It has long been recognized that the second century, despite our relative lack of knowledge, was a time of development and expansion in the writing of Christian documents. Several extracanonical Gospels have been dated to the second century that bear examination for what they can tell us about the state of the New Testament documents. One of these is possibly the so-called Fayyum fragment (P. Vindob. G 2325).[75] This fragment of an extracanonical Gospel is clearly an amalgamation of Mark 14:26–30 and Matthew 26:30–34, in which Peter hears the rooster crow. Another is P. Oxy. LX 4009,[76] thought (erroneously) by some to be a part of the *Gospel of Peter*.[77] This is probably at best an extracanonical writing dependent upon several Gospels. For example, reference to "harvest" in line 4 is dependent upon Matthew 9:37 or Luke 10:2; being "wise as" in lines 5–6, on Matthew 10:16b; mention of "wolf" in line 8, on Luke 10:3; and use of "say," "do," and "kill" in lines 11–16, on Luke 12:4–5.[78]

---

74. See, for example, Bart D. Ehrman, *Lost Scriptures: Books That Did Not Make It into the New Testament* (New York: Oxford University Press, 2005).

75. For edition and bibliography, see Porter and Porter, *Papyri and Parchments*, no. 62, 1:291–94. The usual date for this papyrus is the beginning of the third century, but it has some characteristics of the second century, as noted by Porter and Porter.

76. R. A. Coles et al., *The Oxyrhynchus Papyri, LX*, GRM 80 (London: Egypt Exploration Society, for the British Academy, 1994), 1–5.

77. Egbert Schlarb and Dieter Lührmann, *Fragmente apokryph gewordener Evangelien in griechischer und lateinischer Sprache*, MTS 59 (Marburg: Elwert, 2000), 73.

78. PSI 1200bis may have references to a single Gospel, Matthew, in its language about being first and last, although there is also the chance of reference to Rev. 1:17 (see ibid., 179).

■ *P.EGERTON 2*

The most important apocryphal text for this discussion is the so-called Egerton papyrus (P.Egerton 2 = P.Lond.Christ. 1). There has been much recent discussion regarding the date of P.Egerton 2. The original editors suggested a date of around AD 150, later revised to AD 140–160 for the manuscript, with original composition of the text recorded as no later than AD 110–130.[79] This scheme was later challenged by Michael Gronewald, who posited a date of around AD 200 for transcription, on the basis of the use of the apostrophe in the joined P.Köln VI 255 fragment.[80] However, like Philip Comfort and David Barrett, Gronewald apparently misunderstood Eric Turner's statement regarding the use of the apostrophe. Gronewald seems to think that the use of the apostrophe necessitates a third-century AD date. The apostrophe, however, according to Turner's own evidence, is also found in the second century, not only in the third and after, even if not frequently. I recently made an evidential comparison of P.Egerton 2 with other manuscripts, and I confirm a date no later than around AD 180–190.[81] What is important to note about this extracanonical document, however, is that it is derivative from the four canonical Gospels. There are four major units to the P.Egerton 2 papyrus, each of which appears to be directly derivative from Gospel material.[82]

> Episode 1. Jesus speaks to lawyers and tells them to search the Scriptures, in which they think they have life, because these Scriptures bear witness of him. Jesus says that he did not come to accuse them, but Moses accuses them. They respond by questioning

79. H. I. Bell and T. C. Skeat, *Fragments of an Unknown Gospel and Other Early Christian Papyri* (London: Trustees of the British Library, 1935), 2; *The New Gospel Fragments* (London: Trustees of the British Museum, 1951), 17. For a recent edition of P.Egerton 2 (by Nicklas), see Thomas J. Kraus, Michael J. Kruger, and Tobias Nicklas, eds., *Gospel Fragments* (Oxford: Oxford University Press, 2009), 11–120.

80. Michael Gronewald and Zbigniew Borkowski, eds., *Kölner Papyri (P.Köln) 6*, Papyrologica Coloniensia, vol. 7, no. 6 (Opladen: Westdeutscher Verlag, 1987), 136.

81. See Stanley E. Porter, *Jesus and John's Gospel* (Grand Rapids: Eerdmans, forthcoming).

82. See Bell and Skeat, *Fragments of an Unknown Gospel*, 16–25 (commentary), 26–29 (text and biblical parallels). See also Stanley E. Porter, "Early Apocryphal Gospels and the New Testament Text," in Hill and Kruger, *Early Text*, 350–69, esp. 355–61.

who Jesus is. This passage appears to be dependent upon at least three specific Johannine texts: John 5:39, where Jesus tells his hearers to search the Scriptures, because they think they have eternal life in them, and the Scriptures bear witness to him; John 5:45, where it is not Jesus but Moses who accuses his hearers; and John 9:29, where Jesus's interlocutors know of Moses, but not who Jesus is.

Episode 2. Counsel is given to stone Jesus, and the rulers seek to lay hands on him, but they cannot take him, because his hour has not come. He departs through their midst. A leper comes to him and asks for cleansing, which request Jesus grants. The leprosy goes away, and the man is told to go to the priests. This passage appears to be dependent upon a number of Johannine passages, as well as a number of Synoptic Gospel passages. The Johannine passages include John 8:59; 10:31, which say that they tried to stone Jesus; John 7:30, 44; 10:39, where they seek but fail to capture Jesus. Luke 4:30 states that Jesus passed through the midst of the crowd and went away. The episode with the leper seems to reflect elements of Matthew 8:2–3; Mark 1:40–42; Luke 5:12–13, along with Luke 17:14. The unit closes with wording from a combination of Mark 1:44; Matthew 8:4; Luke 17:14. What is important to note here is that whereas the Synoptic accounts reflect a common incident, P.Egerton 2 appears sometimes to reflect Matthew's account, and then sometimes Luke's. The form of address of the leper to Jesus, "Teacher Jesus," shows later theological interpretation.

Episode 3. After stating that something is shut up, Jesus stands on the edge of the Jordan and stretches out his right hand and sprinkles something on the water, which brings forth fruit.[83] This passage is highly fragmentary and difficult to reconstruct, but the specific episode of standing at the bank of the Jordan is not found in the Gospels, although the language does appear

83. There seems to be a common theme regarding bearing of fruit in a number of the apocryphal gospels (see P.Merton II 51 and P.Oxy. II 210), reflecting the canonical Gospels. See Stanley E. Porter, "POxy II 210 as an Apocryphal Gospel and the Development of Egyptian Christianity," in *Atti del XXII Congresso Internazionale di Papirologia, Firenze, 23–29 agosto 1998*, ed. Isabella Andorlini et al. (Florence: Istituto Papirologico "G. Vitelli," 2001), 2:1095–108, esp. 1105–6.

to reflect the Gospels.[84] The opening may reflect John 12:24, concerning the seed, and similar references to the Jordan River are found in Matthew 3:6; Mark 1:5. Reference to joy at the end of the passage may reflect Luke 2:10.

Episode 4. Jesus's interlocutors attempt to test him with a question. They state that they know he is from God, but then they ask whether it is lawful to give to kings what pertains to their rule. Jesus realizes their thoughts and becomes angry, and he questions their integrity. He notes that Isaiah recognized that people pay honor with their lips but not with their hearts. This passage appears to be dependent upon a mix of passages that supplement the Synoptic episode regarding giving taxes to Caesar. These passages include Matthew 22:16, but also Mark 12:14; Luke 20:21, where people approach Jesus and acknowledge him as master and then ask him about the tax to Caesar. John 3:2 takes a similar approach, recognizing that Jesus is a good teacher (cf. John 10:25). Luke 6:46; 18:19 depict Jesus as responding to interlocutors in terms of why they call him "Lord" or "good." Language in which Jesus condemns hypocrisy is found in Matthew 15:7–9, as well as in Mark 7:6–7 with reference to Isaiah. Jesus is again addressed in P.Egerton 2 as "Teacher Jesus."

Apart from the episode at the river, part of a highly fragmentary section, all of the episodes recorded in P.Egerton 2 clearly reflect a pastiche of Gospel references. As Joachim Jeremias states, "There are contacts with all four Gospels. The juxtaposition of Johannine . . . and Synoptic material . . . and the fact that the Johannine material is shot through with Synoptic phrases and the Synoptic with Johannine usage, permits the conjecture that the author knew all and every one of the canonical Gospels. . . . The text shows no historical knowledge that carries us beyond the canonical Gospels."[85] If this is the case, and the reconstructed date is correct, this exclusive use of the four canonical Gospels goes back to the earliest days of the second century.

84. For the latest discussion, see Kraus, Kruger, and Nicklas, *Gospel Fragments*, 66–75.

85. Joachim Jeremias, "An Unknown Gospel with Johannine Elements," in Edgar Hennecke, *New Testament Apocrypha*, vol. 1, *Gospels and Related Writings*, ed. Wilhelm Schneemelcher, trans. R. McL. Wilson (London: Lutterworth, 1963), 95.

After surveying this range of Gospel and related evidence, where do we stand regarding the textual transmission of the first of the three divisions of the text of the New Testament canon? I think that quite a lot can be said about the transmission of this important part of the New Testament. I have been able to look back to the earliest years of the second century and establish the use of the Gospels as a definable corpus of sacred writings. We can see clear continuity with the first century and observe that by the early years of the second century the four Gospels and possibly Acts were probably already established as an authoritative body of Christian literature, which the noncanonical gospels use in their later depictions of Jesus. This body of authoritative literature was then transmitted through the second and third centuries. By the late second and into the third century, we find $\mathfrak{P}^{45}$, which contains the four Gospels and Acts, and a manuscript such as $\mathfrak{P}^{75}$ with Luke and John, but quite possibly implying the other Gospels if not Acts, if the pattern that I noted above holds true.

In the fourth century the major codexes emerge. The two major deluxe codexes are Codex Sinaiticus (01 $\aleph$) and Codex Vaticanus (03 B). Both of them have the four Gospels and Acts, as well as other New Testament books (and a version of the Old Testament in Greek as well). There appears to be a strong line of continuity from the second century to the fourth, with our four canonical Gospels emerging as a whole together out of the second century.

### The Pauline Epistles

The Pauline Epistles are the second subcorpus for consideration, in terms of reconstructing a history of the transmission of the Greek New Testament before the major codexes. Tradition says that during his lifetime Paul wrote (at least) thirteen letters that we now have in our collection of Pauline Epistles. Critical scholarship since the beginning of the eighteenth century has raised questions about authorship and date of composition. The most extreme critics have doubted Pauline authorship of each and every one of the Pauline Epistles.[86] Since such

---

86. See Werner Georg Kümmel, *Introduction to the New Testament*, trans. Howard Clark Kee, 17th ed. (Nashville: Abingdon, 1975), 250–51. Kümmel briefly surveys various scholars who have doubted, at one time or another, the authenticity of every one of the Pauline Epistles.

skepticism must surely end up doubting one's own existence, such arguments must be doubted as well. More serious have been those who have followed Ferdinand Christian Baur and maintained Pauline authorship of the four main epistles. Today the critical consensus has grown from four to seven letters, including Romans, 1 Corinthians, 2 Corinthians, Galatians, Philippians, 1 Thessalonians, and Philemon. The rest of the letters are often considered pseudonymous, with a date of composition from right after Paul's death in approximately AD 65 to well into the second century for the so-called Pastoral Epistles. For a number of reasons that I cannot explicate here,[87] I believe that the traditional ascription of the thirteen letters to Paul is historically and critically defensible, and I will work from that standpoint in this section. This position actually creates a number of problems for the type of scenario regarding transmission of the New Testament that I will develop further because it includes a larger number of letters (thirteen) within this subcorpus. Nevertheless, I believe that this is explainable within the theory that I am proposing.

In other words, I believe that sometime around AD 65 Paul died, having written at least the thirteen letters ascribed to him, as well as other letters that are not in our Pauline letter collection. As with discussion of the canonical Gospels, the second century is a tunnel period in terms of transmission of the New Testament. Nevertheless, both the second and third centuries merit careful consideration concerning the transmission of Paul's letters. Examination of some of the manuscripts that bear witness to these letters gives us insight into their textual transmission.

■ THE SECOND AND THIRD CENTURIES

The second and third (or early fourth) centuries provide several bodies of evidence regarding the transmission of the Pauline Epistles.

■ 𝔓[92]

By the time of the late third or early fourth century (i.e., by around AD 300), there is firm evidence of gathering of the Pauline Epistles into a single corpus. 𝔓[92], two small fragmentary leaves from a single codex, has portions of Ephesians (1:11–13 on the recto, 1:19–21 on the

---

87. Some of the arguments are found in McDonald and Porter, *Early Christianity*, 388–93.

verso) and 2 Thessalonians (1:4–5 on the verso, 1:11–12 on the recto). When this papyrus was published in 1982, it was titled "Frammenti di un codice con le Epistole di Paolo" ("Fragment of a Codex with the Epistles of Paul").[88] There are no page numbers on the manuscript, but, as Comfort and Barrett state, "The two leaves must have been part of one sheet of a single-quire codex of Paul's epistles. This one sheet may have been somewhere near the middle, with Ephesians and Thessalonians separated only by Philippians and Colossians."[89] Although we do not know the full extent of this Pauline corpus that the manuscript originally contained, it is likely that it contained at least the thirteen letters attributed to Paul, along with quite possibly the book of Hebrews (a topic and book to which I will return immediately below).

- 𝔓⁴⁶

We can go back earlier, however, to the second century. Perhaps as early as the mid-second century and probably by around AD 200, we have tangible documentation in 𝔓⁴⁶ of a gathered corpus of Paul's letters. 𝔓⁴⁶ (most of which is part of the Chester Beatty collection [II], and some of which is at the University of Michigan) is fragmentary in some respects, but it is sufficiently intact for us to recognize that it consists of Romans (beginning in chap. 5), Hebrews, 1 Corinthians, 2 Corinthians, Ephesians, Galatians, Philippians, Colossians, and 1 Thessalonians.[90] Upon observation of this manuscript, three major issues emerge. The first is its ordering of books. Not only does this Pauline collection have Hebrews after Romans and before 1 Corinthians and 2 Corinthians, but it also has Ephesians before Galatians. As noted above, the manuscript ends with 1 Thessalonians, although we know from the codex construction that certainly there was room for 2 Thessalonians and Philemon (2 Thessalonians is clearly included

88. Claudio Gallazzi, "Frammenti di un codice con le Epistole di Paolo," *ZPE* 46 (1982): 117–22.

89. Comfort and Barrett, *Text*, 625.

90. Frederic G. Kenyon, ed., *The Chester Beatty Biblical Papyri: Descriptions and Texts of Twelve Manuscripts on Papyrus of the Greek Bible*, fasc. 3.1, *Pauline Epistles and Revelation, Text*; fasc. 3.1 supplement, *Pauline Epistles, Text*; fasc. 3.2 supplement, *Pauline Epistles, Plates* (London: Emery Walker, 1934–1937); Henry A. Sanders, ed., *A Third-Century Papyrus Codex of the Epistles of Paul* (Ann Arbor: University of Michigan Press, 1935).

in the Pauline letter collection by the third/fourth century, as indicated by $\mathfrak{P}^{92}$). The second issue is its date of composition. When this manuscript was first published, $\mathfrak{P}^{46}$ was dated by Kenyon to the third century, although several other papyrologists, including Günther Zuntz and Ulrich Wilcken, dated it to the second century or at least not past AD 200.[91] It has even been proposed by one scholar that $\mathfrak{P}^{46}$ dates to AD 81–96.[92] Although there is some basis for considering this date, most scholars believe that this is too early on paleographic grounds: the hand of $\mathfrak{P}^{46}$ resembles an early Roman hand in some particulars but not overall. As a result, it has recently been proposed that the date of $\mathfrak{P}^{46}$ is the mid-second century.[93] A date of the mid-second to third century is clearly the range that scholars consider, and in light of the arguments presented, a date of around AD 200 is reasonable. The third issue is contents. The consensus from the time of Kenyon, the manuscript's original editor, has been that $\mathfrak{P}^{46}$ included 2 Thessalonians and Philemon (2 Thessalonians is earliest attested, along with 1 Thessalonians, in the third-century papyrus $\mathfrak{P}^{30}$, and Philemon in the second- or third-century $\mathfrak{P}^{87}$, which closely resembles $\mathfrak{P}^{46}$),[94] but it did not (now or ever) include the Pastoral Epistles. This argument was made on the supposition that the remaining leaves of the codex—it appears that there were fourteen more pages (seven leaves) after 1 Thessalonians—would not have had enough space for the Pastoral Epistles.[95] However, it has also been observed that the scribe was beginning to compress his letters, so that he would have had room to write at least 2 Thessalonians and Philemon with ten or eleven pages to spare, and therefore he would have had room enough for the bulk of 1 Timothy, 2 Timothy, and Titus; and if he ran out of room, he may simply have added an extra sheet or two.[96] The earliest

91. Kenyon, *Chester Beatty Biblical Papyri*, fasc. 3.1 supplement, xiv–xv; Günther Zuntz, *The Text of the Epistles: A Disquisition upon the Corpus Paulinum* (London: Oxford University Press, for the British Academy, 1953), 11.

92. Young Kyu Kim, "Palaeographical Dating of $\mathfrak{P}^{46}$ to the Later First Century," *Bib* 69 (1988): 248–57.

93. Barrett and Comfort, *Text*, 204–6, discussing alternatives.

94. Ibid., 128, 167.

95. See Geoffrey Mark Hahneman, *The Muratorian Fragment and the Development of the Canon*, OTM (Oxford: Clarendon, 1992), 115–16.

96. See Jeremy Duff, "$\mathfrak{P}^{46}$ and the Pastorals: A Misleading Consensus?" *NTS* 44 (1998): 578–90. Contra Jerome D. Quinn, "$\mathfrak{P}^{46}$—The Pauline Canon?" *CBQ* 36 (1974):

attested manuscript with any of the Pastoral Epistles is dated to the second half of the second century, so there is no evidential reason to doubt that the Pastoral Epistles were extant and possibly were even known by the copyist of $\mathfrak{P}^{46}$. David Trobisch also believes that this is the case, as he notes, "There is no manuscript evidence to prove that the letters of Paul ever existed in an edition containing only some of the thirteen letters."[97] From $\mathfrak{P}^{46}$, which is an early Alexandrian text-type,[98] we learn that a likely scenario is that there was a canon of at least thirteen Pauline Epistles by around AD 200, and possibly as early as the mid-second century (if not earlier).

### ▪ MARCION

We can perhaps work back even earlier than $\mathfrak{P}^{46}$, however. As with the Gospels, what little we do know about Marcion offers us some pieces of evidence regarding a consolidated body of Paul's letters.[99] We have Marcionite prologues—written by Marcion's followers but found in early versions of the Vulgate—for ten letters of Paul, including one to the Laodiceans, which probably is Ephesians. The Pastoral Epistles are excluded. Many scholars think, therefore, that Marcion did not know the Pastoral Epistles because they had not yet been written. The fact that the Pastoral Epistles are not included in the Marcionite prologues, however, does not necessarily mean that they had not been written; Marcion may not have known of them, as Tertullian says (*Marc.* 5.21), or may have rejected them, as Marcion's canon is one of exclusion from an existing larger corpus. As

---

379–85. Quinn claims that the Pastoral Epistles were not included because the collection was only of letters to churches. See the discussion by Hahneman (*Muratorian Fragment*, 115–16), who (inadvertently) shows that there was much space to fill, and that the Pastoral Epistles would be the most likely books.

97. David Trobisch, *Paul's Letter Collection: Tracing the Origins* (Minneapolis: Fortress, 1994), 22.

98. Zuntz, *Text of the Epistles*, 254.

99. On Marcion, see George Milligan, *The New Testament Documents: Their Origin and Early History* (London: Macmillan, 1913), 217; Kirsopp Lake and Sylvia Lake, *An Introduction to the New Testament* (London: Christophers, 1938), 96; Bruce, *Canon of Scripture*, 144; Hans von Campenhausen, *The Formation of the Christian Bible*, trans. J. A. Baker (Philadelphia: Fortress, 1972), 148; in Lee Martin McDonald and James A. Sanders, eds., *The Canon Debate* (Peabody, MA: Hendrickson, 2002), see John Barton, "Marcion Revisited," 341–54, esp. 342–43, and Harry Y. Gamble, "The New Testament Canon: Recent Research and the Status Quaestionis," 267–94, esp. 283–84.

Tertullian indicates, Marcion accepted the collection of Paul's letters; however, "he dismembered the Epistles of Paul" (*Praescr.* 27.2 [*ANF* 1.352]). Some of the ones that he may have dismembered, besides excising individual passages, may have been the Pastoral Epistles, as they were clearly addressed to individuals rather than churches. The evidence is that by the mid-second century there was a gathering of Paul's letters, consisting of at least ten letters, and possibly the entire corpus of thirteen (or fourteen if Hebrews were to be included; see pp. 119–20 below for further discussion).

### ▪ CAN WE GO BACK EARLIER?[100]

There have been a number of attempts to go back earlier, even into the first century, to trace the transmission of the Pauline letter collection. Edgar Goodspeed, followed by John Knox, claimed there was widespread neglect of Paul's letters during the first century,[101] on the basis that Acts purportedly does not know Paul's letters, but much of the literature written after Acts, including Revelation 1–3, and every Christian corpus of letters to follow seem to know them. Goodspeed believed that the writing of Acts around AD 90,[102] with its clear and

100. This section is a revised treatment of Stanley E. Porter, "Paul and the Process of Canonization," in *Exploring the Origins of the Bible: Canon Formation in Historical, Literary, and Theological Perspective*, ed. Craig A. Evans and Emanuel Tov, ASBT (Grand Rapids: Baker Academic, 2008), 173–202. Similar arguments have been applied specifically to the second century in Stanley E. Porter, "Paul and the Pauline Letter Collection," in *Paul and the Second Century*, ed. Michael F. Bird and Joseph R. Dodson, LNTS 412 (London: T&T Clark, 2011), 19–36. In a review of this book Joseph Tyson says of my chapter, "Perhaps the most creative essay [in the volume] is that of Stanley Porter on the collection of Paul's letters. . . . In a footnote Porter admits that many scholars will suspect his theory, since it claims the authenticity of the thirteen letters, but he is confident that a case can be made for all of them. This is an essay that should elicit a good deal of conversation, but, to be convincing, conclusions that are so far from mainstream scholarship need and deserve a more extensive treatment" (*RBL* [July 2012]: http://www.bookreviews.org/pdf/8338_9117.pdf). The present treatment within its larger context is designed to go at least some of the way toward this more extensive treatment.

101. See Edgar J. Goodspeed, *New Solutions of New Testament Problems* (Chicago: University of Chicago Press, 1927), esp. 1–103; *The Meaning of Ephesians* (Chicago: University of Chicago Press, 1933); *An Introduction to the New Testament* (Chicago: University of Chicago Press, 1937), esp. 210–21 (relied upon here).

102. See Goodspeed, *New Solutions*, 94–103. Cf. John Knox, "Acts and the Pauline Letter Corpus," in *Studies in Luke-Acts*, ed. Leander E. Keck and J. Louis Martyn (Philadelphia: Fortress, 1966), 279–87.

forceful depiction of Paul, revived interest in Paul. The only thing to be added to such an important volume was a collection of Paul's letters, something that Paul himself had hinted at (see Col. 4:16). Ephesians shows familiarity with the other nine of the Pauline Epistles in a group of ten (excluding the three Pastoral Epistles, which for Goodspeed reflect later knowledge of Paul).[103] By AD 90, Christians in Ephesus, the second most important Christian center (after Antioch), gathered the Pauline Epistles from surrounding cities, and the city became the center for later Christian letter writing.[104] The Pauline corpus, therefore, was circulated from Ephesus with Ephesians, an encyclical letter that drew upon the entire corpus, as the introduction.[105]

The *First Letter of Clement* was written around AD 96 from Rome by the church leader there. It is widely agreed that *1 Clement* quotes Romans and 1 Corinthians for certain.[106] However, *1 Clement* also probably quotes Titus (and Hebrews),[107] with the possibility of at least alluding to Pauline language found in 2 Corinthians, Galatians, Ephesians, Philippians, Colossians, and 1 Timothy.[108] In the light of this evidence, there is no reason to think that Clement did not know 1 Thessalonians, 2 Thessalonians, and 2 Timothy—only that he had no occasion to allude to or quote them. Even if the allusions are only more or less certain, however, the probable or even likely quotation of

103. See Goodspeed, *Meaning of Ephesians*, 82–165.

104. Such as Revelation and the letters of Ignatius, as well as the Gospel and letters of John, works that clearly reflect Pauline influence. Ephesus also had Paul's letter of introduction of Phoebe (Romans 16), according to Goodspeed.

105. For expansions on Goodspeed's theory, see John Knox, *Philemon among the Letters of Paul*, rev. ed. (London: Collins, 1959), 10.

106. See Committee of the Oxford Society of Historical Theology, *New Testament in the Apostolic Fathers* (Oxford: Clarendon, 1905), 37–55. The examples include (I cite the a and b passages in the A category) *1 Clem.* 35:5–6 citing Rom. 1:29–32; *1 Clem.* 33:1 citing Rom. 6:1; *1 Clem.* 37:5; 38:1 citing 1 Cor. 12:12ff.; *1 Clem.* 47:1 citing 1 Cor. 1:11–13; *1 Clem.* 49:5 citing 1 Cor. 13:4–7; *1 Clem.* 24:1 citing 1 Cor. 15:20, 23; *1 Clem.* 24:4–5 citing 1 Cor. 15:36–37 (there are c- and d-rated passages as well).

107. *1 Clem.* 1:3 citing Titus 2:4–5, and possibly *1 Clem.* 2:7; 24:4 citing Titus 3:1; 2:21; 3:17; *1 Clem.* 36:2–5 citing Heb. 1:1–14. On possible echoes of the Pastoral Epistles, see Horacio E. Lona, *Der erste Clemensbrief*, KAV 2 (Göttingen: Vandenhoeck & Ruprecht, 1998), 49–51.

108. *1 Clem.* 36:2 citing 2 Cor. 3:18; *1 Clem.* 2:1 citing Gal. 3:1; *1 Clem.* 5:2 citing Gal. 2:9; *1 Clem.* 36:2 citing Eph. 4:18; *1 Clem.* 46:6 citing Eph. 4:4–6; *1 Clem.* 59:3 citing Eph. 1:18; *1 Clem.* 3:4; 21:2 citing Phil. 1:27; *1 Clem.* 47:1–2 citing Phil. 4:15; *1 Clem.* 59:2 citing Col. 1:12–13; *1 Clem.* 61:2 citing 1 Tim. 1:17.

Romans, 1 Corinthians, and Titus indicates knowledge of an extensive corpus of Paul's letters by the end of the first century in Rome. While many would dispute the allusions, the number and distribution of them points to knowledge by Clement of a corpus of Pauline writings very similar to that found in $\mathfrak{P}^{46}$ already in existence by the closing years of the first century.

Theodor Zahn and Adolf von Harnack[109] believed that interest in the Pauline Epistles existed from the time of their writing. After examining the evidence of Marcion, *1 Clement*, Polycarp, Ignatius, and later canonical lists, Zahn concluded[110] that the consistent references among various early writers, and reference to the letters in churches separated in distance (e.g., Rome, Smyrna, Antioch, and Corinth, where the process of collection may have occurred),[111] indicated that the Pauline Epistles were collected early on and served a vital liturgical purpose. Zahn's Pauline corpus consisted of ten letters (excluding the Pastoral Epistles) and was completed after the writing of Acts but before the writing of *1 Clement*, around AD 80 to 85.[112] Harnack, drawing upon Pauline passages referring to the letter-writing process,[113] saw this as evidence of an early collection of Paul's letters, with the process occurring around AD 100 and including the Pastoral Epistles.[114] Recent study of the book of Acts may push this date even earlier, however, as it has been argued that the author of Acts did know a number of Paul's letters. Richard Pervo claims that he can find significant evidence that Luke used Paul's letters in the

---

109. See Theodor Zahn, *Forschungen zur Geschichte des neutestamentlichen Kanons und der altkirchlichen Literatur* (Erlangen: Deichert, 1888), 1:811–39; Adolf von Harnack, *Die Briefsammlung des Apostels Paulus und die anderen vorkonstantinischen christlichen Briefsammlungen* (Leipzig: Hinrichs, 1926), 6–27. The encapsulation here also draws upon Brevard S. Childs, *The New Testament as Canon: An Introduction* (Valley Forge, PA: Trinity Press International, 1994), 423; C. L. Mitton, *The Formation of the Pauline Corpus of Letters* (London: Epworth, 1955), 15; Gamble, "New Testament Canon," 267–68.

110. He was anticipated by Westcott, *General Survey*, 19–63.

111. See F. F. Bruce, "New Light on the Origins of the New Testament Canon," in *New Dimensions in New Testament Study*, ed. Richard N. Longenecker and Merrill C. Tenney (Grand Rapids: Zondervan, 1974), 3–18, esp. 10.

112. Zahn, *Geschichte des neutestamentlichen Kanons*, 1:835.

113. Harnack, *Die Briefsammlung des Apostels Paulus*, 7–8. For example, exalting Paul as a letter writer, or warning against false letters, and so on, as in 2 Thess. 2:2; 3:17; 1 Cor. 7:17; 2 Cor. 3:1; 10:9–10.

114. Ibid., 6.

writing of Acts. He contends that there are verbal, thematic, setting, and content indicators of the use of Romans, 1 Corinthians, 2 Corinthians, Galatians, Ephesians, Philippians, and Colossians, as well as indicators of Paul's itinerary.[115] Others have found elements of other letters in Acts, such as 1 Thessalonians in the Miletus speech (Acts 20:18–35).[116] If this is true and the date of Acts is not in the second century but instead either AD 85 or earlier,[117] then the gathering of the Pauline letter collection would need to have occurred even earlier.

A number of scholars have recognized that it is probable that a single, significant follower of Paul was responsible for the gathering and creation of the Pauline corpus. Claiming that Acts does not seem to know of the Pauline Epistles, C. F. D. Moule believed that after Paul's death Luke gathered the corpus when he revisited the major Pauline cities.[118] Donald Guthrie proposed that Timothy collected Paul's letters, claiming that all of the major churches associated with Pauline Epistles had either direct or indirect Pauline foundations or strong personal connections to him at the time of his death.[119] To support such remembrance of Paul, Guthrie notes such factors as the exchange of Paul's letters (Col. 4:16), their public reading (1 Thess. 5:27) and wider distribution (see 1 Corinthians), the circular character of some of the letters (e.g., Romans, Ephesians), and the respect shown for Paul's writings by early church writers, such as Clement (*1 Clem.* 5:5–7).

115. Richard Pervo, *Dating Acts: Between the Evangelists and the Apologists* (Sonoma, CA: Polebridge, 2006), 51–147. Pervo, however, wishes to date Acts in the second century, a conclusion that does not necessarily follow. A few others have argued unnecessarily similarly.

116. See Steve Walton, *Leadership and Lifestyle: The Portrait of Paul in the Miletus Speech and 1 Thessalonians*, SNTSMS 108 (Cambridge: Cambridge University Press, 2000), 201–13.

117. See Porter, "Was Paulinism a Thing?," 9–12. For a survey of recent approaches to Paulinism, see Stanley E. Porter, "The Portrait of Paul in the Acts of the Apostles," in *The Blackwell Companion to Paul*, ed. Stephen Westerholm (Oxford: Blackwell, 2011), 124–38.

118. C. F. D. Moule, *The Birth of the New Testament*, 3rd ed. (San Francisco: Harper & Row, 1982), 263–65.

119. Donald Guthrie, *New Testament Introduction*, 3rd ed. (Downers Grove, IL: InterVarsity, 1970), 653. That is, outside of Palestine, since relations with the Jerusalem church near the end of Paul's life were strained. See Stanley E. Porter, *The Paul of Acts: Essays in Literary Criticism, Rhetoric, and Theology*, WUNT 115 (Tübingen: Mohr Siebeck, 1999), 172–86.

Accepting personal involvement in the collection of Paul's letters and concentrating upon the first four letters, Trobisch posits Paul's own involvement in the letter-collection process.[120] This idea is not new.[121] E. Randolph Richards has also argued that Paul used a secretary (much like Cicero's secretary, Tiro). Hence, Paul had copies made of his letters, and these letters constituted the origin of the Pauline letter collection, possibly then assembled by Paul's secretary, Luke.[122] Trobisch claims that Paul's letters are public letters that were kept in copies, whereas a private letter is never a copy but the original. But in fact, even private letters regularly were copied (e.g., Cicero, *Fam.* 9.26.1; 7.18.1; *Att.* 13.6.3).[123] This process of copying would follow the pattern of many ancient writers—such as Seneca and Cicero as literary authors (indicating that actual letters were involved, not composites of the fragments of earlier letters), and Zenon as a documentary writer, among them—who made copies of their letters before having them dispatched.[124] Many of the early manuscripts, especially the early codexes,[125] follow essentially modern canonical order for the Pauline Epistles.[126]

120. See David Trobisch, *Die Entstehung der Paulusbriefsammlung: Studien zu den Anfängen christlicher Publizistik*, NTOA 10 (Freiburg: Universitätsverlag; Göttingen: Vandenhoeck & Ruprecht, 1989); *Paul's Letter Collection* (1994), noted above; and now *The First Edition of the New Testament* (New York: Oxford University Press, 2000).

121. See Guthrie, *New Testament Introduction*, 657, citing R. L. Archer, "The Epistolary Form in the New Testament," *ExpTim* 63 (1951–1952): 296–98, esp. 297.

122. E. Randolph Richards, *The Secretary in the Letters of Paul*, WUNT, 2nd ser., vol. 42 (Tübingen: Mohr Siebeck, 1991), esp. 164–65, 187–88; *Paul and First-Century Letter Writing: Secretaries, Composition and Collection* (Downers Grove, IL: InterVarsity, 2004), 218–23; "The Codex and the Early Collection of Paul's Letters," *BBR* 8 (1988): 151–66; followed by E. Earle Ellis, "Pastoral Letters," *DPL* 658–66, esp. 660.

123. Jerome Murphy-O'Connor, *Paul the Letter-Writer: His World, His Options, His Skills* (Collegeville, MN: Liturgical Press, 1995), 12–13.

124. See Richards, *Paul and First-Century Letter Writing*, 156–65, 214–15. Paul is considered one of the great letter writers of the ancient world. If that is true—and his corpus of letters argues that it is—then it is logical to think that Paul followed the conventions of ancient letter writing, including producing and retaining copies. However, this does not necessarily imply that we can identify the autographs, since (as noted in chap. 1) the published (or preserved or authenticated) version is considered the original.

125. Such as Codexes Sinaiticus (01 ℵ), Alexandrinus (02 A), Vaticanus (03 B), and Ephraemi Rescriptus (04 C).

126. Trobisch, *Paul's Letter Collection*, 17–26; *Die Entstehung der Paulusbriefsammlung*, 56–62.

However, 𝔓⁴⁶, the oldest intact Pauline letter collection, arranges the Pauline Epistles essentially according to length, so Ephesians precedes Galatians, and Hebrews appears after Romans. Trobisch believes that the common form of title of the Pauline Epistles implies their having been gathered together under Paul's name.[127] He also notes that the overall arrangement of the letters in 𝔓⁴⁶ is based upon the addressees, with the letters to churches preceding the letters to individuals, and within these two categories they are organized by decreasing length,[128] with letters to the same place or person kept together.[129] He posits a three-stage process to the formation of Paul's letter collection: Romans to Galatians is a single early unit,[130] with it "highly probable that this old collection was edited and prepared for publication by Paul himself."[131] Paul edited the four authentic letters[132] so as to unite them together in thought and amount of personal detail.[133] The second stage was expansion of the corpus, and the third stage was comprehensive and inclusive editions.[134] Ephesians serves as the introductory letter for the pseudepigraphal appendix to the authentic Pauline corpus.[135] These three stages led to the canonical Pauline collection.[136]

127. Trobisch, *Paul's Letter Collection*, 24.

128. See ibid., 52–54.

129. Ibid., 25. For example, 1 and 2 Corinthians; 1 and 2 Thessalonians; and 1 and 2 Timothy.

130. Ibid., 25–47; i.e., Romans, 1 and 2 Corinthians, and Galatians.

131. Ibid., 54.

132. See ibid., 55–96; cf. Trobisch, *Die Entstehung der Paulusbriefsammlung*, 100–104, 128–32.

133. See Trobisch, *Paul's Letter Collection*, 62–70. For example, personal greetings are important only in terms of travel plans, and one of their common ideas is the collection.

134. Ibid., 54. Trobisch claims to provide inadvertent support for Goodspeed's hypothesis, with the thirteen-letter corpus an expansion upon the original four letters.

135. Ibid., 101n22.

136. Murphy-O'Connor (*Paul the Letter-Writer*, 120–30) adopts a similar three-stage collection process: collection A consists of Romans, 1 Corinthians, 2 Corinthians, and Galatians, which originated at Corinth; collection B consists of those letters from neighboring churches in Asia Minor and Greece; and collection C, the personal letters, was added to collection B. Murphy-O'Connor (ibid., 121, 123) uses violations of the consistent decrease in length (e.g., from Galatians to Ephesians, and 2 Thessalonians to 1 Timothy), reinforced by the varying placement of Hebrews, as indicators of section breaks. He also minimizes problems over the different canonical orderings on the basis that other possible determiners of length besides number of characters, such as stichoi and Euthalian numbers, indicate very similar lengths between the books

This reconstruction plausibly shows that Paul may well have been responsible for gathering the first four letters of the Pauline letter collection, but Trobisch neglects other evidence provided by his own examples that allows us to push this theory further. The evidence of $\mathfrak{P}^{46}$ itself points toward Paul's involvement in more than simply the gathering of Romans, 1 Corinthians, 2 Corinthians, and Galatians, which are not the first four books in $\mathfrak{P}^{46}$. As Trobisch has noted, manuscript variations in the Pauline corpus occur within relatively narrow parameters; the corpus of Paul's letters originated in a particular location at the instigation of a small group of people, possibly including Paul and some of his closest associates. The variations in the manuscripts revolve around placement of the book of Hebrews (found in a number of manuscripts),[137] the alternating of Ephesians and Galatians (e.g., $\mathfrak{P}^{46}$), some uncertainty over the order of Colossians and Philippians (e.g., Codex Claromontanus [06 Dp]), and whether the Pastoral Epistles are included (e.g., $\mathfrak{P}^{46}$).[138] As Jerome Murphy-O'Connor has shown, however, if one does not rely simply upon counting characters but uses other evident ancient forms of measurement, such as the indicated stichoi,[139] the fluctuation in placement of Hebrews is the only real variable; there is otherwise virtual fixity to the manuscript ordering, at least in the early stages.[140] The placement of Colossians before Philippians is understandable, as they are within two hundred characters of each other and have similar stichoi in some traditions.

---

of Galatians, Ephesians, Colossians, and Philippians. On stichometry, see J. Rendel Harris, *Stichometry* (London: Clay, 1893); on the Euthalian numbers, see Louis Charles Willard, *A Critical Study of the Euthalian Apparatus*, ANTF 41 (Berlin: de Gruyter, 2009). The result is a very consistent pattern of division of the Pauline corpus that strengthens Trobisch's analysis. However, Murphy-O'Connor (ibid., 130) sees possibly Timothy and more likely Onesimus, rather than Paul, as instigating this process.

137. Apart from $\mathfrak{P}^{46}$, Hebrews appears only either at the juncture of the church and personal letters (i.e., between 2 Thessalonians and 1 Timothy) or at the end of the Pauline corpus (or at the beginning). A possible exception is the numbering of the chapters in Codex Vaticanus (03 B). But, as Trobisch (*Paul's Letter Collection*, 21–22) notes, it is only the numbering of the chapters that places Hebrews after Galatians, since the manuscript itself has Hebrews after 2 Thessalonians.

138. Walther Schmithals, *Paul and the Gnostics*, trans. John E. Steely (Nashville: Abingdon, 1972), 256.

139. Stichometry is an ancient practice of dividing texts into individual sense or structural units (stichoi) often used to measure the length of a text according to the number of stichoi. See J. Rendel Harris, *Stichometry* (London: Clay, 1893), 2–3.

140. Murphy-O'Connor, *Paul the Letter-Writer*, 125.

In any event, this transposition from the normal order only occurs in Codex Claromontanus (06 Dp) and a fourteenth-century minuscule (5).[141] The placement of Ephesians before Galatians only occurs in $\mathfrak{P}^{46}$, but this ordering does reflect actual length, with Ephesians being seven hundred to nine hundred letters longer, depending upon whose count is followed.[142] The ordering in $\mathfrak{P}^{46}$ may in fact be the original ordering, which may have implications for Paul's involvement in his letter collection. In other words, the evidence seems to point toward complete consistency in the compositional ordering of the entire Pauline corpus (whether one accepts $\mathfrak{P}^{46}$ or not), not just within three groups of letters. The Pauline corpus follows the principle of decreasing size[143] from Romans to 2 Thessalonians, what might be called the "church letters," and then begins again with an ordering in decreasing size from 1 Timothy to Philemon, what might be called the "personal letters."[144] This same differentiation of church and personal letters is found in the Muratorian Canon.[145] There is some debate over the date of the Muratorian Canon. Those who contend for a fourth-century date claim that there are no parallels of lists of New Testament books from the second century.[146] However, this may not be entirely correct.

141. Murphy-O'Connor (ibid., 123) unwisely dismisses this as "an error without historical significance."

142. The number of stichoi in some traditions, however, is similar. Murphy-O'Connor (ibid., 124) again unwisely dismisses this transposition as "an insignificant error." Cf. Trobisch, *Paul's Letter Collection*, 17, where he notes that $\mathfrak{P}^{46}$ in its entirety is arranged according to length, with Hebrews placed before 1 Corinthians, which is longer, so as not to separate the two Corinthian letters.

143. This pattern is thus found not only in modern arrangements of the Pauline canon (Bruce, *Canon of Scripture*, 130n50), but also in ancient times.

144. Philemon is typically considered a personal letter, even if it is more than that (Joseph A. Fitzmyer, *The Letter to Philemon: A New Translation with Introduction and Commentary*, AB 34C [New York: Doubleday, 2000], 23). The Pastoral Epistles were given that name only by the nineteenth century. Dispute over their authenticity often concerns the personal elements found in the letters (for an older but representative survey of opinion, see E. Earle Ellis, *Paul and His Recent Interpreters* [Grand Rapids: Eerdmans, 1961], 49–57). See also Jeffrey T. Reed, "To Timothy or Not? A Discourse Analysis of 1 Timothy," in *Biblical Greek Language and Linguistics: Open Questions in Current Research*, ed. Stanley E. Porter and D. A. Carson, JSNTSup 80 (Sheffield: JSOT Press, 1993), 90–118. Reed notes the clear indications of the personal nature of the correspondence addressed to Timothy.

145. Lee Martin McDonald, *The Biblical Canon: Its Origin, Transmission, and Authority* (Peabody, MA: Hendrickson, 2007), 370, for quotation of the Muratorian Canon.

146. Ibid., 371–78.

No fourth-century list of authoritative New Testament writings, so far as I can tell, differentiates church and personal letters.[147] The parallel of the Muratorian Canon with the listing in 𝔓⁴⁶ seems to indicate a second-century date, like the date of 𝔓⁴⁶.

As noted above, Hebrews is the one book of the Pauline group that varies significantly regarding ordering. Trobisch claims that the amount and type of variation in the placement of Hebrews, along with other internal and external differences, indicate that Hebrews was not part of the original thirteen-letter Pauline corpus but rather was added later to a relatively fixed corpus.[148] In other words, if Hebrews is removed from the Pauline letter collection,[149] then the corpus from earliest times seems to have been intact.

If one does not remove Hebrews from the collection, however, but instead considers the implications of its placement within the Pauline letter collection, interesting possibilities may be suggested. Hebrews appears after Romans in 𝔓⁴⁶ and quite possibly in 𝔓¹³ (dates vary, but AD 225–250 to early fourth century have been suggested for 𝔓¹³).[150] 𝔓¹³ has portions of Hebrews (2:14–5:5; 10:8–22; 10:29–11:13; 11:28–12:17), but the columns are enumerated.[151] Hebrews 2:14 starts on column 47, indicating that text was found in the same manuscript before Hebrews. In 𝔓⁴⁶, Hebrews 2:14 is on page 44. The manuscripts are similar enough in configuration with regard to line length and lines per column that it is very possible that 𝔓¹³ was part of a similar Pauline manuscript with Hebrews after Romans. Hebrews appears after 2 Thessalonians and before 1 Timothy in Codexes Sinaiticus (01 ℵ), Alexandrinus (02 A), Vaticanus (03 B), and Ephraemi Rescriptus (04 C) (fourth to fifth centuries). In the fifth-century Codex Claromontanus (06 Dp) and in the Byzantine text-type, Hebrews appears at the

147. See ibid., 445–51.
148. Trobisch, *Paul's Letter Collection*, 20. This point was made by Zuntz, *Text of the Epistles*, 15–16.
149. If one accepts that this variation indicates that Hebrews was a later addition, it appears to have been added at the end of the corpus to indicate ambivalence over its authorship, or at the end of the church letters (after 2 Thessalonians) because it is not a personal letter, but in this case still reflecting indecision over authorship.
150. See Comfort and Barrett, *Text*, 83.
151. Bernard P. Grenfell and Arthur S. Hunt, *The Oxyrhynchus Papyri, IV* (London: Egypt Exploration Fund, 1904), 36–48; with a fragment by Vittorio Bartoletti and M. Norsi, *Papiri greci e latini della Società Italiana* 12 (1951): 209–10.

end of the Pauline Epistles—that is, after Philemon.[152] The evidence, rather than indicating uncertainty as to whether Hebrews belongs to the Pauline corpus, points to Hebrews being included in the Pauline corpus in the earliest manuscripts but indecision on what type of letter it is—that is, whether it is one of the major church letters ($\mathfrak{P}^{46}$), either a church or a personal letter (most major codexes), or uncertainty as to its type (Codex Claromontanus [06 Dp]). Although Hebrews is cited by Clement of Rome, the earliest clear reference to Pauline authorship is in the late second century by Clement of Alexandria (Eusebius, *Hist eccl*. 6.14). Scholarship today rejects Pauline authorship of Hebrews, but its inclusion with Paul's letters in the early manuscripts keeps open the possibility that the book was considered in some way Pauline—either directly Pauline (Hebrews is formally anonymous) or indirectly Pauline, such as by a companion of Paul under his influence; the product of similar scribal influence upon the letter's composition (whether the same scribe or a similar process); or edited by someone from Pauline material.[153] The ending of the letter certainly has a Pauline character to it (Heb. 13:22–25).

The Pauline corpus, once formed in the first century, quite possibly by Paul himself, began to be used and copied widely, so that it is likely that a complete compilation of Paul's letters was circulating by the end of the second century ($\mathfrak{P}^{46}$) and throughout subsequent centuries ($\mathfrak{P}^{13}$), probably with Hebrews considered a part of the Pauline letter collection.

### The Rest of the New Testament

We have now examined the Gospels and Acts and the Pauline corpus and seen that we can reconstruct the transmissional history of these two subcorpora back to the second and even first centuries respectively. What about the rest of the New Testament books? Due to much more limited textual evidence, it is far more difficult to retrace

---

152. Trobisch, *Paul's Letter Collection*, 20.
153. James Moffatt, *An Introduction to the Literature of the New Testament*, 3rd ed. (Edinburgh: T&T Clark, 1918), 433. For a recent discussion, see Andrew W. Pitts and Joshua F. Walker, "The Authorship of Hebrews: A Further Development in the Luke-Paul Relationship," in *Paul and His Social Relations*, ed. Stanley E. Porter and Christopher D. Land, PSt 7 (Leiden: Brill, 2013), 143–84.

the transmissional history of the rest of the New Testament than it is to trace it for the Gospels and Acts and the Pauline corpus. As a result, such reconstructions must be highly speculative. I will mention three examples, however, that point at least in part toward an early gathering of this part of the New Testament corpus.

■ 0232

The first example concerns the Johannine corpus. There is little transmissional or manuscript evidence to indicate a usual gathering of the Johannine writings as a subcorpus—even in the major codexes, which did not keep John's Gospel, the three Johannine Epistles, and the book of Revelation together. However, there is one manuscript that may indicate that a Johannine corpus was gathered together fairly early. Majuscule manuscript 0232, which is a fragmentary parchment, has a small portion of 2 John 1–9 on the front and back of a single page.[154] What is significant is that these pages are numbered 164 and 165. The editor of the manuscript, C. H. Roberts, dated this parchment to the third century. Later, Kurt Aland redated it to the fifth or the sixth century.[155] However, Comfort and Barrett, in the original edition of their volume of early New Testament manuscripts, date it to the late third or the early fourth century (around AD 300).[156] According to Roberts, the page numbers, which appear in a second hand, in relation to the text of 2 John provide intriguing possibilities. Roberts's calculation of the words per page leads him to believe that there is too much material in the Pauline corpus and too little in the Catholic Epistles and the Pastoral Epistles to fill the previous 160-plus pages. He concludes that it is likely that the Gospel of John, Revelation, and 1 John preceded 2 John, though acknowledging that the

154. C. H. Roberts, *The Antinoopolis Papyri, I* (London: Egypt Exploration Society, 1950), 24–26.

155. Kurt Aland, ed., *Kurzgefasste Liste der griechischen Handschriften des Neuen Testaments*, ANTF 1 (Berlin: de Gruyter, 1963), 56.

156. Philip W. Comfort and David P. Barrett, *The Complete Text of the Earliest New Testament Manuscripts* (Grand Rapids: Baker Academic, 1999), 648. I note, however, that Comfort and Barrett do not include this manuscript in their revised edition (2001), nor is it in Philip Comfort, *Encountering the Manuscripts: An Introduction to New Testament Paleography and Textual Criticism* (Nashville: Broadman & Holman, 2005), perhaps indicating that they have subsequently been convinced that the Aland date is correct.

spacing is not entirely amenable to his solution. Thus, it is possible that there was a separate and distinct gathering of the Johannine writings by the year AD 300 or even earlier.[157]

- $\mathfrak{P}^{72}$

The second example concerns the Petrine corpus. $\mathfrak{P}^{72}$ is part of a number of Bodmer papyri (P.Bodmer VII and VIII).[158] Textual critics frequently overlook that biblical manuscripts are sometimes found with other nonbiblical manuscripts. Such is the case with $\mathfrak{P}^{72}$. This manuscript, which consists of 1 Peter, 2 Peter, and Jude from the New Testament, was bound together with the *Nativity of Mary*, the apocryphal letter 3 Corinthians, *Odes of Solomon* 11, Melito's *Homily on the Passion*, a fragment of a liturgical hymn, the *Apology of Phileas*, and Psalm 33:2–34:16 (LXX).[159] There have been several attempts to reconstruct the origin and relationship of what Tommy Wasserman calls the "Bodmer codex."[160] Issues to be considered include the several different scribes involved (probably four), the different pagination schemes evidenced, the ability to link together the various parts of this codex (it has now been split up and published in separate parts), and the evidence for binding. Wasserman's recent study concludes that 1 Peter, 2 Peter, and Jude, though they are separated within the codex, were written by the same hand, even if they follow different originals—1 Peter being closest to Codex Vaticanus (03 B), and 2 Peter and Jude having Western readings.[161] Wasserman sees a process of collection taking place that brought the various manuscripts together into the codex, which was bound together in the early fourth century. The date of $\mathfrak{P}^{72}$, including 1 Peter, 2 Peter, and Jude by the same scribe, could reasonably be the third century.[162] The manuscript appears to have

---

157. There is, if Aland is correct, evidence showing nothing more than such a gathering by the fifth or the sixth century, which we already know from major codexes such as Sinaiticus (01 א) in the fourth century and Alexandrinus (02 A) in the fifth century.

158. Michel Testuz, *Papyrus Bodmer VII–IX: L'Epître de Jude, les deux Epîtres de Pierre, les Psaumes 33 et 34* (Cologny-Geneva: Bibliotheca Bodmeriana, 1959).

159. See ibid., 8.

160. Tommy Wasserman, *The Epistle of Jude: Its Text and Transmission*, ConBNT 43 (Stockholm: Almqvist & Wiksell, 2006), 31.

161. Wasserman, *Epistle of Jude*, 42–50 (who concludes that the scribe copied all of the books in the Bodmer Codex); Comfort and Barrett, *Text*, 479.

162. Testuz, *Papyrus Bodmer VII–IX*, 7; Wasserman, *Epistle of Jude*, 30–50, esp. 33, 40. Wasserman clearly refutes the inadequate analyses of (the former student of Bart

been prepared not for liturgical use but rather for private use, and it is part of the Dishna Papers, found near the Pachomian headquarters, probably as part of a "Pachomian monastic library."[163] If this is true, it indicates that by as early as the third century, 1 Peter, 2 Peter, and Jude were considered a subcorpus and copied together, even if they were later bound with other manuscripts for particular theological purposes.

■ $\mathfrak{P}^{23}$

The third example concerns the Catholic Epistles. $\mathfrak{P}^{23}$,[164] a fragmentary manuscript of the letter of James (1:10–12, 15–18) that dates possibly to the late second or the third century (though Grenfell and Hunt dated it to the fourth century) and agrees with Codexes Sinaiticus (01 ℵ), Alexandrinus (02 A), and Ephraemi Rescriptus (04 C), followed by Vaticanus (03 B) and $\mathfrak{P}^{74}$, has page numbers on both the front and the back of the leaf (2 and 3).[165] Similar though probably later is $\mathfrak{P}^{100}$, also a manuscript of the letter of James (3:13–4:4; 4:9–5:1),[166] which dates to the late third or early fourth century, resembles primarily Codex Vaticanus (03 B) and then Codex Sinaiticus (01 ℵ) and Codex Alexandrinus (02 A) and has page numbers on both sides of the leaf (6 and 7).[167] These page numbers in both instances indicate that page 1 was the beginning of the Epistle of James. Since Hebrews probably was included with the Pauline Epistles, it is possible either that both $\mathfrak{P}^{23}$ and $\mathfrak{P}^{100}$ were manuscripts of just the Epistle of James or that they were the first book in a collection of the Catholic (or General) Epistles.[168] We cannot know for sure, although the use of page numbers may indicate that a larger collection of texts was included. If the latter is the

---

Ehrman) Kim Haines-Eitzen, *Guardians of Letters: Literacy, Power, and the Transmitters of Early Christian Literature* (Oxford: Oxford University Press, 2000), 96–104.

163. Wasserman, *Epistle of Jude*, 32, citing James M. Robinson, *The Pachomian Monastic Library at the Chester Beatty Library and the Bibliothèque Bodmer*, OPIAC 19 (Claremont, CA: Institute for Antiquity and Christianity, 1990), 2–6 (on the library), 19–21 (for an inventory).

164. Bernard P. Grenfell and Arthur S. Hunt, *The Oxyrhynchus Papyri*, X (London: Egypt Exploration Fund, 1914), 16–18.

165. Comfort and Barrett, *Text*, 111. They discuss date, noting that Aland and Aland (*Text of the New Testament*, 97) date it to the third century.

166. M. W. Haslam et al., *The Oxyrhynchus Papyri*, LXV, GRM 85 (London: Egypt Exploration Society, 1998), 20–25.

167. See Comfort and Barrett, *Text*, 111, 633.

168. Ibid., 633.

case, there is evidence of the Catholic Epistles being gathered together possibly by the second century and almost assuredly by the third.

As we can see from this survey of the papyri, the evidence is much more slender for this third subcorpus of the New Testament. Nevertheless, three pieces of disparate evidence, admittedly subject to question, are of potential relevance. They indicate the possibility that by the late second century and probably by the third century, at least parts of even this portion of the New Testament were being gathered together into recognizable groupings. By the time of the fourth century, the existence of the Catholic Epistles as a group—with James at the head, followed by 1 Peter, 2 Peter, and Jude (in that order, though separated by the Johannine Epistles)—is well established.[169]

## The Major Codexes

The fourth and fifth centuries were the centuries of production of deluxe codexes that contained the entire Bible.[170] The history that I reconstructed above gave evidence of early gathering of subcorpora of the New Testament, including the four Gospels and possibly Acts, the Pauline Epistles including Hebrews, and even the Catholic Epistles. By the fourth century all of these major parts of the New Testament had been brought together into one large book, along with the Old Testament. Various New Testament books, possibly as part of larger gatherings, but certainly individually, continued to be copied onto papyrus and parchment. However, with the conversion of Constantine and the institutionalization of Christianity, one of the major results was the production of major Bibles, in a form that is very much recognizable as similar to the Bible that we use today. There are four such great codexes extant that originally had both Testaments. A brief description of them gives further insight into the transmissional unity of the New Testament.

169. This is found in Codex Sinaiticus (01 ℵ) and Codex Vaticanus (03 B), Athanasius (fourth century), Epiphanius (fourth century), Philastrius (fourth century), Rufinus (fourth century), Gregory of Nazianzus (c. 390), Amphilochius (fourth century), Council of Carthage (397), Jerome (fourth/fifth century), and Augustine (fourth/fifth century). See Moffatt, *Introduction*, 14; McDonald, *Biblical Canon*, 446–48.

170. See Parker, "Majuscule Manuscripts."

## Codex Sinaiticus and Codex Vaticanus

The two earliest major codexes are Codex Sinaiticus (01 ℵ) and Codex Vaticanus (03 B).[171] Codex Vaticanus (03 B),[172] dated to the fourth century, has been in the Vatican library since at least 1481, when a catalogue records its presence. The manuscript now consists of 759 leaves out of an original total of 820—617 of which are the Old Testament and the rest the New Testament. In the Old Testament, 31 leaves at the beginning of the manuscript, containing Genesis 1:1–46:28, and 10 leaves, containing Psalms 105:27–137:6, are missing, and the leaves containing 2 Samuel 2:5–67, 10–13 are mutilated. The Old Testament includes all the books of the Greek Bible except Maccabees and follows Athanasius's *Festal Letter*, with the poetical books before the prophets. The New Testament includes the four Gospels, Acts, James to Jude, Romans to 2 Thessalonians, and Hebrews.[173] The original hands of the manuscript end at Hebrews 9:14, but the manuscript continues

171. Original publication of Codex Sinaiticus was Constantin Tischendorf, *Bibliorum Codex Sinaiticus Petropolitanus*, 4 vols. (St. Petersburg, 1862), of which only three hundred copies were printed. Further editions of the New Testament include Constantin Tischendorf, *Novum Testamentum Sinaiticum sive Novum Testamentum cum epistula Barnabae et fragmentis Pastoris* (Leipzig: Brockhaus, 1863). Photographic reproductions include Helen and Kirsopp Lake, *Codex Sinaiticus Petropolitanus*, 2 vols. (Oxford: Clarendon, 1911, 1922); *Codex Sinaiticus* (Peabody, MA: Hendrickson; London: British Library, 2010), the latter including virtually all of the known fragments. The publishing history of Codex Vaticanus is less clear and accessible. Editions include Angelus Mai, *Vetus et Novum Testamentum ex antiquissimo Codice Vaticano* (Rome, 1857), with the New Testament appearing alone as *Novum Testamentum ex vetustissimo Codice Vaticano secundis curis editum* (Rome, 1859), and in England as *Codex Vaticanus: Η ΚΑΙΝΗ ΔΙΑΘΗΚΗ, Novum Testamentum Graece* (London: Williams & Norgate, 1860) (generally considered an unreliable edition); Constantin Tischendorf, *Novum Testamentum Vaticanum* (Leipzig: Giesecke & Devrient, 1867). Photographic reproductions include *Bibliorum sacrorum Graecorum Codex Vaticanus B: Bibliothecae Apostolicae Vaticanae Codex Vaticanus Graecus 1209* (Vatican: Istituto Poligrafico e Zecca dello Stato, 1999). For some of the information above and other references, see J. K. Elliott, *A Bibliography of Greek New Testament Manuscripts*, 2nd ed., SNTSMS 109 (Cambridge: Cambridge University Press, 2000), 43–45, 47–49 (though not always accurate); Stephen Pisano, "The Text of the New Testament," in *Prolegomena*, 27–41, esp. 31–32 (accompanying volume to *Bibliorum sacrorum Graecorum Codex Vaticanus B*, noted above).

172. General information on Codex Vaticanus (03 B) is from Kenyon, *Text*, 43–44, 85–88.

173. This placement of Hebrews is also found in later manuscripts: Codex 016/I (fifth century), Codex 015/H (sixth century), Minuscule 5 (fourteenth century).

in a minuscule hand from the fifteenth century and includes the rest of Hebrews and Revelation (Minuscule 1957).[174] The assumption is that Vaticanus originally had the three Pastoral Epistles, Philemon, and Revelation. Skeat thought that Codex Vaticanus (03 B), as well as Codex Sinaiticus (01 ℵ), was one of the fifty manuscripts commissioned by the emperor Constantine in AD 335 (Eusebius, *Vit. Const.* 4.36–37), and that possibly Sinaiticus was rejected.[175] I agree with Metzger, who takes his cue from Skeat, that it is also possible that Vaticanus was rejected, as Vaticanus lacks the Eusebian table numbers and the books of Maccabees, in addition to having many corrections and having later been reinscribed.[176]

Codex Sinaiticus (01 ℵ), discovered by Constantin Tischendorf and published by him in 1862, is also now dated to the fourth century.[177] The manuscript, consisting of 411 extant leaves, once contained 743 leaves, but the Old Testament has been severely damaged, so that only 293 Old Testament leaves survive (43 in Leipzig and 197 in the British Museum, along with all or parts of 36 pages in St. Catherine's Monastery in Sinai and parts of 8 pages in the National Library of Russia in St. Petersburg). The Old Testament contains fragments and parts of Genesis, Leviticus, Numbers, Deuteronomy, Joshua, Judges, 1 Chronicles (including a large duplicate section), 2 Esdras, and Lamentations, and the virtually complete texts of Esther, Tobit, Judith, 1 Maccabees, 4 Maccabees, the prophets and the poetical writings, Wisdom of Solomon, Sirach, and Job.[178] The parts that are

174. Parker, *New Testament Manuscripts*, 234.

175. T. C. Skeat, "The Codex Sinaiticus, the Codex Vaticanus and Constantine," *JTS* 50 (1999): 583–625; repr. in J. K. Elliott, ed., *The Collected Biblical Writings of T. C. Skeat*, NovTSup 113 (Leiden: Brill, 2004), 193–237. Parker (*Codex Sinaiticus*, 19–22) questions this.

176. Metzger, *Text*, 48 (4th ed., 68–69).

177. Tischendorf had earlier published the forty-three leaves that had been given to him and taken to Leipzig. See Constantin Tischendorf, *Codex Friderico-Augustanus sive fragmenta Veteris Testamenti* (Leipzig: Sumtibus Caroli Francisci Koehleri, 1846).

178. General information on Codex Sinaiticus (01 ℵ) is from Kenyon, *Text*, 41–42, 78–83; Parker, *Codex Sinaiticus*, esp. 7–10; Dirk Jongkind, *Scribal Habits of Codex Sinaiticus* (Piscataway, NJ: Gorgias, 2007), esp. 5–21; and the booklet that accompanies the photographic reproduction. The only exception regarding early dating is that the German paleographer Viktor Gardthausen dated it to the early fifth century (*Griechische Palaeographie* [Leipzig: Veit, 1913], 2:122–34). Parker's book is one of the results of a project instituted in 2005 by the British Library, the

mostly missing (especially most of Genesis, all of Exodus, much of Leviticus, two-thirds of Numbers, and most of Deuteronomy and Joshua) are compatible with Tischendorf's account of finding the manuscript in a basket and being told that two previous baskets (presumably with the earlier parts of the Old Testament) had already been thrown in the fire.[179] The New Testament is complete on 150 leaves, as well as the *Letter of Barnabas* and part of the *Shepherd of Hermas* (all of the New Testament and Barnabas are in the British Library with the exception of two leaves—one at St. Catherine's and one in the National Library of Russia). The New Testament order is the four Gospels, the Pauline Epistles from Romans to Philemon (with Hebrews after 2 Thessalonians), Acts, the Catholic Epistles, and then Revelation, before *Barnabas* and *Shepherd of Hermas*—a point I will return to below.

---

University of Leipzig, St. Catherine's Monastery, and the National Library of Russia to digitize and publish online and in print form the entire Codex Sinaiticus (01 א). This was accomplished in 2009. In the late 1990s I made a proposal on behalf of Dr. Jeffrey T. Reed and myself to a curator of the British Library to digitize Codex Sinaiticus, including providing funding for the digitization. The British Library apparently had not at that time even considered such an idea, but nevertheless rejected the offer, claiming that it would require restoration of the manuscript before they could proceed. When the project was instigated, we were not part of the discussions, and no effort was made to include us in it, apart from general information sent to scholars worldwide.

179. See Constantin Tischendorf, *When Were Our Gospels Written? An Argument, with a Narrative of the Discovery of the Sinaitic Manuscript* (London: Religious Tract Society, 1896), esp. 23. There has been much controversy regarding the factuality of Tischendorf's account, most recently again raised by Parker (*Codex Sinaiticus*, 127–48). In fact, Parker drags a number of red herrings across the argument, regarding things such as orientalism versus continentalism, colonialism, linguistic competence, and some other issues related to political correctness. Even if Tischendorf did not save the manuscript from being burned (I still think that this is the best explanation of the facts), other indications are that the monks may well have already split up the manuscript, did cut parts of it up to be used in bookbinding or even as bookmarks, did lose track of at least some of it in a room no longer used, and indisputably gave Tischendorf forty-three leaves to take with him in 1844 (see Parker, *Codex Sinaiticus*, 3–4, 121–24, 133). I also believe, along with Christoph Böttrich and others, that Tischendorf played a significant role in ensuring that the situation with the monks at St. Catherine's was duly and legally settled, as the most recently published documentation seems to indicate. See Christoph Böttrich, "Constantin von Tischendorf und der Transfer des Codex Sinaiticus nach St. Petersburg," in *Die Theologische Fakultät der Universität Leipzig: Personen, Profile und Perspektiven aus sechs Jahrhunderten Fakultätsgeschichte*, ed. Andreas Gössner, BLUW 2A (Leipzig: Evangelische Verlagsanstalt, 2005), 253–75.

## Codex Alexandrinus

The third manuscript is Codex Alexandrinus (02 A).[180] This fifth-century manuscript once contained 820 leaves. It passed from the Patriarch of Alexandria to Constantinople and then was offered to James I of England, but it finally came into English hands in 1627 when Charles I was king. The Old Testament is virtually intact, missing only ten leaves, although some pages have been mutilated. The Old Testament consists of the entire Greek Bible, including 3 Maccabees and 4 Maccabees. The New Testament has the Gospels and Acts, the Catholic Epistles, the Pauline Epistles from Romans to Philemon (with Hebrews after 2 Thessalonians), and Revelation. The New Testament lacks part of Matthew and of John (Matt. 1:1–25:6; John 6:50–8:52, probably without the episode of the woman caught in adultery on the basis of spacing) and 2 Corinthians 4:13–12:6. The books of *1 Clement* and *2 Clement* follow the New Testament (though they have lost probably one leaf of *1 Clement* and two leaves of *2 Clement*),[181] and *Psalms of Solomon* was (apparently) appended at the end (per a table of contents at the beginning of the manuscript).[182]

## Codex Ephraemi Rescriptus

The fourth manuscript is Codex Ephraemi Rescriptus (04 C).[183] This manuscript is a palimpsest—that is, a manuscript that has been erased and then written over with a new text—that was deciphered by Tischendorf in 1843 (New Testament) and 1845 (Old Testament).[184] In the

180. Editions include B. H. Cowper, *Codex Alexandrinus: Η ΚΑΙΝΗ ΔΙΑΘΗΚΗ, Novum Testamentum Graece* (revised from C. G. Woide) (London: Williams & Norgate, 1860). General information on Codex Alexandrinus (02 A) is from Kenyon, *Text*, 42–43, 83–85.

181. E. Maunde Thompson, ed., *Facsimile of the Codex Alexandrinus* (London: British Museum, 1883), 4:4.

182. A photograph of this table of contents is included in Trobisch, *First Edition*, 42.

183. General information on Codex Ephraemi Rescriptus (04 C) is from Kenyon, *Text*, 88–89.

184. The edition is Constantin Tischendorf, *Codex Ephraemi Syri rescriptus, sive fragmenta utriusque Testamenti e codice Graeco Parisiensi celeberrimo quinti ut videtur post Christum seculi* (Leipzig: Bernhard Tauchnitz, 1843). In 2005 I had the privilege of examining Tischendorf's notes and the manuscript that he prepared for publication of this manuscript, held in the University of Leipzig library. I thank Steffen Hoffmann for this opportunity.

twelfth century the works of Ephraim of Syria were written over a fifth-century manuscript of the Old and New Testaments. The Old Testament now has only 64 leaves, while the New Testament has 145. The Old Testament is so fragmentary that one cannot determine its original size, but the New Testament probably had about 238 leaves. The New Testament is itself fragmentary, but it includes portions of every New Testament book except 2 Thessalonians and 2 John.

## Contents of the Major Codexes

It is a commonplace in much discussion of the transmission of the New Testament to note that both Codex Sinaiticus (01 ℵ) and Codex Alexandrinus (02 A) include works not now in our usual New Testament canon,[185] and to claim that their inclusion indicates their

185. See, for example, McDonald, *Biblical Canon*, 67. McDonald claims, "Later, Codex Constantinoplitanus (C) included *1–2 Clement*, *Barnabas*, *Didache*, and the letters of Ignatius." I think that McDonald must be confused at this point. The only other reference I can find to Codex Constantinoplitanus is in his own article, where he states, "Later in Codex Constantinoplitanus (C) includes [*sic*] 1 and 2 Clement, *Barnabas*, the *Didache*, and an interpolated text of the letters of Ignatius" (Lee Martin McDonald, "The First Testament: Its Origin, Adaptability, and Stability," in *The Quest for Context and Meaning: Studies in Biblical Intertextuality in Honor of James A. Sanders*, ed. Craig A. Evans and Shemaryahu Talmon, BIS 28 [Leiden: Brill, 1997], 295). Codex C is Codex Ephraemi Rescriptus (04), already discussed above. I think that McDonald is referring not to a codex, but to the catalogue of biblical books (both Old and New Testaments) included between Philemon and Hebrews in the bilingual Codex Claromontanus (06 Dp), dating to the sixth century. The catalogue, which probably is independent of the codex, lists the four Gospels, the Pauline Epistles (excluding Philippians, 1 Thessalonians, and 2 Thessalonians), the Catholic Epistles, *Barnabas*, Revelation, Acts, *Shepherd of Hermas*, *Acts of Paul*, and *Revelation of Peter* (I am not sure how the letters of Ignatius figure into all of this). *Barnabas*, *Shepherd of Hermas*, *Acts of Paul*, and *Revelation of Peter* have a horizontal line placed before them. This line, not mentioned by McDonald, almost certainly indicates disputed status about these four works, as one might expect (see the argument below). For discussion of the catalogue, see Hahneman, *Muratorian Fragment*, 140–41. Hahneman agrees that the line perhaps indicates disputed works, and he thinks that the catalogue may date to the fourth century (which would make sense as to why these works were still listed but disputed). For the catalogue itself, see Alexander Souter, *The Text and Canon of the New Testament* (London: Duckworth, 1912), 211–12 (Souter notes that Adolf von Harnack dated the catalogue to around AD 300, again consonant with inclusion of these disputed books). McDonald also lists "Codex Claromantanus [*sic*]" alongside Vaticanus, Sinaiticus, and Alexandrinus as providing "New Testament Lists from Biblical Manuscripts of the Fourth and Fifth Centuries" (*Biblical Canon*, 451), which I believe is misleading, as the catalogue in

authoritative scriptural status. In this book I do not present a discussion of the canon per se, but I would argue that such statements may go further than they need to or should. For example, with reference to Codex Sinaiticus (01 ℵ), one scholar states that the "*Shepherd of Hermas* and the *Letter of Barnabas* eventually dropped away from the church's sacred Scriptures after having been included by some Christians for centuries."[186] Similarly, regarding Codex Alexandrinus (02 A), one author states that "the epistles of Clement [are] reckoned with the canonical books."[187]

A closer examination of the two manuscripts involved may prompt us to moderate these conclusions, at least insofar as the transmission of manuscripts is concerned. The first observation to make is that the books that we would now consider noncanonical are placed at the end of their respective manuscript. *Barnabas* and *Shepherd of Hermas* appear after Revelation in Codex Sinaiticus (01 ℵ), and *1 Clement* and *2 Clement* appear after Revelation in Codex Alexandrinus (02 A). I noted above that there may be some manuscript variations in the order of the Gospels, Acts, the Pauline Epistles, and the Catholic Epistles, as well as some internal variation within these, most noteworthy being that the book of Hebrews occurs in different places within the Pauline corpus. However, the books often promoted as indicating an "open" canon invariably appear at the end of the major codexes (which probably would also be the case with Codex Vaticanus [03 B] if it included other books, since the Paulines probably would have been completed, then Revelation, and then any others, if they were included at all).

The second, and perhaps even more important, observation is that the two codexes themselves appear to recognize some type of

---

Claromontanus is a separate list, not connected to the manuscript contents itself. This mistake and confusion persists in one of McDonald's latest works, where he states, "Codex Claramontanus [*sic*] (Dp, sixth century) includes most of Paul's Letters but also *Epistle of Barnabas*, *Shepherd of Hermas*, *Acts of Paul*, and *Apocalypse of Peter*; however, it lacks Philippians, 1–2 Thessalonians, and Hebrews" (*Forgotten Scriptures: The Selection and Rejection of Early Religious Writings* [Louisville: Westminster John Knox, 2009], 169).

186. McDonald, *Biblical Canon*, 67. Larry Hurtado (*The Earliest Christian Artifacts: Manuscripts and Christian Origins* [Grand Rapids: Eerdmans, 2006], 32–33) indicates that *Shepherd of Hermas* was a very popular work in early Christianity, with the largest number of manuscripts of noncanonical works in the second and third centuries.

187. Cowper, introduction to *Codex Alexandrinus*, xiv.

differentiation among the books included. The organization of Codex Sinaiticus (01 א) falls into three distinguishable parts. The first part, including the four Gospels, ends with John's Gospel and is followed by a blank sheet. The second part includes the Pauline Epistles, with Hebrews after 2 Thessalonians, and ends after Philemon, followed by a blank sheet. The third section consists of Acts, the Catholic Epistles, and then Revelation (a pattern of organization that seems to have become prominent from the seventh century on, especially in Byzantine manuscripts),[188] before *Barnabas* and *Shepherd of Hermas*. There are blank sheets that distinctly separate the Gospels and the Pauline Epistles. I think this may well indicate that these units—the very ones that I traced transmissionally above—are thought of as fixed units. There is no further blank sheet dividing the rest of the New Testament books from *Barnabas* and *Shepherd of Hermas*. However, another telling feature may well serve a similar purpose. At the end of every book in the New Testament (and Old Testament as well) of Codex Sinaiticus (01 א), there is a colophon that includes the title of the book and a coronis (a decorative mark used to indicate the end of a textual unit) written in the ink of the manuscript. Ever since the fundamental work of H. J. M. Milne and T. C. Skeat on the hands of Sinaiticus (as well as the colophons of Codex Alexandrinus [02 A]), there has been a strong linkage of the colophons, and the accompanying corona, with the scribal hands, so that scribe A has a particular way of drawing his coronis, and so on.[189] I believe this is probably generally correct, but three exceptions are worth noting that help us to understand the organization and content of Codex Sinaiticus (01 א). At the end of Revelation and of *Barnabas* there is a more ornate coronis used than is found elsewhere. Both Revelation 1:5 to the end and *Barnabas* were written by scribe A, whose "coronis is the simplest, consisting of a crossed pair of wavy lines,

---

188. Parker, *New Testament Manuscripts*, 283.
189. H. J. M. Milne and T. C. Skeat, including contributions by Douglas Cockerell, *Scribes and Correctors of the Codex Sinaiticus* (London: British Museum, 1938), 27–29, with an appendix of the colophons on plates 1–9. This is followed by Parker, *Codex Sinaiticus*, 74. I am not convinced, however, that all that can be said about the use of the colophons, especially the corona, has been said. Some of my comments below indicate further directions for possible study. For the latest study of the manuscript, see Jongkind, *Scribal Habits*. Jongkind concentrates on the scribes but in some areas does not go beyond Milne and Skeat.

sometimes ornamented with tendrils."[190] However, the corona at the end of Revelation and *Barnabas* are considerably more elaborate in their written forms, with more ornamentation of the tendrils. These corona in the hand of scribe A are unparalleled in the New Testament, although there are corona approaching this elaboration by scribe A at the end of Psalms, Proverbs, and 1 Maccabees.[191] The corona are more complex in their written form, but more noteworthy is the fact that they may well have been partially written in red ink. The online version and the recent printed version of Codex Sinaiticus (01 ℵ) do not note the coloring of these corona (although they do indicate uses of red elsewhere, including in the Psalms and for Eusebian and Ammonian numbers),[192] but such coloring is found in the facsimile edition of Tischendorf. It is possible that Tischendorf fabricated this coloring himself (as he is often, though I think grossly unjustly, accused of fabricating other things), but the places where he indicates red ink in the corona match more darkly colored ink in the photographs. I suspect that the red ink was observed by Tischendorf and captured in his facsimile, but has now faded to a dark brown.[193] The only other place where a more developed coronis is found in the New Testament of Codex Sinaiticus (01 ℵ) is at the end of Mark's Gospel. This coronis is usually simply attributed to scribe D, who uses more elaborate corona. However, there are only four examples of corona by scribe D in extant Sinaiticus, and this is by far the most elaborate and the only one that also uses red ink (visible in the photograph as well as in Tischendorf's facsimile). In my view, it is probable that the scribes used these colored corona to indicate the location of known textual irregularities and to differentiate them from the rest of the

---

190. Milne and Skeat, *Scribes and Correctors*, 28.

191. I think that Milne and Skeat underestimate the variety of corona used by scribe A, and the potential places where various corona might be used. The case in point is the uses in the Old Testament noted above, where it is possible (the evidence on the basis of the fragmentary nature of the Old Testament precludes certain judgment) that more elaborate corona were used to differentiate groupings within the Testament. For example, Psalms and Proverbs are differentiated from the other poetical works (written in two-column format), and 1 Maccabees is differentiated from 4 Maccabees (Sinaiticus did not contain 2 Maccabees and 3 Maccabees).

192. See Parker, *Codex Sinaiticus*, 48.

193. The corona have undoubtedly faded on many pages of the manuscript to the point of being nearly undetectable (e.g., at the end of 1 Corinthians).

text.[194] Thus, the scribe of Codex Sinaiticus (01 ℵ) realized that after Revelation there was something extraordinary about *Barnabas* and *Shepherd of Hermas*, hence their placement at the end of the manuscript, even after the third and least well-fixed textual grouping, and differentiation with the colored corona at the end of Revelation and *Barnabas* to indicate the following textual ambiguity. The scribes also, it seems to me, realized that there was a known alternative ending to Mark (the long ending), though they did not include it but indicated their knowledge with the elaborate and colored coronis.[195]

This analysis has a correlative in Codex Alexandrinus (02 A) that indicates that the scribes recognized some type of distinction between the books included in that manuscript. Portions of *1 Clement* and *2 Clement* are included at the end of the manuscript, then, according to the table of books at the beginning of the manuscript,[196] to be followed by *Psalms of Solomon*, not now present. In the table of books of the manuscript written in ancient times, the New Testament books are listed as follows: Gospels: according to Matthew, according to Mark, according to Luke, according to John; Acts of the Apostles; Catholics, six; Epistles of Paul, fourteen (I note, including Hebrews after 2 Thessalonians); Apocalypse of John; Epistle of Clement 1; Epistle of Clement 2. Then there is a space of about two blank lines before these words: "Along with Books . . . Psalms of Solomon." B. H. Cowper believes that originally these two lines read, "Along with the 29 Books, Psalms of Solomon."[197] He may be right. It is clear by

194. One might find an analogy with the umlaut used in Codex Vaticanus (03 B), which may be used to indicate a textual variant. See Parker, *New Testament Manuscripts*, 73.

195. This is consonant with the fact that scribe D wrote a bifolium (four pages—the front and back of a single sheet inserted in the middle of a quire) apparently to replace a bifolium by scribe A that was defective. Milne and Skeat (*Scribes and Correctors*, 9–11) discuss the possibilities and conclude that the problem probably was that scribe A had included extra material at the end of Mark, but they rule out that it could be the long ending of Mark (16:9–20). However, this does not mean that scribe A did not include an intermediate-length ending, or that the long ending was not known and that there was some other dispute about the ending of Mark. In any case, the scribe indicates that something unusual pertains to the ending of Mark.

196. According to Thompson (*Facsimile of the Codex Alexandrinus*, 1:9), the table of books is written in a slightly larger hand, though it appears to be contemporary with copying of the manuscript.

197. Cowper, introduction to *Codex Alexandrinus*, xiii–xiv. Thompson says, "In the Table of Books the Clementine Epistles are included among the canonical

this that *Psalms of Solomon* is an appendix to the manuscript, and clearly not part of the New Testament, possibly even of the other books of the Bible.[198] More important is the inclusion of *1 Clement* and *2 Clement* in the table of books. There is evidence of the "reverential use" of the Clementine letters into the fourth century.[199] However, we must note how the New Testament books are arranged even in Codex Alexandrinus (02 A). They are listed under the rubric of Gospels, then the four listed; Acts; six Catholic Epistles; fourteen Epistles of Paul; Apocalypse of John; but then each letter of Clement. They are not listed as "Letters of Clement, two." In other words, there is a differentiation made in the way that the letters of Clement are listed in relation to the rest of the New Testament books. Second, the two Clementine letters are included after the book of Revelation, and not with the other letters, which are grouped one after the other.[200] Finally, in the manuscript itself, the various groupings of books are indicated by major colophons, often accompanied by starting the next section on a new page, with the books within a group represented by smaller colophons. The two letters of Clement are grouped together but separated by only a small colophon and the second letter following on the next column.[201] I contend that the scribe both recognized that these Clementine letters were to be distinguished (probably as not by the same author) and wanted to make clear that they were not of the same status as the other New Testament books.

works" (*Facsimile of the Codex Alexandrinus*, 1:6 [cf. 4:4]). For why I think this is inaccurate, see below.

198. See Thompson, *Facsimile of the Codex Alexandrinus*, 1:6. Thompson notes that the "interval" before the title *Psalms of Solomon* is "separately added." Thompson also says that the *Psalms of Solomon* "were not counted among the canonical books" (ibid., 4:4).

199. Cowper, introduction to *Codex Alexandrinus*, xvi. See *Apostolic Canons* 85 (c. AD 380). See McDonald, *Biblical Canon*, 447.

200. As Metzger (*Canon of the New Testament*, 295) makes clear, the book of Revelation is invariably the final book in most canonical groupings, apart from a few very late manuscripts (twelfth and thirteenth centuries) and possibly Codex Bezae (05 D), but this is highly debatable. Of course, the issue might be raised whether Codexes Sinaiticus (01 ℵ) and Alexandrinus (02 A) are exceptions, but there are other indications, as noted above, that the scribes believed that the New Testament "ended" with Revelation.

201. Thompson, *Facsimile of the Codex Alexandrinus*, vol. 4, on the basis of my personal observation. The colophons in Codex Alexandrinus (02 A) are reproduced in Milne and Skeat, *Scribes and Correctors*, plates 10–43.

The third observation concerns the structure of the New Testament and its subcorpora. It may well be that *Barnabas, Shepherd of Hermas,* and *1 Clement* and *2 Clement,* possibly among other books, were still reverenced in certain circles even in the fourth and fifth centuries AD. I think, however, that even if this is the case, the textual evidence is that the scribes of these two codexes recognized that there was still a distinction among the books, a recognition perhaps of deuterocanonical New Testament books. Looking at the books of the New Testament, we see that by the time of Codex Sinaiticus (01 א) the subcorpora of the Gospels and the Pauline Epistles were firmly established. The third subcorpus was the last to be firmly established, and it is perhaps no coincidence that this group was included last and was the one to which *Barnabas* and *Shepherd of Hermas* were attached, even if being distinguished. Similarly with Codex Alexandrinus (02 A), we see that all of the subcorpora—Gospels, Acts, Pauline Epistles, Catholic Epistles, Revelation—were firmly established, but that the two Clementine letters were attached at the end. In other words, there may have been a couple of books floating on the edges of the New Testament by the fourth and fifth centuries, but the major subcorpora, and even the other books, were firmly established by this time.

The majuscule manuscripts continued to be produced until the tenth or the eleventh century. Some of these are very beautiful and elegant manuscripts, highly ornate and decorated, while others are more functional. However, few of them contain the entire Greek New Testament. Codex Bezae (05 D), dated to the fifth century, is a bilingual Greek and Latin manuscript that contains the Gospels (in the order Matthew, John, Luke, Mark), the book of Acts, and part of 3 John in Latin only.[202] Bezae included all of the Catholic Epistles at one time. The label "Codex D" has also been given to Codex Claromontanus (06 Dp), mentioned above, a sixth-century bilingual Greek and Latin manuscript containing the Pauline Epistles, with Hebrews as an appendix after three blank pages.[203]

---

202. The edition is Frederick H. Scrivener, *Bezae Codex Cantabrigiensis, Being an Exact Copy, in Ordinary Type, of the Celebrated Uncial Graeco-Latin Manuscript of the Four Gospels and Acts of the Apostles* (Cambridge: Deighton, Bell, 1864). See D. C. Parker, *Codex Bezae: An Early Christian Manuscript and Its Text* (Cambridge: Cambridge University Press, 1992).

203. Trobisch, *Paul's Letter Collection,* 20. The edition is Constantin Tischendorf, *Codex Claromontanus, sive Epistulae Pauli omnes Graece et Latine ex codice Parisiensi*

This may be the earliest evidence of Hebrews being awkwardly added to or distinguished from an established collection of thirteen Pauline letters. Many of the later majuscule documents evidence the rise of the Byzantine text-type, until this text-type becomes ascendant by the turn of the millennia.

## Liturgical Use of Manuscripts

Over the course of the centuries during which these majuscule manuscripts were transmitted, they were put to a variety of uses. One of these is liturgical. It is often noted that the early papyri evidence only haphazard punctuation and breathing marks, the occasional diaeresis, and related diacritical marks. As manuscripts continued to be copied, and no doubt as they were increasingly copied and used in contexts where the indigenous language was not Greek, punctuation and other diacritical marks were used with increased frequency. At the same time, Greek musical notation had already been developed as early as the third century BC, and the earliest Christian hymn, with original words and music, dates to the third century AD (P.Oxy. XV 1786).[204] Nevertheless, diacritical annotation of biblical texts for liturgical use appears to have taken longer and developed more gradually. In the process of editing the New Testament papyri and parchments of the Vienna National Library papyrus collection, my wife, Wendy, and I observed an increase in such diacritical marks that is probably typical of development in New Testament manuscripts. Wendy Porter writes,

> What we observe is a gradual but progressive inclusion of a larger and more frequent range of markings. Of the fourth-century manuscripts that use some form of punctuation, or other marks, all use the raised dot, some use double dots and the low dot, some use the spiritus asper

---

celeberrimo nomine Claromontani plerumque dicto sexti ut videtur post Christum saeculi (Leipzig: Brockhaus, 1852).

204. Wendy J. Porter, "The Use of Ekphonetic Notation in Vienna New Testament Manuscripts," in Akten des 23. Internationalen Papyrologenkongresses, Wien, 22.–28. Juli 2001, ed. Bernhard Palme, Papyrologica Vindobonensia 1 (Vienna: Verlag der Österreichischen Akademie der Wissenschaften, 2007), 582. Cf. Egert Pöhlmann and Martin L. West, Documents of Ancient Greek Music: The Extant Melodies and Fragments (Oxford: Clarendon, 2001).

and diaresis, as well as diastrophe to separate the palatal sounds of two side-by-side kappas, and some introduce a few other less distinguishable marks, possibly of accentuation. The fifth-century manuscripts use raised dots with frequency, while some use medial, low or double dots; marks for rough breathing and diaresis are found; and some diacritical marks are used that may indicate accent or intonation, sometimes in combination with the end of a unit. Eleven of the sixth-century manuscripts have numerous prosodic marks, which may indicate accent, intonation, unit endings, and possibly, in some cases, all of these, especially at the end of a section. In the seventh-century manuscripts, we see one that has many diacritical marks and the distinctive use of the teleia [+, small cross].[205]

As these manuscripts continued to be copied and were used in liturgical contexts, especially by those who did not use Greek indigenously, the system of ekphonetic marks was developed to indicate the musical-rhetorical intonation of the text. Eventually these marks were developed into a system of marks called "neumes," which were widely used in later lectionary texts.[206]

What is interesting to note from the study of biblical majuscule manuscripts is that biblical manuscripts clearly were used in liturgical contexts, and sometimes these manuscripts were not only copied for their text but also annotated with diacritical marks to indicate how they were to be intoned. One fascinating case is Austrian National Library Suppl. Gr. 121 (0105).[207] This ninth- or tenth-century manuscript now consists of eight pages of text from John's Gospel, consisting of most of chapter 7.[208] The text found on these eight pages has been divided into four lectionary units (by means of the words αρχη, *archē* ["beginning"] and τελος, *telos* ["end"]) of approximately thirteen to sixteen verses each. Each of these units is roughly a complete pericope. These pericopes consist of Jesus at the Feast of Tabernacles (John

205. Porter, "Ekphonetic Notation," 583–84.
206. See Egon Wellecz, *A History of Byzantine Music and Hymnography*, 2nd ed. (Oxford: Clarendon, 1961).
207. See Stanley E. Porter, "What Do We Know and How Do We Know It? Reconstructing Christianity from Its Earliest Manuscripts," in Porter and Pitts, *Christian Origins*, 66–69.
208. See Porter, "Ekphonetic Notation," 584–85; Porter and Porter, *Papyri and Parchments*, no. 40, 1:162–86; cf. no. 24, 1:94–102, from the eighth century.

7:1–13), Jesus teaching at the feast (vv. 14–30), a discussion about who the Christ is (vv. 31–36), and Jesus speaking about thirsting and the response of the guards (vv. 37–46 [and beyond?]). The first two and the last pericope have ekphonetic notation, but the third does not. The annotation includes indications of units, of rising and falling voice pitch, of vocal intervals, and of emphasis and accentuation, among others. Wendy Porter speculates, "This manuscript appears to have been used in three liturgical contexts. The third pericope, the unnotated one, is also the least visually depictable of the four"[209]—that is, a discussion about who Jesus is.

Thus, the musical-rhetorical annotation and use of the text were also important dimensions of textual transmission.

### Minuscules and Lectionaries

Two further categories of manuscripts important in transmission of the New Testament merit mention: the minuscules and the lectionaries.[210]

#### *Minuscules*

Minuscules, as we have already noted, consist of a style of handwriting that includes cursive characteristics and the use of two hundred different letter combinations to facilitate ease of writing. Despite these conventions to make writing easier and faster, as well as more compact, the number of complete biblical manuscripts written in a minuscule hand is surprisingly small. Out of nearly three thousand minuscule manuscripts (2,911 or so), only about seven have a complete Bible (although that number is perhaps growing due to recent discoveries), and all of them date to after the tenth century. Most of the minuscules contain the four Gospels. The overwhelming majority of minuscules reflects the Byzantine or Majority text-type.

Several of the minuscules merit brief mention. One of these is Minuscule 1. This twelfth-century manuscript, now housed in the Basel

---

209. Porter, "Ekphonetic Notation," 584.
210. See, in Ehrman and Holmes, *Text of the New Testament*, Barbara Aland and Klaus Wachtel, "The Greek Minuscule Manuscripts of the New Testament," 43–60; Carroll D. Osburn, "The Greek Lectionaries of the New Testament," 61–74.

University library, was one of the manuscripts that Erasmus had but did not widely use in creating his text of the Greek New Testament. The manuscript includes the Gospels, Acts, the Catholic Epistles, and the Pauline Epistles—all but Revelation. The text of this manuscript is distinct from the Byzantine text-type that Erasmus ended up following, and is one of the group of four or five manuscripts that make up what is designated as Family 1 (the others are 118, 131, 209, possibly 1582). Family 1 and Family 13 (13, 69, 124, 174, 230, 346, 543, 788, 826, 828, 983, 1689, 1709) are part of what has been designated in the past as the Caesarean text, along with Codex Koridethi (038 Θ).[211] If Erasmus had chosen to follow this manuscript, he still would have had to deal with the problem of Revelation, but there would have been some notable differences from the text that he created. For example, the Family 1 manuscripts indicate the following textual readings: the long ending of Mark 16:9–20 perhaps would have been marked as being omitted in some manuscripts; Luke 1:28 with "blessed are you among women" would have been omitted, as it is in Codex Sinaiticus (01 ℵ) and Codex Vaticanus (03 B); the shorter form of the Lord's Prayer (Luke 11:2–4) would have been read; and the pericope of the woman caught in adultery would have been found at the end of John's Gospel rather than at John 7:53.[212] But this was not to be. Instead, Erasmus used a number of manuscripts that followed the Byzantine text-type: Minuscule 2, a twelfth-century manuscript of the Gospels; Minuscule 2ap (now 2815), a twelfth-century manuscript with the Pauline Epistles and Acts; and Minuscule Ir (now 2814), a damaged and incomplete twelfth-century manuscript of Revelation. One can only wonder how the entire controversy over the Textus Receptus, and especially dispute over certain passages, would have been different if Erasmus had chosen Minuscule 1.

### Lectionaries

The last type of text to discuss is lectionary texts. Lectionary texts have been a neglected area of study, even though there are over 2,400 of them (2,453 at last count). They range in age from the fourth

---

211. Kenyon, *Text*, 105.
212. The above information is from ibid., 188–89.

century to beyond the fifteenth century, and they were designed to be used in services to provide biblical readings according to a designated plan. The usual definition of a lectionary text is that it is not a continuous-text manuscript of a book of the New Testament but one that is "divided into separate pericopes, arranged according to their sequence as lessons appointed for the church year."[213] We can already see a problem with such a definition. The Alands note that with "only a few exceptions," "all the papyri, all the uncials, and all the minuscules" qualify as continuous text.[214] Eldon Epp is even bolder: "All of the papyri are continuous-text MSS, that is, MSS containing (originally) at least one NT writing in continuous fashion from beginning to end."[215] However, for many of the papyri, the extant text that we have is shorter than some of the readings in lectionaries. The fragmentary nature of these papyri does not indicate whether they are continuous text of an entire book of the New Testament or whether they are in fact a smaller excerpt or pericope. The Alands themselves have identified some papyri that in varying ways are not continuous text because they resemble talismans, selections, commentaries, lectionaries, and the like.[216] Further, there are continuous biblical manuscripts, such as the John manuscript noted above, that have been marked for liturgical use, including the designation of pericope openings and closings.

A case that illustrates the difficulties that have repeatedly been ignored in handling lectionaries is seen in Lectionary 1043.[217] This lectionary is one of the earliest, probably dated to the fifth century (although some date it to the seventh or the eighth century), the only earlier lectionary being 1604, dated to the fourth century. This now-fragmentary manuscript contains Matthew 3:7–17 (it begins in the midst of the unit), Matthew 4:23–5:12; 7:13–20; 10:37–42, a unit beginning with Matthew 9:35, Mark 6:18–29 (it begins in the midst of

213. Aland and Aland, *Text of the New Testament*, 163.
214. Ibid.
215. Eldon J. Epp, "The Papyrus Manuscripts of the New Testament," in Ehrman and Holmes, *Text of the New Testament*, 5.
216. Aland and Aland, *Text of the New Testament*, 85.
217. See Porter and Porter, *Papyri and Parchments*, no. 58, 1:246–76. The original edition was Carl Wessely, *Griechische und koptische Texte theologischen Inhalts III*, SPP 12 (Leipzig: Haessel, 1912), 231–40, no. 184.

a unit), Luke 2:1–20; 11:27–32; 24:36–38 (it ends in the midst of the unit), and John 20:1–18; 20:24–27 (it ends in the midst of the unit). Whereas some lectionaries have introductions to the individual lectional units (incipits) or markings with αρχη, *archē* and τελος, *telos*, this manuscript simply records biblical text continuously within the identifiable and distinct unit, as such lectionary features apparently were not used until the eighth century.[218] The individual complete lections included here vary from seven verses up to twenty verses, and some are at least as long as the readings found in a vast number of papyri that are considered continuous text.[219] I am not suggesting that all of these papyri be considered lectionaries. Instead, I am suggesting two things: first, at least some of them may have been lectionaries, but we cannot tell because of their fragmentary nature; second, lectionaries may have a use in textual criticism because, in some instances at least, the "continuous" text of many papyri is shorter in length than are some of the lectional units found in a lectionary such as 1043.

## A Proposal regarding Textual Transmission of the Greek New Testament

As a result of the evidence given above, including discussion of lectionaries, I have come to believe that we need a more nuanced method of discussing the manuscripts that we use in textual criticism of the Greek New Testament. I believe that there should be two major categories of manuscripts, rather than the one that is currently used.[220]

218. Aland and Aland, *Text of the New Testament*, 167.
219. These include 𝔓[1], 𝔓[2], 𝔓[3], 𝔓[9], 𝔓[17], 𝔓[18], 𝔓[19], 𝔓[20], 𝔓[21], 𝔓[23], 𝔓[26], 𝔓[28], 𝔓[31], 𝔓[32], 𝔓[35], 𝔓[37], 𝔓[39], 𝔓[48], 𝔓[51], 𝔓[52], 𝔓[56], 𝔓[57], 𝔓[68], 𝔓[71], 𝔓[73], 𝔓[81], 𝔓[82], 𝔓[85], 𝔓[86], 𝔓[87], 𝔓[88], 𝔓[89], 𝔓[90], 𝔓[91], 𝔓[93], 𝔓[94], 𝔓[95], 𝔓[96], 𝔓[97], 𝔓[98], 𝔓[101], 𝔓[102], 𝔓[103], 𝔓[104], 𝔓[105], 𝔓[107], 𝔓[108], 𝔓[109], 𝔓[110], 𝔓[111], 𝔓[112], 𝔓[113], 𝔓[114], 𝔓[116], 𝔓[117], 𝔓[118], 𝔓[120], 𝔓[121], 𝔓[122], 𝔓[123], 𝔓[124], 𝔓[125], 𝔓[126].
220. This is a proposal I first made in Stanley E. Porter, "Why So Many Holes in the Papyrological Evidence for the Greek New Testament?" in *The Bible as Book: The Transmission of the Greek Text*, ed. Scot McKendrick and Orlaith A. O'Sullivan (London: British Library Publications and Oak Knoll Press, 2003), 176; repeated and expanded in Stanley E. Porter, "Textual Criticism in the Light of Diverse Textual Evidence for the Greek New Testament: An Expanded Proposal," in *New Testament Manuscripts: Their Texts and Their World*, ed. Thomas J. Kraus and Tobias Nicklas, TENTS 2 (Leiden: Brill, 2006), 305–37, esp. 313–36; and mentioned again in Porter and Porter, *Papyri and Parchments*, 1:xiv.

The first category should include those manuscripts that consist of continuous text of what was originally clearly establishable as at least one New Testament book, and the second category should include those manuscripts that are not clearly continuous text of the New Testament. The purpose of this proposal is to recognize the ambiguous nature of some manuscripts and, further, to recognize that there are manuscripts without "continuous text," as traditionally defined, that can and should play a part in informing textual criticism of the Greek New Testament. This is not a "negligible" matter, as the Alands assert,[221] as it may affect up to 20 percent of papyrus manuscripts, as well as others. Here I will say something more about each of these categories of manuscripts and then give some examples of the additional manuscripts that may play a part in textual criticism of the Greek New Testament.

### Continuous Text Manuscripts

The first category would include any manuscript—whether on papyrus or parchment, whether majuscule or minuscule—that contains continuous text of one book of the New Testament or more. Many, if not most, of those currently designated as papyri probably would still belong here, but those that have been shown not to be continuous text would need to be transferred to the second category. Most of the majuscules and minuscules mentioned above would be included here as well.

### Noncontinuous Text Manuscripts

The second category would include manuscripts that are noncontinuous text of the New Testament. There are a number of subcategories of manuscripts to include within this second category. I recognize that these categories could be further divided into various other levels, depending upon the manuscripts' closeness to being continuous text and their usefulness for textual reconstruction.[222]

---

221. Aland and Aland, *Text of the New Testament*, 85. In fact, in some ways it goes to the very heart of their view of manuscripts, especially the papyri.

222. For information on many of the following manuscripts, see Elliott, *Bibliography*; van Haelst, *Catalogue*.

## ▪ LECTIONARY AND LITURGICAL TEXTS

Examples of this type of text are $\mathfrak{P}^2$, with only three verses of John 12:12–15 in Greek with Luke 7:50 in Coptic above it on one side, clearly not continuous text, and Luke 7:22–26 in Coptic on the other; $\mathfrak{P}^3$, formerly Lectionary 348,[223] with two Lukan pericopes, 7:36–45 and 10:38–42, on a single sheet;[224] $\mathfrak{P}^{34}$, with the end of 1 Corinthians 16 (vv. 4–7, 9–10) on one page, and a page with 2 Corinthians 5 (vv. 18–19, 19–21) on the next, apparently discontinuous text that lacks the early part of 2 Corinthians;[225] $\mathfrak{P}^{44}$, with passages from Matthew (17:1–3, 6–7; 18:15–17, 19; 25:8–10) and John (9:3–4; 10:8–14; 12:16–18); Lectionary 1043 (see above); and other formal lectionary texts, as well as other papyri and possibly other manuscripts.

## ▪ MINIATURE CODEXES AND MAGICAL PAPYRI/AMULETS

Examples here are P.Oxy. VIII 1077, with Matthew 4:23–24 written over five columns and three ranks, along with ornamentation;[226] $\mathfrak{P}^{50}$, with Acts 8:26–32, 10:26–31, one following the other, though with a space between them;[227] $\mathfrak{P}^{78}$, with Jude 4–5, 7–8, an "extraordinary" miniature codex or amulet;[228] $\mathfrak{P}^{105}$, with Matthew 27:62–64, 28:2–5, and a string from binding still attached, thus "proving that the text was used as an amulet";[229] PSI VI 719, with John 1:1, Matthew 1:1, John 1:23, Mark 1:1, Luke 1:1, Psalm 90:1, and Matthew 6:9 on one side; P.Vindob. G 29831, with John 1:5–6.[230]

---

223. See Gregory, *Griechischen Handschriften*, 45.

224. See Porter and Porter, *Papyri and Parchments*, no. 4, 1:13–17.

225. See ibid., no. 20, 1:76–84.

226. See Arthur S. Hunt, *The Oxyrhynchus Papyri, VIII* (London: Egypt Exploration Fund, 1911), 10–11, with plate.

227. This according to the edition in John F. Oates, Alan E. Samuel, and C. Bradford Welles, *Yale Papyri in the Beinecke Rare Book and Manuscript Library I* (New Haven: American Society of Papyrologists, 1967), 20.

228. The wording is that of Peter Parsons, in L. Ingrams et al., *The Oxyrhynchus Papyri, XXXIV*, GRM 49 (London: Egypt Exploration Society, 1968), 4.

229. So J. David Thomas, in E. W. Handley et al., *The Oxyrhynchus Papyri, LXIV*, GRM 84 (London: Egypt Exploration Society, 1997), 12.

230. See G. H. R. Horsley, "Reconstructing a Biblical Codex: The Prehistory of MPER n.s. XVII. 10 (P.Vindob. G 29831)," in *Akten des 21. Internationalen Papyrologenkongresses, Berlin, 13.–19.8.1995*, ed. Bärbel Kramer et al., APVG 3 (Stuttgart: Teubner, 1997), 1:473–81.

■ **Commentaries, Especially Johannine Manuscripts with Hermēneia**

Some examples are $\mathfrak{P}^{55}$, $\mathfrak{P}^{59}$, $\mathfrak{P}^{63}$, $\mathfrak{P}^{76}$, $\mathfrak{P}^{80}$, 0145, 0210, all of which are Johannine manuscripts but prepared with Johannine text above the word ἑρμηνεια, *hermēneia* ("interpretation"), and apparently some type of biblically inspired commentary wording below.[231]

■ **Apocryphal Texts**

Some examples of apocryphal texts are P.Egerton 2 = P.Lond. Christ. 1,[232] with passages reflecting Matthew, Mark, Luke, and especially John (see above); P.Oxy. II 210,[233] reflecting Matthew, Mark, Luke, John, Romans, 1 Corinthians, 2 Corinthians, and Colossians; P.Vindob. G 2325 (Fayyum fragment);[234] and even P.Oxy. IV 840, with only John 10:23.[235]

■ **Excerpts and Occasional Texts**

Examples here include $\mathfrak{P}^7$, which is actually two papyrus fragments, one with Matthew 6:33–34 and possibly Matthew 7:12, and the other with some kind of homily and then Luke 4:1–2;[236] $\mathfrak{P}^{10}$, with Romans 1:1–7, "no doubt a schoolboy's exercise";[237] $\mathfrak{P}^{12}$, with Hebrews 1:1 at

231. See Stanley E. Porter, "The Use of Hermeneia and Johannine Papyrus Manuscripts," in Palme, *Akten des 23. Internationalen Papyrologenkongresses*, 573–80. For a fuller exposition of how such manuscripts can aid in reconstructing early Christianity, see Porter, "What Do We Know?" 60–63.

232. See Stanley E. Porter, "Apocryphal Gospels and the Text of the New Testament before AD 200," in *The New Testament Text in Early Christianity: Proceedings of the Lille Colloquium, July 2000* [= *Le texte du Nouveau Testament au début du christianisme: Actes du colloque de Lille, juillet 2000*], ed. C.-B. Amphoux and J. K. Elliott, HTB 6 (Lausanne: Éditions du Zèbre, 2003), 235–59; "Early Apocryphal Gospels," 355–61.

233. See Porter, "POxy II 210 as an Apocryphal Gospel."

234. Porter and Porter, *Papyri and Parchments*, no. 62, 1:291–94.

235. See discussion in Michael J. Kruger, *The Gospel of the Savior: An Analysis of P.Oxy. 840 and Its Place in the Gospel Traditions of Early Christianity*, TENTS 1 (Leiden: Brill, 2005), 156–61.

236. See Gregory, *Griechischen Handschriften*, 46.

237. Bernard P. Grenfell and Arthur S. Hunt, *The Oxyrhynchus Papyri, II* (London: Egypt Exploration Fund, 1899), 8–9, here 8, with plate. For the latest study, confirming this, see AnneMarie Luijendijk, "A New Testament Papyrus and Its Documentary Context: An Early Christian Writing Exercise from the Archive of Leonides (P.Oxy. II 209/$\mathfrak{P}^{10}$)," *JBL* 129 (2010): 575–96.

the top of the middle column of an early Christian letter;[238] $\mathfrak{P}^{25}$, with fragments of Matthew 18:32–34 and Matthew 19:1–3, 5–7, 9–10, including Tatianic glosses;[239] $\mathfrak{P}^{42}$, with Luke 1:54–55, the prayer of Mary, and Luke 2:29–31, the song of Simeon, along with eleven other biblical songs from the Old Testament;[240] $\mathfrak{P}^{43}$, with Revelation 2:12–13 and Revelation 15:8–16:2 on front and back in different hands; $\mathfrak{P}^{62}$, with Matthew 11:25–30 and Daniel 3:51–53, 55 on a miniature codex with the Matthean passage followed by the one from Daniel; 0212, with a harmony of Matthew 27:56–57, Mark 15:40, 42, Luke 23:49–51, 54, and John 19:38 (see above for discussion); 0153, twenty ostraca with text of the New Testament from the four Gospels;[241] Petrie Ostraka, thirteen ostraca with passages from Acts, Romans, Galatians, James, Jude and 1 John;[242] P.Aberd. 3, an ostracon with Matthew 3:14, 15, 17, obviously not continuous text on the basis of the limitations of the writing material (and probably part of a collection of ostraca with hymns, including P.Aberd. 4, 5, 6); and possibly $\mathfrak{P}^{72}$, with 1 Peter, 2 Peter, and Jude, along with other books, probably assembled for private use (see discussion above).

■ UNKNOWN WORKS

An example here would be the 7Q fragments, such as 7Q5. This highly controversial and sensational text deserves fair treatment for what it is, rather than being treated at the extremes of scholarship.[243]

238. For the text of Hebrews (P.Amh. III[b]) and Genesis 1:1–5 (P.Amh. III[c]) found on the back of the papyrus, see Bernard P. Grenfell and Arthur S. Hunt, *The Amherst Papyri, I* (London: Oxford University Press, 1900), 30–31; for the Christian letter (P.Amh. III[a]), see 28–30. For a photograph, see Adolf Deissmann, *Light from the Ancient East*, trans. Lionel R. M. Strachan, 4th ed. (London: Hodder & Stoughton, 1927), between 208 and 209. Aland and Aland (*Text of the New Testament*, 85) label these as notes, but this does not explain why they are given a papyrus number.

239. Otto Stegmüller ("Ein Bruchstück aus dem griechischen Diatessaron," *ZNW* 37 [1938]: 23–29) first labeled it a portion of the *Diatessaron*, but this was revised by C. Peters ("Ein neues Fragment des griechischen Diatessaron?" *Bib* 21 [1940]: 51–55) as biblical with Tatianic glosses.

240. Porter and Porter, *Papyri and Parchments*, no. 3, 1:10–12.

241. Found in Gregory's list of New Testament manuscripts under majuscule manuscripts (*Griechischen Handschriften*, 43), but deleted from Aland's.

242. Cornelia Römer, "Ostraka mit Christlichen Texten aus der Sammlung Flinders Petrie," *ZPE* 145 (2003): 183–201, with plates.

243. There has been much controversy over the identity of these 7Q fragments, with some positing that they are biblical manuscripts. For discussion and references,

In establishing the text of the New Testament, and in tracing its transmission, the fullest range of manuscripts should be included in the discussion, not to necessarily use category-two (noncontinuous text manuscripts) documents to establish the Greek New Testament, but to provide possible insight into its development and transmission.

## Conclusion

The transmission of the New Testament is clearly related to the text of the New Testament. I have chosen to cast the discussion first in terms of the materials and writing that is used for the manuscripts of the New Testament. Once one is familiar with these manuscripts and their individual characteristics, it is possible to examine them and to retrace the transmissional history of both individual manuscripts and collections of manuscripts. Through primarily manuscript evidence, occasionally supplemented by the evidence from other statements in early church history, it is possible to trace the development of the four-Gospel and Pauline letter corpora back to the second century. It is even possible to find some indications that the remaining parts of the New Testament were also being gathered during this time. Once we emerge from this tunnel period of limited evidence, we encounter the major majuscule codexes and the other codex manuscripts that followed them. In these manuscripts we trace not only textual transmission but also the growth of the use of these New Testament manuscripts for liturgical purposes. The liturgical use also helps account for the development of formal liturgical texts such as are found in lectionaries. The variety of the types of manuscripts identified, including the fact that many manuscripts apparently have been misclassified in the course of doing New Testament textual criticism, pushes for expansion of the system of manuscript classification used in New Testament studies. The two categories of manuscripts would include those that are continuous-text New Testament manuscripts and those that, though not continuous texts, have possible value for establishing the text and transmission of the New Testament.

see Porter, "Why So Many Holes?" 184–85, esp. nn. 67, 68; "Textual Criticism," 335–36, and nn. 89, 90.

# 3

# The Translation of the New Testament

## Introduction

The modern translation of the Bible, especially the New Testament, has been one of the great feats of Christian outreach and mission since the invention of the printing press. Statistics from the latest *Ethnologue* of Wycliffe Bible Translators, as of the 2009 sixteenth edition, indicate that the Bible has been translated, in whole or in part, into 2,546 languages and dialects (of 6,909 living languages in existence). This represents 37 percent of the identified languages of the world.[1] The result of such translational work is that the Bible, in some translated form, exists in the various languages of well over 95 percent of the world's population,[2] and it remains the "most widely published book in the world."[3]

In the fifteenth century, when movable type printing was invented in the Western world, the world was a different place in terms of translation. At that time, only thirty-three languages had a portion

1. This information is from M. Paul Lewis, ed., *Ethnologue: Languages of the World*, 16th ed. (Dallas: SIL International, 2009), 15; also available online at www .ethnologue.com.
2. Eugene A. Nida, "Principles of Translation as Exemplified by Bible Translating," in *On Translation*, ed. Reuben A. Brower, HSCL 23 (Cambridge, MA: Harvard University Press, 1959), 11.
3. Lewis, *Ethnologue*, 15.

or more of the Bible. During the nineteenth century, four hundred more languages gained a portion of the Bible. During the first half of the twentieth century, five hundred more languages received scriptural texts. A mere fifty years ago, only 1,109 languages had a portion of the Bible.[4] The last fifty years, so I have been told, have seen a doubling of the languages that have received a portion of the Bible. Now, although over two thousand languages or dialects, representing 380 million people, still lack a translation, there are 1,953 such translation projects worldwide. These incredible statistics might make us think that interlingual translation of the Bible is a recent phenomenon.[5] No doubt for many language groups this is certainly the case, as the Scriptures, through recent translation efforts, have been rendered into languages and dialects in which no such writings previously existed. However, the translation of the Christian Scriptures is not a new phenomenon at all.

In the previous chapters I discussed the text of the Greek New Testament, including the various text-types and how we got the Greek New Testament, and the transmission of the Greek New Testament, including its origins and development into manuscripts that we would recognize as the Bible. In this chapter I will discuss the translation of the New Testament, as an important dimension of how we got the New Testament—that is, how it has been conveyed to us down through the years. First I will trace the history of translation of the New Testament, from earliest times up to contemporary English translations. Then I will examine some of the issues in translation, including various schools of thought on translation, various controversial issues, and some suggestions for future efforts in Bible translation.

## The History of Translation of the New Testament

Interlingual translation of the New Testament has a long, complex, and even intriguing history. I begin here with the earliest Bible

4. Nida, "Principles of Translation," 11.
5. The distinction of interlingual from intralingual ("rewording" or paraphrase) and intersemiotic ("transmutation" or the change of sign systems) translation is attributable to Roman Jakobson, "On Linguistic Aspects of Translation," in Brower, *On Translation*, 233.

translations into ancient languages, the so-called ancient versions, and then work forward to the most recent in English. The history of Bible translation is one of the most fascinating ever told. I hope to offer a brief glimpse into this important task, as it is vitally important to how many, if not most, Christians today come into contact with their Bible: through translation.

## Ancient Versions

We begin with some of the ancient versions.[6] There was one translation that preceded the New Testament, but that provided a model for later translations: the translation of the Old Testament into Greek. Three translations occurred early in the history of Christianity: Syriac, Latin, and Coptic. Each of these is worth noting because of its significance in discussion of the development and transmission of the Greek New Testament. I begin with the Septuagint as a backdrop for discussing the Syriac, Latin, and Coptic translations of the New Testament.

### ▪ THE SEPTUAGINT

The first Christians may not have thought much about it, but translation of their sacred writings was something that most of them accepted without hesitation. The first Bible of Christians was the Old Testament, and the form in which most of them used it was the Greek translation that has come to be known as the Septuagint (or Old Greek, which describes everything but the Pentateuch, the first five books of the Old Testament that are often called the Torah). The vast majority of Jews, especially in the Diaspora but also many in Palestine (as evidenced by the use of the Septuagint by the Gospel writers and Paul), probably used the Septuagint as well.[7]

6. For a detailed overview of the ancient versions, see Bruce M. Metzger, *The Early Versions of the New Testament: Their Origin, Transmission and Limitations* (Oxford: Clarendon, 1977) (except the Septuagint). For a popular version of the topic of ancient and modern versions, see Philip W. Comfort, *The Essential Guide to Bible Versions* (Wheaton: Tyndale, 2000).

7. On some of these and related issues, see R. Glenn Wooden, "The Role of 'the Septuagint' in the Formation of the Biblical Canons," in *Exploring the Origins of the Bible: Canon Formation in Historical, Literary, and Theological Perspective*, ed. Craig A. Evans and Emanuel Tov, ASBT (Grand Rapids: Baker Academic, 2008),

The translation of what we call the "Septuagint" out of Hebrew and into Greek (most of the books were translated, but some were originally written in Greek) is probably the greatest translational accomplishment of the ancient world. As Julio Trebolle Barrera states, "This version is the first example of the translation of the complete corpus of sacred, legal, historical and poetic literature of one people, in a language of the Semitic cultural world, to the language of classical Greek culture."[8] There are various accounts given of the origins of the Septuagint.[9] These narratives include the well-known account in the *Letter of Aristeas* that seventy-two translators from Jerusalem, six from each of the twelve tribes of Israel, were requested to come to Alexandria by King Ptolemy Philadelphus's librarian, and they performed the translational task. Whether or not this account has a factual basis, it is agreed that the Pentateuch was translated in the third century BC. The rest of the books were either translated over time, some in Alexandria (e.g., Pentateuch, Judges, 1–4 Kingdoms, 1–2 Chronicles, Proverbs, Job, the Twelve Prophets, Jeremiah, Baruch, Letter of Jeremiah, Ezra, and probably Isaiah) and some in Palestine (e.g., Ruth, Esther, Ecclesiastes, Song of Songs, Lamentations, Judith, 1 Maccabees),[10] or were written originally in Greek (e.g., Wisdom of Solomon, 2–4 Maccabees), some of them in Palestine.[11] By the time

129–46; Stanley E. Porter, "The Greek of the Jews and Early Christians: The Language of the People from a Historical Sociolinguistic Perspective," in *Far from Minimal: Celebrating the Work and Influence of Philip R. Davies*, ed. Duncan Burns and J. W. Rogerson, LHBOTS 484 (London: T&T Clark, 2012), 350–64.

8. Julio Trebolle Barrera, *The Jewish Bible and the Christian Bible: An Introduction to the History of the Bible*, trans. Wilfred G. E. Watson (Leiden: Brill; Grand Rapids: Eerdmans, 1998), 301. See also discussion in Stanley E. Porter, *Verbal Aspect in the Greek of the New Testament, with Reference to Tense and Mood*, SBG 1 (New York: Peter Lang, 1989), 117–18, 141–56. See also Stanley E. Porter, "Septuagint," in *Encyclopedia of Ancient Greek Language and Linguistics*, ed. Georgios Giannakis et al. (Leiden: Brill, forthcoming).

9. References to the origin of the Septuagint are found in, especially, *Letter of Aristeas*; Aristobulus as summarized in Eusebius, *Praep. ev.* 13.12.1–2; Philo, *Moses* 2.26–44; Josephus, *Ant.* 12.11–118; *Ag. Ap.* 2.45–47. These views are summarized and assessed in Stanley E. Porter, "Septuagint/Greek Old Testament," *DNTB* 1099–106, esp. 1100–101.

10. Trebolle Barrera, *Jewish Bible*, 303.

11. Martin Hengel with Roland Deines, *The Septuagint as Christian Scripture: Its Prehistory and the Problem of Its Canon*, trans. Mark E. Biddle, OTS (Edinburgh: T&T Clark, 2002), 93.

of the New Testament, the Pentateuch and the Prophets, and at least portions of the Writings, such as Psalms, were well-established as Scripture, and it is this Greek form of the Scriptures that usually was employed by early Christians.

There has been much and continued discussion of the translational technique and resulting Greek of the Septuagint books. Henry St. John Thackeray divides the books of the Greek Old Testament into six categories, three reflecting types of translation, one paraphrase, and two free Greek. Translations include good Koine Greek found in the Pentateuch, parts of Joshua, Isaiah, and 1 Maccabees; indifferent Greek found in parts of Jeremiah, Ezekiel, and the Twelve Prophets, most of 1–2 Chronicles, portions of 2–3 Kingdoms, Psalms, Sirach, and Judith; and literal translation found in portions of Jeremiah and Baruch, Judges, Ruth, parts of 2–4 Kingdoms, Song of Songs, Lamentations, Daniel (Theodotion), 2 Esdras, and Ecclesiastes. Paraphrase is found in 1 Esdras and Daniel (Old Greek), Esther, Job, and Proverbs. Free Greek of a literary or Atticistic type is found in Wisdom of Solomon, the Letter of Jeremiah, part of Baruch, and 2–4 Maccabees. Vernacular Greek is found in Tobit.[12] Trebolle Barrera differentiates between literal and free translation, equating literal with "formal equivalence" and free with "functional equivalence."[13] It is hard to equate his categories with his descriptions of the individual books, however, as these descriptions seem to resemble Thackeray's more variegated categories. This has been a tendency in Septuagint studies—namely, to reduce the translational technique to literal versus free.[14] Nevertheless, what we see from this is that during the first century, when the authors of the New Testament were writing, they were

12. Henry St. John Thackeray, *A Grammar of the Old Testament in Greek according to the Septuagint* (Cambridge: Cambridge University Press, 1909), 13. For a recent linguistic perspective on the Septuagint, see David G. Burke, "The First Versions: The Septuagint, the Targums, and the Latin," in *A History of Bible Translation*, ed. Phillip A. Noss, HBT 1 (Rome: Edizioni di Storia e Letteratura, 2007), 59–89, esp. 61–75; Harry Sysling, "Translation Techniques in the Ancient Bible Translations: Septuagint and Targum," in Noss, *History of Bible Translation*, 279–305, esp. 281–92. See also Theo A. W. van der Louw, *Transformations in the Septuagint: Towards an Interaction of Septuagint Studies and Translation Studies*, CBET 47 (Leuven: Peeters, 2007), although his bibliography is limited in some areas for a work such as this.

13. I deal with these terms below.

14. As Jennifer M. Dines points out in *The Septuagint*, ed. Michael A. Knibb (London: T&T Clark, 2004), 119–21; see also van der Louw, *Transformations*, 9–12.

already familiar with translation of sacred writings. More than that, they were using—though whether they were aware of this, one cannot tell—texts that varied in their translational technique and style.[15]

The influence and importance of the Septuagint cannot be overstated. It had an impact certainly on the writers of the New Testament and probably on future translations of the New Testament into various languages. In fact, translation of the New Testament began surprisingly quickly after the writing of the New Testament books. The first translations seem to have been made in the late second century, or at least sometime after AD 180. They came about for a number of reasons. These factors include the early and ambitious missionary efforts of Christians who took Christianity to new areas where there were other indigenous languages[16] and diminution over time of the use of Greek, especially in the western areas of the Roman Empire.[17] These early translations seem, at least at first glance, to hold great promise for helping us trace the development and transmission of the Greek New Testament. However, debate over the value of translations in reconstructing the text of the Greek New Testament continues. Although the ancient versions are early, in fact earlier than most Greek manuscripts, several prohibitive factors are to be considered when using them, including whether the translation was made from a Greek original or is derivative,[18] the level of linguistic competence of the translators (both in Greek, the source language, and in the target language),[19] whether the target language has linguistic transparency in relation to Greek,[20] and whether the translation reflects intralingual translational issues.[21] These issues will be kept in view

15. See H. B. Swete, *An Introduction to the Old Testament in Greek* (Cambridge: Cambridge University Press, 1902), 382–86. Swete notes the quotations of the Septuagint in the New Testament.

16. Bruce M. Metzger, *The Text of the New Testament: Its Transmission, Corruption, and Restoration*, 2nd ed. (New York: Oxford University Press, 1968; 4th ed., with Bart D. Ehrman, 2005), 67 (4th ed., 94). See Stephen Neill, *A History of Christian Missions*, 2nd ed., revised by Owen Chadwick (London: Penguin, 1986), 24–52.

17. Kurt Aland and Barbara Aland, *The Text of the New Testament: An Introduction to the Critical Editions and to the Theory and Practice of Modern Textual Criticism*, trans. Erroll F. Rhodes, 2nd ed. (Grand Rapids: Eerdmans, 1989), 52.

18. Ibid., 185.

19. Metzger, *Text*, 67 (4th ed., 95).

20. Ibid., 67–68 (4th ed., 95).

21. Aland and Aland, *Text of the New Testament*, 185.

as I briefly examine several important early translations of the Greek New Testament.

## ■ SYRIAC TRANSLATION

The Syriac translation not only reflects the early spread of Christianity but also has played a significant role in debate over establishing the Greek text of the New Testament. There are five Syriac versions of the New Testament. These include the Old Syriac, with two major manuscripts, the Cureton (Syr$^c$) and the Sinai (Syr$^s$); the Peshitta or Syriac Vulgate (Syr$^p$); the Philoxenian (Syr$^{ph}$); the Harclean (Syr$^h$); and the Palestinian (Syr$^{pal}$). The Palestinian is considered independent of the others and dates to the fifth century AD. The Philoxenian and Harclean are either two versions of the same original text or one version that was revised; in either case, they date to the sixth century and later. The Sinai Old Syriac version probably was made in the fourth century, and the Cureton in the fifth, but with both reflecting a Greek text from the late second or early third century. The Peshitta version, which became the version of the Bible used in the Syriac church and dates to after AD 400, has been known for centuries, and many manuscripts of it are available.[22]

As recently as the beginning of the twentieth century it was thought by some that the Peshitta reflected the earliest version of the Syriac Bible. John Burgon, defender of the Textus Receptus, believed that the Peshitta was to be dated to the second century and that the Cureton, Philoxenian, and Harclean versions were later versions of the Syriac tradition—a tradition, he contended, that went back to the second century or, even earlier, to the autographs themselves. The dating of the Peshitta was important to Burgon because the Peshitta, and the other versions such as the Palestinian, contained the long ending of Mark's Gospel (16:9–20).[23]

The date of the Syriac version was an important factor in the debate over the relative merits of the Textus Receptus and the Revised Version

22. See Metzger, *Text*, 68–71 (4th ed., 96–100); J. Neville Birdsall, "The Recent History of New Testament Textual Criticism (from Westcott and Hort, 1881, to the Present)," *ANRW* II.26.1 (1992): 123–32; F. G. Kenyon, *The Text of the Greek Bible*, rev. A. W. Adams, 3rd ed., ST (London: Duckworth, 1975), 129–30.

23. John W. Burgon, *The Last Twelve Verses of the Gospel according to S. Mark* (1871; repr., Ann Arbor, MI: Sovereign Grace Book Club, 1959), 110–12.

of 1881 (to be discussed below). The Textus Receptus was defended against the Revised Version in a well-known debate in 1897 on textual criticism of the New Testament. The debate took place between, on one side, Burgon's successor in the defense of the Textus Receptus, Edward Miller, along with G. H. Gwilliam, who edited the Peshitta for Clarendon Press, and Albert Bonus, who had collated the Cureton, Sinai, and Peshitta versions, in part on the basis of the early date of the Peshitta, and on the other side, the successors of Westcott and Hort, William Sanday, Arthur C. Headlam, and W. C. Allen, all of them members of the seminar run by Sanday that produced the now famous book on the Synoptic Gospels.[24] Sanday acknowledged that the date of the Peshitta was crucial for the case by Miller. The debate was not clearly settled for either side, but soon after the debate, however, Francis Conybeare published an analysis of the Sinai and Peshitta versions in which he concluded that the Armenian and Georgian versions of the New Testament, which can be dated to AD 325–400, seem to know the former but not the latter. Therefore, he concluded that the Peshitta version was not yet in existence at this time.[25] This confirmed that the earliest Syriac tradition, reflective of the Western text-type in the Old Syriac, can be dated to the late second century at the very earliest (and probably not that early for the versions themselves) and was not as early as the Alexandrian text-type.

Even if the Syriac is early, there are difficulties in using it as an early source of the New Testament. The translatability of Greek into Syriac is highly problematic. Sebastian Brock, the well-known Syriologist, has noted a number of incommensurabilities between the two languages: no formalized case for Syriac, differing verbal systems, different functions of the article, parataxis (rather than hypotaxis)[26]

24. J. L. North, "The Oxford Debate on the Textual Criticism of the New Testament, Held at New College on May 6, 1897: An End, Not a Beginning, for the Textus Receptus," in *Studies in the Early Text of the Gospels and Acts: The Papers of the First Birmingham Colloquium on the Textual Criticism of the New Testament,* ed. D. G. K. Taylor, SBLTCS 1 (Atlanta: Society of Biblical Literature, 1999), 5–16. See the article for an account of the debate. See W. Sanday, ed., *Studies in the Synoptic Problem, by Members of the University of Oxford* (Oxford: Clarendon, 1911).

25. F. C. Conybeare, "The Growth of the Peshitta Version of the New Testament, Illustrated from the Old Armenian and Georgian Versions," *AngJT* 1 (1897): 883–912.

26. Parataxis is when units, such as clauses, are connected on equal terms (e.g., "and"), while hypotaxis is when units are connected on unequal or subordinate terms.

in Syriac, lack of formal equivalence for some phrases in Syriac, fewer adjectives in Syriac, different conjunction systems, and few particles in Syriac.[27] These elements of discontinuity would appear to represent the major difficulties for rendering Greek into Syriac that would accurately reflect the original. However, Brock has noted that the "most problematical cases" are when the Syriac seems to indicate formal correspondence with the Greek original. As Brock states, "Formal identity can by no means be used as evidence that the Syriac supports the Greek variant in question."[28] He cites the example of Greek δέ, *de* (a conjunction, often translated either "and" or "but"), where, despite apparent similarity, there is "no exact equivalence in usage between [Greek] δέ and [Syriac] *den*."[29]

■ LATIN TRANSLATION

The second language to discuss is Latin. There are two important features of the Latin versions and tradition. The first is the Old Latin translations themselves, probably first made in northern Africa in the late second century, and later in Italy and elsewhere.[30] The Old Latin version, which is thought to resemble the Western text-type, has numerous fragmentary manuscripts, but they are highly divergent in their readings. Bruce Metzger cites Luke 24:4–5 as an example where there are more than twenty-seven variants in the surviving Old Latin manuscripts.[31] Two of these manuscripts merit mention. The bilingual Codex Bezae (05 D), dating probably to the fifth century, has both Greek and Latin. The Old Latin is thought by most scholars to represent a manuscript tradition that dates to the early third century, as the manuscript occasionally agrees with readings in two earlier Latin manuscripts, designated "k" and "a." The manuscript k, though it dates to around AD 400, has a text that agrees with the third-century text of the Latin father Cyprian.[32] The other Latin manuscript is Codex Gigas (gig). This is a large manuscript, with pages twenty inches

27. Sebastian P. Brock, "Limitations of Syriac in Representing Greek," in Metzger, *Early Versions*, 83–84.
28. Ibid., 98.
29. Ibid., 93.
30. Metzger, *Text*, 72 (4th ed., 101).
31. Ibid.
32. Ibid., 73–74 (4th ed., 102).

across and thirty-six inches high. This manuscript, though not early (it dates to the thirteenth century), was written in Bohemia and came into the possession of the government in Prague. However, during the conquest of Prague in 1648 by the Swedes it was taken, and a year later it was presented to the Royal Library in Stockholm,[33] where it is still on display, much to the consternation of the Czech government.

The second feature of the Latin tradition is the important influence on it of Jerome's edition of the Latin Bible, the Vulgate. Jerome (347–420) was asked by Pope Damasus around AD 382 to revise the Old Latin Bible. This request came about in light of the chaotic state of affairs regarding Old Latin manuscripts. Jerome himself observed that there were nearly as many versions of the Latin text as there were manuscripts themselves.[34] Jerome, as the most accomplished biblical scholar of his day, was commissioned to prepare a revision of the Latin Bible, using the Greek manuscripts available to him. By AD 384 Jerome had prepared the four Gospels by comparing the existing Latin manuscripts with the Greek ones and correcting the Latin where it was problematic. There is serious question as to whether or to what extent Jerome actually revised the rest of the New Testament. Like Augustine, his near contemporary, Jerome in his commentaries uses a different text than is found in the Vulgate. Further, it appears that his degree of revision decreased as his work progressed. It is possible that if he did revise the rest of the New Testament, he less and less corrected the Old Latin. In any case, we unfortunately do not know what manuscripts, either Latin or Greek, Jerome used in his revision. However, at least for the Gospels, it appears that he used a form of Alexandrian text-type, quite possibly a text that was similar in nature to Codex Sinaiticus (01 ℵ).[35] The Latin version that Jerome began (if not finished) underwent numerous revisions during the course of the Middle Ages by a number of scholars, resulting in much textual corruption and mixing of the Latin text-types.[36] Whether Jerome finished his task or not, this version was the Bible of the Western church for a thousand years, enshrined as the authoritative edition of the Bible for the Roman Catholic Church by papal bull in 1592 (Pope

33. Ibid., 74 (4th ed., 103–4).
34. Ibid., 72 (4th ed., 101).
35. Kenyon, *Text*, 158.
36. Metzger, *Text*, 76 (4th ed., 106).

Clement VIII). It formed the basis of all English translations of the Bible until the sixteenth century and the translation work of William Tyndale, who was the first English translator to use the Greek and Hebrew.[37] The Vulgate continued to be the basis of the major English translations of the New Testament used by Roman Catholics, including the Douai-Rheims (1610, 1749) and Ronald Knox (1955) versions, until 1966 with publication of the Jerusalem Bible (a revision of a French translation produced in 1948) and 1970 with publication of the New American Bible.

Apart from the problems with transmission of the Latin text, there are a number of difficulties with using the Latin text as a means of establishing the Greek original. Bonifatius Fischer, though noting the suitability of Latin for rendering Greek, also notes certain clear limitations. These include the following: there is no differentiation in Latin between the Greek aorist and perfect tense-forms, forms of imperatives, double negatives and negative sense, or negative particles; Latin lacks an article; there are differences in Latin in rendering the same Greek word; Latin has difficulties in rendering Greek prepositions; and there are numerous phonological ambiguities between the two languages.[38] Thus, even Latin does not provide as useful a guide to establishing the Greek text as one would like.

### ▪ COPTIC TRANSLATION

The third language to consider is Coptic. Coptic is the last form of the native Egyptian language, which began first with hieroglyphics and continued with hieratic and demotic, until Coptic developed in the late first and early second centuries. The earliest Coptic manuscript is dated perhaps as early as the late first century.[39] Coptic adopted the twenty-four letters of the Greek alphabet and supplemented them with seven characters from demotic.[40] The development of Coptic is directly linked to the spread of Christianity in Egypt, which seems to have occurred very early and very rapidly, moving from Alexandria outwards, as attested by a number of Greek manuscripts found in

37. Kenyon, *Text*, 145; Birdsall, "Recent History," 118.
38. Bonifatius Fischer, "Limitations of Latin in Representing Greek," in Metzger, *Early Versions*, 365–74.
39. Kenyon, *Text*, 135.
40. Metzger, *Early Versions*, 107.

various places in Egypt. For example, $\mathfrak{P}^{52}$, dated to the first half of the second century (see above) and possibly discovered in the Fayyum, gives evidence of a Christian community in the early second century well beyond Alexandria,[41] as does $\mathfrak{P}^{46}$, with the Pauline Epistles, also possibly found in the Fayyum, or possibly near ancient Aphroditopolis.[42] $\mathfrak{P}^{64}$ (linked to $\mathfrak{P}^4$ and $\mathfrak{P}^{67}$) was discovered even farther south in Coptos, in the Upper Nile region.[43] By the third century, Christianity had penetrated the native population, and by the fourth century the country had been Christianized.[44] By the time the country was Christianized, however, there had been a major transition from the use of Greek to the use of Coptic in the church. Athanasius (296/298–373) tells the story of St. Anthony (251–356 [also called "Anthony the Great"]), who apparently did not know Greek, hearing and understanding the Scriptures being read around AD 270–275.[45] In order for this to have happened, either there was a translation provided for the occasion or, more likely, there was already a translation of the Gospel passage (Matt. 19:21) into Coptic at that point. The rise of Christianity among the native population led to the translation of the Bible into Coptic, so that by the early fourth century, Pachomius, who founded a monastic order in Egypt, required his monks to be able to read in Coptic.[46]

Coptic appears in a number of different dialects into which the New Testament is translated. These include the following: the Sahidic, which, though having some characteristics of the Western text-type but being closer to the Alexandrian, has been identified more recently as used in many of the Egyptian papyri and seems to date to the third century as the earliest of the dialects;[47] the Bohairic, which, though it

41. Kenyon, *Text*, 136. The date of $\mathfrak{P}^{52}$ has recently been called into question, but see Stanley E. Porter, "Recent Efforts to Reconstruct Early Christianity on the Basis of Its Papyrological Evidence," in *Christian Origins and Greco-Roman Culture: Social and Literary Contexts for the New Testament*, ed. Stanley E. Porter and Andrew W. Pitts, TENTS 9 (Leiden: Brill, 2013), 71–84.

42. Philip W. Comfort and David P. Barrett, *The Text of the Earliest New Testament Greek Manuscripts*, corrected ed. (Wheaton: Tyndale, 2001), 203.

43. Ibid., 47.

44. Metzger, *Early Versions*, 103.

45. Ibid., 104–5; cf. Kenyon, *Text*, 136.

46. Metzger, *Early Versions*, 105; cf. Kenyon, *Text*, 136.

47. Kenyon, *Text*, 137–39; Metzger, *Text*, 79 (4th ed., 110).

has been known for a longer time, reflects the Alexandrian text-type even more closely than the Sahidic, but is later;[48] the Achmimic, in which there is little New Testament evidence; the sub-Achmimic, in which there have been few findings, though there are some of significance (see below);[49] Middle Egyptian, in which the Gospel of Matthew has been found (Codex Scheide), dating to the fifth century and resembling Codexes Sinaiticus (01 א) and Vaticanus (03 B), while a portion of Acts in Codex Glazier follows the Western text;[50] and the Fayyumic, in which there is little New Testament material, although what exists is significant (see below).

Three manuscripts of the Gospel of John merit attention here.[51] The first is a manuscript of most of John's Gospel written in the Bohairic dialect and dated to the fourth century. In this manuscript two textually disputed passages are absent. These passages include John 5:3b–4, where the angel troubles the water, and John 7:53–8:11, the pericope of the woman caught in adultery.[52] A second manuscript is of John's Gospel written in the Fayyumic dialect and dated to the early fourth century. This manuscript contains John 6:11–15:11. It is missing four folios (eight pages) between John 7:42 and 8:39.[53] However, on the basis of the number of lines per page and the number of verses, it appears that this manuscript did not have the pericope of the woman caught in adultery.[54] A third manuscript is in the sub-Achmimic dialect, datable to the mid-fourth century (AD 350–375) and found at Qau el Kebir, one of few manuscripts with specific provenance. This manuscript also omits John 5:3b–4 and the pericope of the woman caught in adultery.[55]

48. Kenyon, Text, 141; Metzger, Text, 80 (4th ed., 112).

49. Metzger, Early Versions, 116.

50. Ibid., 117–19.

51. Due to these findings, some might wish to observe that the Gospel of John has particular affinities with Egyptian gnosticism. See, in refutation, Charles E. Hill, The Johannine Corpus in the Early Church (Oxford: Oxford University Press, 2004), 205–93.

52. Rodolphe Kasser, Papyrus Bodmer III: Évangile de Jean et Genèse I–IV, 2 en bohaïrique, vol. 1, CSCO 177 (Louvain: Secrétariat du CorpusSCO, 1958).

53. Elinor M. Husselman, The Gospel of John in Fayumic Coptic (P.Mich. Inv. 3521), Kelsey Museum of Archaeology Studies 2 (Ann Arbor, MI: Kelsey Museum of Archaeology, 1962), 61.

54. The four folios (eight pages) would have held a total of approximately forty verses. There are thirty-nine verses between John 7:42 and 8:39 without the pericope.

55. Herbert Thompson, The Gospel of St. John according to the Earliest Coptic Manuscript (London: British School of Archaeology in Egypt, 1924).

Regarding the use of Coptic to reconstruct the original Greek text, J. Martyn Plumley states, "One important and overriding fact about the Coptic language must always be borne in mind. Coptic, like the ancient Egyptian language from which it is the direct descendant, is a language of strict word order. This is so since there are no case endings."[56] Coptic furthermore has two genders, uses asyndeton (connecting clauses without conjunctions), does not differentiate negative particles, and does not form the passive voice, among other features,[57] which make it difficult to use in determining the underlying source language.

Other ancient translations could be discussed as well—for example, Armenian, Georgian, Ethiopic, Gothic, and Old Church Slavonic[58]—but these are sufficient to show the difficulties in development even of ancient translations. As noted above, the major translation in the Western world was the Latin Vulgate, with the Greek Bible remaining in use in the East until at least the fall of Constantinople in 1453. This has a direct bearing upon the development of English New Testament translations.

### English New Testament Translations

No language has seen as many Bibles translated into its language as has English. Bible translation into English is a major industry, for good or for bad, with new translations being produced at an alarming rate. Some of these translations come into being with little comment, while others have caused tremendous stir, to the point of some even costing their translators their lives. Other languages can tell somewhat similar stories, if not to the same voluminous extent. Nevertheless, there are a number of important modern translations of the New Testament to note, especially those in English, and especially in relation to the Greek text that they have translated. Several of these translations merit mention, although this can only be brief. There were well over one hundred New Testament translations produced in the twentieth century alone, so I can mention in passing only a few in the history of English Bible translation.[59]

56. J. Martyn Plumley, "Limitations of Coptic (Sahidic) in Representing Greek," in Metzger, *Early Versions*, 143.
57. Ibid., 146–49.
58. These are discussed in Metzger, *Early Versions*.
59. There are several serviceable accounts of the Bible in English. The best, even though now showing their age, are F. F. Bruce, *History of the Bible in English*, 3rd ed.

## ■ JOHN WYCLIFFE (1320–1384)

The first English translation of the New Testament is attributed to the English scholar and theologian John Wycliffe, but probably it actually was done by John Purvey, his secretary. There are two versions of the Wycliffe Bible. The earlier one (1380–1384) was made during Wycliffe's lifetime and was literalistically based upon the Latin Vulgate that it translated; that is, these were hand-copied manuscripts that needed to be compared to each other, as they often contained transcriptional errors (printing did not come until 1456). The later version, done after Wycliffe's death, is more idiomatic and reflects principles of translation laid out by Purvey in his General Prologue (1495–1496), although it includes the "Letter of Paul to the Laodiceans," a fourth-century pseudepigraphal work. It is this second version that became very popular as Wycliffe's Bible.[60]

## ■ WILLIAM TYNDALE (1492–1536)

Arguably, the greatest translation of the New Testament into English was that of William Tyndale.[61] Tyndale came to Cambridge to study soon after Erasmus left, having already graduated from Oxford. Tyndale used Erasmus's second and third editions of the Greek New

(Guildford: Lutterworth, 1979); David Ewert, *From Ancient Tablets to Modern Translations: A General Introduction to the Bible* (Grand Rapids: Zondervan, 1983). Probably the most beautiful treatment, full of excellent photographs, is Donald L. Brake, *A Visual History of the English Bible: The Tumultuous Tale of the World's Bestselling Book* (Grand Rapids: Baker Academic, 2008). Others include Brooke Foss Westcott, *A General View of the History of the English Bible*, 2nd ed. (London: Macmillan, 1872), for an excellent older perspective; E. H. Robertson, *The New Translations of the Bible* (London: SCM, 1959); Sakae Kubo and Walter Specht, *So Many Versions? Twentieth Century English Versions of the Bible* (Grand Rapids: Zondervan, 1975); Philip W. Comfort, *The Complete Guide to Bible Versions*, rev. ed. (Wheaton: Tyndale, 1996); Steven M. Sheeley and Robert N. Nash Jr., *The Bible in English Translation: An Essential Guide* (Nashville: Abingdon, 1997); Bruce M. Metzger, *The Bible in Translation: Ancient and English Versions* (Grand Rapids: Baker Academic, 2001). Not all of these are of equal worth. See also Stanley E. Porter, "Translations of the Bible (Since the KJV)," *DBCI* 362–69, as well as my several other articles cited below.
60. Bruce, *History of the Bible*, 13–22.
61. I realize that this is bound to arouse the ire of those who are particularly fond of the Authorized Version, especially those who hold to the virtual inspiration of this translation. The fact that so much of the Authorized Version uses Tyndale's wording, and that Tyndale made the translation (at least of the New Testament) on his own under such horrible circumstances, speaks for itself.

Testament (1519, 1522) as the basis of his translation, which he made in Hamburg, Germany, finally getting it published in 1526, and then revised in 1534.[62] Tyndale followed Luther's order of the New Testament, with Hebrews, James, Jude, and Revelation at the end.[63] He also included, along with the New Testament, "Epistles from the Old Testament," excerpted poetic and prophetic passages translated out of Hebrew or Greek (from the Apocrypha).[64]

Having fled England, done much of his publishing work in Germany, and then taken refuge in Antwerp, Tyndale was kidnapped by the Belgian king Charles V and executed in 1536, praying that the king of England's eyes would be opened. Henry VIII's eyes had been opened, and he was already circulating throughout England a Bible translated in 1535 by Miles Coverdale based on Tyndale's.[65]

How significant was Tyndale's translation? Consider such recognizable biblical phrasing as "and God shall wipe away all tears from their eyes" (Rev. 7:17); "ask, and it shall be given you; seek, and ye shall find; knock, and it shall be opened unto you" (Matt. 7:7); "with God all things are possible" (Matt. 19:26); "in him we live, and move, and have our being" (Acts 17:28); "be not weary in well doing" (2 Thess. 3:13); "fight the good fight of faith; lay hold on eternal life" (1 Tim. 6:12); "looking unto Jesus the author and finisher of our faith" (Heb. 12:2); "behold, I stand at the door, and knock" (Rev. 3:20); "the salt of the earth" (Matt. 5:13); "the signs of the times" (Matt. 16:3); "where two or three are gathered together" (Matt. 18:20); "the spirit is . . . willing, but the flesh is weak" (Matt. 26:41); "eat, drink, and be merry" (Luke 12:19); "clothed, and in his right mind" (Luke 8:35); "there fell from his eyes as it had been scales" (Acts 9:18); "a law unto themselves" (Rom. 2:14); "the powers that be" (Rom. 13:1); and "the patience of Job" (James 5:11). All of these memorable verses and phrases, many of them part of our English idiom to this day, are from the Authorized Version of the Bible, but they are taken directly from William Tyndale (with only

62. David Daniell, introduction to William Tyndale, *Tyndale's New Testament* (New Haven: Yale University Press, 1989), xvii.
63. See Martin Luther, *Die gantze Heilige Schrifft Deudsch Wittenberg 1545*, 2 vols. (Bonn: Lempertz, 2004), esp. 2:1966, for the table of contents.
64. Bruce, *History of the Bible*, 48.
65. Ibid., 52; Ewert, *Ancient Tablets*, 190.

slight changes).[66] In fact, it has been estimated that nine-tenths of the Authorized Version came from Tyndale's Bible, and that in some places where the Authorized Version departed from Tyndale, it was restored in later translation.[67]

## ■ PREDECESSORS TO THE AUTHORIZED VERSION

Besides Tyndale's New Testament, there were a number of translations that appeared before the Authorized Version and paved the way for it. These include that of Miles Coverdale (1488–1569), who quaintly rendered Psalm 91:5 as "thou shalt not need to be afrayed for eny bugges by night";[68] Thomas Matthew's Bible (the name being a pseudonym), a completion in 1537 of Tyndale's Bible by a man named "Rogers" (Tyndale did not finish the Old Testament);[69] the Great Bible, great because of its size and not its translation, as it is a 1539 revision by Coverdale of Matthew's Bible; the Geneva Bible, a Calvinistically oriented Bible, as one might expect on the basis of its origins, containing marginal notes such as reference to the beast in Revelation 11:7 as "the Pope which hath his power out of hell and cometh hence," and in its many subsequent editions (160 in all) with typographical errors such as "blessed are the placemakers" in Matthew 5:9 and "Jesus Church" for "Jesus Christ" in John 5:20;[70] and the Bishops' Bible, a revision in 1568 of the Great Bible by a team led by the archbishop of Canterbury, Matthew Parker, with such memorable renderings as "lay thy bread upon wet faces" for "cast thy bread upon the waters" taken from the Great Bible in Ecclesiastes 11:1.[71]

## ■ AUTHORIZED VERSION

There is little that needs to be said about the Authorized Version of 1611 (also known as the King James Version) that has not already been said elsewhere.[72] King James, not sharing the Calvinistic theology of

---

66. Daniell, introduction to Tyndale, *Tyndale's New Testament*, ix–x.
67. Ewert, *Ancient Tablets*, 188–89.
68. Ibid., 190.
69. Ibid., 191.
70. Ibid., 194–95. This is the Bible of Elizabethan England, including the Bible of Shakespeare and the Puritans. Its influence was tremendous.
71. Ibid., 195.
72. The year 2011 celebrated the four-hundredth anniversary of the first publication of the Authorized Version. As a result, many works were written about it in the

the Geneva Bible, welcomed the proposal in 1603 of a new translation. He commissioned six groups of translators, involving roughly
fifty-seven translators in all, to perform the translational work. Three
groups worked on the Old Testament, two on the New Testament,
and one on the Apocrypha. Their drafts were revised by a smaller
group and then published. Common names and ecclesiastical wording
were retained, while added words were put in italics. Although the
Authorized Version is a translation in its own right, in the sense that
the scholars involved probably used Beza's fifth edition for the Greek
New Testament (according to F. H. A. Scrivener, though some think
that a version of Stephanus from 1550 was used),[73] it is also a major
revision in that it was based upon the Bishops' Bible and ended up
retaining such a high percentage of Tyndale's wording.[74] The early
editions of the Authorized Version were full of all kinds of mistakes,
such as rendering Matthew 23:24 with "strain at a gnat" instead of
"strain out a gnat," a mistake that was retained in subsequent editions. The edition of 1631 left the word "not" out of the seventh com-
mandment, "You shall not commit adultery," for which the printer
was fined, and this Bible became known as the "Wicked Bible." In

---

years leading up to the celebration. Some are exercises in hagiography rather than
historical, cultural, or linguistic investigation. The translators' own words are cap-
tured in Erroll F. Rhodes and Liana Lupas, eds., *The Translators to the Reader: The
Original Preface of the King James Version of 1611 Revisited* (New York: American
Bible Society, 1997). A reasonable history is Adam Nicolson, *God's Secretaries: The
Making of the King James Bible* (New York: HarperCollins, 2003). A linguistic treatment by a significant linguist is David Crystal, *Begat: The King James Bible and the
English Language* (Oxford: Oxford University Press, 2010). A specialized treatment
of the individuals involved is Gustavus S. Paine, *The Men behind the King James
Version* (Grand Rapids: Baker, 1959). Two collections of essays on various related
issues are David G. Burke, ed., *Translation That Openeth the Window: Reflections
on the History and Legacy of the King James Bible*, BSNA 23 (Atlanta: Society of
Biblical Literature, 2009) (unfortunately, the photo on the cover is not of a portion
of Hampton Court Palace in existence during the time of James, but a portion added
under William and Mary); David Lyle Jeffrey, ed., *The King James Bible and the World
It Made* (Waco, TX: Baylor University Press, 2011). A fascinating book is Ward Allen,
trans. and ed., *Translating for King James* (London: Allen Lane Penguin, 1970), an
edition of the only set of notes taken by a member involved in the revision stage of
the Authorized Version.
    73. Stanley E. Porter, "Language and Translation of the New Testament," in *The
Oxford Handbook of Biblical Studies*, ed. John W. Rogerson and Judith M. Lieu
(Oxford: Oxford University Press, 2006), 197.
    74. Bruce, *History of the Bible*, 97–98.

an edition of 1795 Mark 7:27 was rendered "Let the children first be killed" (instead of "filled"). Another has "the dogs liked his blood" in 1 Kings 22:38 (rather than "licked up"), and, finally (for my list, not finally for the list of all errors and misprints!), Psalm 119:161 is rendered "Printers [rather than "princes"] have persecuted me without a cause." Despite these difficulties, the Authorized Version, because of its official support—though no one has any official record of its being "authorized" by the government—and the quality of its resulting language, in large part because of Tyndale's prior work but also because of the intentions of those involved, became the Bible of the English-speaking world, only finally being challenged in the nineteenth century. Even so, there have been a number of efforts to revise it and keep it current, including the New King James Version (1979)[75] and the 21st Century King James Version (1994).

■ REVISED VERSION[76]

In the nineteenth century two major factors influenced Bible translation. The first, as discussed in chapter 1, was the discovery of new, early manuscripts of the New Testament and the development of new texts of the Greek Bible that reflected these earlier manuscripts. The second was the realization that the language found in the Authorized Version was increasingly archaic and in need of revision. As a result, and in response, there began a movement to produce new Bible translations.

The first major effort to revise the Authorized Version was the Revised Version (1881), or the American Standard Version (1901) as it

75. Arthur L. Farstad, *The New King James Version: In the Great Tradition* (Nashville: Nelson, 1989).
76. For what follows, see Stanley E. Porter, "Modern Translations," in *The Oxford Illustrated History of the Bible*, ed. John Rogerson (Oxford: Oxford University Press, 2001), 135–47. I note that often, at least in the past, a book in defense or explanation of the translation often accompanied a new translation, especially by a committee. I refer to some of those below. However, one must remember that these are sometimes exercises in self-justification (often written by the head of the translation committee!), and frequently they do not address the heart of matters involved in translation. One essay that does address some of these issues, although it is clear that the author's respondents fail to grasp the essence of his statement, is D. A. Carson, "New Bible Translations: An Assessment and Prospect," in *The Bible in the Twenty-First Century: Symposium Papers*, ed. Howard Clark Kee (New York: American Bible Society, 1993), 37–67.

was called in the United States. The translators tried to avoid making unnecessary changes to the Authorized Version,[77] but they used the Greek text of Westcott and Hort—being developed at the time, with Westcott on the translation committee—as the basis of their work.[78] Though this version was popular at first, selling over two million copies in the first few days, it failed to replace the Authorized Version because of its lack of literary quality (quite frankly, it is rather wooden and cumbersome to read). It also aroused great antipathy in those who supported the Textus Receptus or Majority text, as this revised Bible "eliminated" a number of passages not found in earlier manuscripts, such as John 5:3b–4 and 1 John 5:7, and indicated that others (e.g., Mark 16:9–20, the long ending; John 7:53–8:11, the woman caught in adultery) were not in the earliest manuscripts.

■ INDIVIDUAL TRANSLATIONS

In some ways, the history of English Bible translation has been the history of individual translations. It has been estimated that as many as seventy private versions of the Bible were published in English from 1611 to 1881,[79] including one in 1775 by the evangelist and scholar John Wesley (1703–1791), one in 1833 by the lexicographer Noah Webster (1758–1843), and one in 1860 by the Bible scholar Henry Alford (1810–1871).[80] As a result of the failure of the Revised Version

77. Nevertheless, people were aware of the differences, to the point that two different versions of Greek texts were published, one with the reconstructed Authorized Version with Revised Version variants and the other with the reconstructed Revised Version with Authorized Version variants. See F. H. A. Scrivener, *The New Testament in Greek according to the Text Followed in the Authorised Version Together with the Variations Adopted in the Revised Version* (Cambridge: Cambridge University Press, 1908); E. Palmer, ed., *Η Καινη Διαθηκη: The Greek Testament with the Readings Adopted by the Revisers of the Authorised Version* (Oxford: Clarendon, 1897).

78. See Brooke Foss Westcott, *Some Lessons of the Revised Version of the New Testament* (London: Hodder & Stoughton, 1897). Westcott's journals of the translation discussions have now become available, and they appear to contain much interesting information on what actually went on in the committee work. See Alan Cadwallader, "The Politics of Translation of the Revised Version: Evidence from the Newly Discovered Notebooks of Brooke Foss Westcott," *JTS* 58 (2007): 415–39.

79. Porter, "Modern Translations," 135.

80. One of the most notorious translations, which really is not a translation but rather an edition, is by Thomas Jefferson. His thoroughly expurgated New Testament, begun while he was president of the United States, was completed in 1819 but not published until 1904. See Donald S. Harrington, foreword in O. I. A. Roche, ed., *The*

to capture the Bible-reading public's favor, a number of individual translations were produced in the first part of the twentieth century. These versions were produced by scholars such as Richard Weymouth (1882–1902), whose translation (published posthumously in 1903) was based on his Resultant Greek Testament (1886), where the now familiar disputed passages were either deleted or indicated as not in the earliest manuscripts; James Moffatt (1870–1944), who produced two translations, the first (1901) ordered according to his theory of New Testament development (called the Historical New Testament),[81] and either deleting or indicating the lateness of the usual passages, and the second (1913) based upon Hermann von Soden's Greek New Testament (1913) indicating the same; Edgar J. Goodspeed (1871–1962), who produced an American English translation (1923) based upon the text of Westcott and Hort (1881); and J. B. Phillips (1906–1982), who, out of a desire to communicate with those who lacked biblical background, produced a literarily sensitive rendering (1958, entire New Testament based on Westcott and Hort; 1972 revised, based on the United Bible Societies *Greek New Testament*).[82]

### ■ REVISED STANDARD VERSION[83]

The next major revisionist effort by a team of scholars was more successful than the first. The Revised Standard Version (RSV) was based upon the American Standard Version while retaining as much of the Authorized Version as possible. A committee was established

*Jefferson Bible with the Annotated Commentaries on Religion of Thomas Jefferson* (New York: C. N. Potter, 1964), 9–13, esp. 10.

81. This must have been a trend of the time, as the popular British Everyman series published a similar New Testament: *The New Testament of Our Lord and Saviour Jesus Christ Arranged in the Order in Which Its Parts Came to Those in the First Century Who Believed in Our Lord* (London: Dent; New York: Dutton, 1906).

82. C. S. Lewis (1898–1963), the great British literary scholar, apologist, and lay theologian, wrote the introduction to the first installment of Phillips's translation. See C. S. Lewis, introduction to J. B. Phillips, *Letters to Young Churches: A Translation of the New Testament Epistles* (New York: Macmillan, 1957, 1st ed., 1947), vi–ix.

83. Luther A. Weigle, ed., *An Introduction to the Revised Standard Version of the New Testament* (Chicago [?]: The International Council of Religious Education, 1946), with essays by various committee members. Some may be interested to know that A. T. Robertson was on the American Standard Bible Committee (which eventually became the committee that produced the RSV) from 1930 until his death in 1934. A similar book was published on the Old Testament: Luther A. Weigle, ed., *An Introduction to the Revised Standard Version of the Old Testament* (Nashville: Nelson, 1952).

in 1937 to oversee this revision, using the sixteenth and seventeenth
editions of Nestle's Greek New Testament (1936, 1941). Reintroducing
some practices from the Authorized Version (such as rendering the
same Greek word with different English words), eliminating "thee"
and "thou," and using quotation marks (a practice not used in the
Authorized or Revised Versions), the RSV New Testament was published in 1946 to both great acclaim and vitriolic reaction. The reac-
tions included a minister burning the Bible with a blowtorch in his
pulpit. As one writer has sardonically remarked, at least it "is better
than burning the translators, which they did in the days of Tyndale."[84]
The RSV was published by Thomas Nelson, and one person wrote
to the translators, "Who is this Tom Nelson who has written a new
Bible? I don't want Tom Nelson's Bible. I want the Bible the way the
Apostle James wrote it."[85] The RSV has been revised (New Testament
in 1962; entire Bible in 1971), with both a Catholic version (1965)
and an Orthodox version (1973), as well as the gender-sensitive New
Revised Standard Version (NRSV [1989], using the United Bible Societies *Greek New Testament* corrected third edition plus information
about changes to the critical apparatus to be introduced in UBS[4]).[86]

■ NEW ENGLISH BIBLE/REVISED ENGLISH BIBLE[87]

In Britain a team of scholars was established in 1947 to produce
a Bible for a variety of church groups, the committee headed by the
well-known New Testament scholar C. H. Dodd (1884–1973) and
later by the equally well-known Old Testament scholar G. R. Driver
(1892–1975). This committee produced the New English Bible (1961),
having developed their own eclectic text based on the Nestle text
(1964).[88] The goal of the translation was to render passages by sense

84. Ewert, *Ancient Tablets*, 229.
85. Ibid., noting the confusion over whether King James or the apostle James
wrote the Bible.
86. See Bruce M. Metzger, Robert C. Dentan, and Walter Harrison, *The Making
of the New Revised Standard Version of the Bible* (Grand Rapids: Eerdmans, 1991),
although this volume is a disappointment compared to the similar volume for the RSV.
87. Geoffrey Hunt, *About the New English Bible* (Oxford: Oxford University
Press; Cambridge: Cambridge University Press, 1970).
88. The edition was edited by the evangelical scholar R. V. G. Tasker, *The Greek
New Testament* (Oxford: Oxford University Press; Cambridge: Cambridge University
Press, 1964).

or meaning, and not literalistically or word for word. The result was deemed a mixed result, at least in part because the translation followed too closely many of the suggested textual emendations of Driver on the basis of comparative Semitic philology.[89] Consequently, the translation underwent a revision in 1989 to produce the Revised English Bible, which seems far less innovative in today's climate than did its earlier form.

■ NEW AMERICAN STANDARD BIBLE

In reaction to some of the free renderings found in translations since the American Standard Version, a foundation in California published the New American Standard Bible in 1963, based upon the twenty-third edition of the Nestle-Aland Greek New Testament, with the translation being revised in 1995. This translation, which tends to be literalistic and awkward in its English at points (e.g., translating so-called historic presents in Greek, which are present in form but refer to past action, with English present tenses), returns to some of the conventions found in the Authorized Version, such as italics for added words and lack of paragraphing. Many, especially students, find this version helpful to use when studying the original biblical languages because the target text is so closely aligned with the source text.

■ GOOD NEWS TRANSLATION AND CONTEMPORARY ENGLISH VERSION[90]

The Good News Translation (originally Today's English Version, then the Good News Bible) was an attempt to enshrine in translated form the "dynamic equivalence" translation principles of the great linguist and organizer of translation projects Eugene Nida (1914–2011), about which and whom I will say more below. The New Testament was produced by Robert Bratcher (1920–2010) in 1966, based upon the

---

89. John Rogerson, "Can a Translation of the Bible Be Authoritative?" in *Bible Translation on the Threshold of the Twenty-First Century: Authority, Reception, Culture and Religion*, ed. Athalya Brenner and Jan Willem van Henten, JSOTSup 353 (London: Sheffield Academic Press, 2002), 24. Apparently, these aberrations were called "Driverisms."

90. Eugene A. Nida, *Good News for Everyone: How to Use the Good News Bible* (Waco, TX: Word, 1977); Barclay M. Newman et al., *Creating and Crafting the Contemporary English Version: A New Approach to Bible Translation* (New York: American Bible Society, 1996).

United Bible Societies *Greek New Testament* first edition (in that sense, it is an individual translation). This translation, produced under the auspices of the American Bible Society, has been widely used by Bible translators as a template of a dynamic rendering. The translation still reads today as the innovative communicative translation that it was when first published. The Contemporary English Version (1995) is in some ways the next stage of development of the Good News Translation, in the sense that every new generation needs its own Bible in its own language. Based upon the third and fourth editions of the United Bible Societies *Greek New Testament* (1975, 1993), this translation is dynamic, but with an eye on the tradition of the Authorized Version. A number of accusations were aimed at the Contemporary English Version when it appeared, such as that it was the first Bible to use a number of words thought inappropriate for a Bible translation, or (in a British context) that it had succumbed to using too many distinctive Americanisms. In virtually all cases, previous translations had used these same words, revealing that such criticisms were emotive rather than substantive in nature.[91] The American Bible Society, now through its Nida Institute for Biblical Scholarship, continues to support the work of Bible translation, of which these are two products.

### ■ NEW INTERNATIONAL VERSION[92]

The New International Version (NIV) was a translation that developed out of a concern by some American denominations for a more conservative general-purpose Bible in contemporary English. An international team of translators produced the New Testament in 1973 using the standard eclectic Greek New Testament. It was later

---

91. Stanley E. Porter, "The Contemporary English Version and the Ideology of Translation," in *Translating the Bible: Problems and Prospects*, ed. Stanley E. Porter and Richard S. Hess, JSNTSup 173 (Sheffield: Sheffield Academic Press, 1999), 18–45, esp. 37–38.

92. Richard Kevin Barnard, *God's Word in Our Language: The Story of the New International Version* (Colorado Springs: International Bible Society, 1989); Kenneth L. Barker, ed., *The NIV: The Making of a Contemporary Translation* (Grand Rapids: Zondervan, 1986). Cf. Kenneth L. Barker, "Bible Translation Philosophies with Special Reference to the New International Version," in *The Challenge of Bible Translation: Communicating God's Word to the World: Essays in Honor of Ronald F. Youngblood*, ed. Glen G. Scorgie, Mark L. Strauss, and Steven M. Voth (Grand Rapids: Zondervan, 2003), 51–64.

published in a gender-neutral version, wherever this neutrality can arguably be supported by the original language, first in the United Kingdom and Canada (1995) after much debate and dispute in the United States led to its not being released there, and later in North America as Today's New International Version (2005). However, the controversy over this translation continues, with the NIV translation committee having undertaken what appears to be a thorough revision of the translation (2011) in an attempt to mediate the dispute over a variety of issues, including translational technique and gender inclusivity. Despite continuing controversy over the consistency of its translation, the NIV continues to sell well as the Bible of the evangelical Christian church in North America.[93] Debate over the NIV generally centers on how much and to what degree it is a formal equivalence or dynamic equivalence translation (terms that I will discuss further below). This middle road has generated criticism from both sides.

### ■ Other Recent Translations

A number of other recent translations have been produced. The New English Translation (or NET Bible) was developed in both electronic and then print form (from 1996 on). This translation uses a form of modified dynamic equivalence, with the Greek text based upon $NA^{27}/UBS^4$. The translation, which is more dynamic, comes with hyperabundant notes that are more literalistic and sometimes highly repetitive. They are not always to be relied upon for issues of Greek grammar. The Holman Christian Standard Bible (2000), based upon the same Greek text as the NET Bible, advocates a position between formal and dynamic equivalence, what its editors call "optimal equivalence." The English Standard Version (2001), which perhaps not too surprisingly has caught on in especially conservative theological circles, is a reversion to a literalistic translational technique based upon the Revised Standard Version, including rejection of gender-neutral language.[94] The latest translation to note is the

---

93. See my comments in Stanley E. Porter, "New International Version Still Selling after 30 Years," *Christian Week Ontario Edition*, vol. 22, no. 12, September 1, 2008, p. 8.

94. Porter, "Language and Translation," 207. I find it ironic that the ESV is basically a "theologically corrected" RSV (I understand that the publisher of the ESV bought the copyright for the original RSV). Leland Ryken (*The Word of God in English: Criteria for Excellence in Bible Translation* [Wheaton: Crossway, 2000], 55) says that about 6

Common English Bible, with the New Testament published in 2010 and the entire Bible in 2011. This product of the work of 120 different translators, according to the preface, tries to be readable. It probably misses the mark with "the Human One" for titular "son of man," but some of its other renderings are fully communicative.

A number of personal translations have also appeared in the latter part of the twentieth century. The following are worthy of note: the Berkeley Version (1945); the 1955 translation by the Jewish scholar Hugh Schonfield (1901–1988); the 1952 translation of the Gospels by the classical scholar E. V. Rieu (1887–1972) and the 1957 translation of Acts by his son, C. H. Rieu (1916–2008); the translation of the New Testament (1962 for the Gospels, 1982 for Acts and the Epistles) by another classical scholar, Richmond Lattimore (1906–1984); the translation of the Daily Study Bible (1968–1969) by William Barclay (1907–1978); the Living Bible (1971), produced by the publisher Ken Taylor (1917–2005) in a simplified version for his children, revised in 1996 on the basis of the NA²⁷/UBS⁴ Greek text; the 1989 translation of the New Testament by the Jewish convert Heinz W. Cassirer (1903–1979); and *The Message: The New Testament in Contemporary Language* (1993), a highly idiomatic and often persuasive rendering by pastor and pastoral theologian Eugene Peterson (1932–).[95]

Of course, many more translations could be discussed here, such as the New Testament in Basic English, based upon the list of 850 basic English words devised by the linguist C. K. Ogden (1941; complete Bible in 1949), the Children's Bible (1962), the Cotton Patch Version (1968), and the Reader's Digest Bible (1982), among many others. However, the ones I have chosen show the development and progress of translation, at least in English, from the time of Erasmus's publication of the Greek New Testament to today.

---

percent was changed. I would imagine that some of its biggest supporters today would have been the same type of people who protested when the original RSV appeared. The ESV represents what Ryken has called "essentially literal Bible translation" (9–10), to be discussed further below. See also Wayne Grudem, Leland Ryken, C. John Collins, Vern S. Poythress, and Bruce Winter (all members of the ESV oversight committee), *Translating Truth: The Case for Essentially Literal Bible Translation* (Wheaton: Crossway, 2005). See also Leland Ryken, *The ESV and the English Bible Legacy* (Wheaton: Crossway, 2011).

95. Porter, "Modern Translations," 139.

In light of this brief survey, several concluding observations are necessary. First, the next generation always seems to find the previous generation deficient in its translations and hence the church in need of a new translation. This is probably both a good and a bad thing, but also inevitable. We need to be careful not to dismiss what has gone before, but also to recognize that the Bible we use now must function in our current context. This should make us cautiously optimistic about many recent translations, while also just plain cautious about several others. Second, the production of new translations sometimes means a completely new translation (if such a thing is possible), but often it means revision of a previous one or even regression to a previous translational perspective, even if the language is brought up to date. One of the distinctives of being a Bible translation, apparently, is that it is expected to sound like what we expect the Bible to sound like, so it is hard to depart very far from the translational tradition. Third, the Textus Receptus is no longer the text used for modern English translations of the Bible, having been replaced for the most part by the eclectic Greek text, usually the one created by Nestle-Aland and the United Bible Societies, with a few early on using Westcott and Hort's edition, and one using von Soden (Moffatt). The few exceptions to the use of these standard editions are the development by Weymouth of his own edition, which does take into account the Textus Receptus, and the reconstructed text edited by Tasker of one used in translation of the New English Bible, based on Nestle's text. None of these is recent, however. The result is translation of what amounts in some ways to a new Greek "received text." Based on what I said at the close of the previous chapter, this issue may well be worth revisiting, with all of the consequences that it implies for Bible translation.

## Major Issues in Translation of the New Testament

As I have already discussed, translations of the Bible have been produced since the earliest days of Christianity. A variety of both translation practices and theories about translation have been propounded. There have been those who have reflected upon translation from Christian times forward. In light of many of the recent translation controversies, some of the comments seem surprisingly progressive, and perhaps they merit further consideration.

## Comments on the Nature of Translation

Comments on the nature of translation span the time from the writing of the New Testament to the present, by translators of all types of literature, including (but not limited to) the Bible.[96] The range of opinions is worth noting, given what I have discussed above and will discuss below. This list, like the one recounted in the first chapter, constitutes a whirlwind tour of opinions on translation, but the cumulative effect of these voices is relevant to my subsequent discussion, especially in light of the way that some people are advocating for particular theories of translation.

The Latin orator Cicero (106–43 BC), referring to his own translation work, states, "I did not translate them [orations] as an interpreter but as an orator . . . not . . . word for word, but I preserved the general style and force of the language."[97] The Latin poet Horace (65–8 BC), in his *Ars Poetica* of 20 BC, similarly states, "Nor will you as faithful translator render word for word." So much for any thought that dynamic and nonliteralistic translations are a recent development!

John Dryden (1631–1700), the poet and literary theorist, in 1680 indicates that there are three types of translation: metaphrase, which is "word for word" and "line for line"; paraphrase, where words are "not so strictly followed as is the sense," which, he says, "may be amplified but not altered"; and imitation, which he thought may not constitute translation at all. This is reminiscent of a commonly heard distinction between formal, paraphrastic, and dynamic translation.

Alexander Tytler (1747–1813), the Edinburgh professor and friend of Robert Burns, in 1790 defines a "good translation" as "that, in

96. Some very handy collections of such statements are found in Hans Joachim Störig, ed., *Das Problem des Übersetzens* (Darmstadt: Wissenschaftliche Buchgesellschaft, 1963) (unfortunately, with even those statements that originally appeared in English now in German translation); Rainer Schulte and John Biguenet, eds., *Theories of Translation: An Anthology of Essays from Dryden to Derrida* (Chicago: University of Chicago Press, 1992); Lawrence Venuti, ed., *The Translation Studies Reader* (London: Routledge, 2000).

97. For this and the following quotations, see Bayard Quincy Morgan, "A Critical Bibliography of Works on Translation," in Brower, *On Translation*, 274–81.

which the merit of the original work is so completely transfused into another language, as to be as distinctly apprehended, and as strongly felt, by a native of the country to which that language belongs, as it is by those who speak the language of the original work." This formulation consciously notes the role of understanding in translation, to which I will return below.

The poet William Cowper (1731–1800) says in his preface to the *Iliad* (1791), "The tr[anslation] which partakes equally of fidelity and liberality . . . promises fairest," akin to the distinction the Holman Christian Standard Bible makes. The German polymath (as well as linguist) Wilhelm von Humboldt (1767–1835) writes in a letter (1796) to the German poet August Wilhelm Schlegel (1767–1845), "All translating seems to me simply an attempt to accomplish an impossible task." The philosopher Arthur Schopenhauer (1788–1860) recognizes (1851) that "a word in one language seldom has a precise equivalent in another one."

The classicist John Conington (1825–1869) says (1861) that a translator "ought to endeavor not only to say what his author has said, but to say it as he has said it." Benjamin Jowett (1817–1893), the classicist and biblical scholar, says that the first requirement of a translation into English is "that it be English. Further the translation being English, it should also be perfectly intelligible in itself without reference to the Greek, the English being really the more lucid and exact of the two languages."[98]

The poet and musician Sidney Lanier (1842–1881), writing in 1897, states, "It is words and their associations which are untranslatable, not ideas; there is no idea . . . which cannot be adequately produced as idea in English words." Ulrich von Wilamowitz-Moellendorff (1848–1941), a renowned classicist, says (1902), "The new verses should produce the same effect upon their readers as the originals did upon their contemporaries," repeating a theme that others have promoted regarding translation. Flora Amos, a professor of literature, writing in 1920, says that translation theory cannot be reduced to a simple formula, but must be modified as new facts come along. Finally, J. B. Postgate, a comparative philologian, says, "The Faithful Translator

---

98. Porter, "Contemporary English Version," 40, citing Fredrick C. Grant, *Translating the Bible* (Edinburgh: Nelson, 1961), 136.

will give the letter where possible, but in any case the spirit." With this brief journey through time, we have covered nearly two millennia of comments on translation.

This chronologically arranged selection of statements by those commenting on translation reveals a number of important insights. The first is the obvious one: serious thought about translation is not a recent phenomenon. To the contrary, serious thought has been given to the nature of the translational process long before the present time. Another insight is that there is always a decision to be made between literalism and freedom of expression. This tension has been recognized by intelligent theorizers regarding translation since at least the time of the writing of the New Testament itself.[99] In fact, we have seen that this tension goes back to the Septuagint, the Scriptures of the early Christians. Another observation is that there is an always shifting balance between the source text and the target text. This too has been recognized since ancient times, as translators shift between obligations to writers and readers. A fourth insight is that there is a question of how well one can render one language into another. This difficulty is felt in terms of both sense and structure, and often it requires compromise between the two. A fifth point is that there is more to consider than just the words, but also things such as the audience and the original author. A sixth and final observation is that there are constraints on translation, provided by the source and the target text.

All of the varied yet surprisingly confluent statements cited above were made long before Eugene Nida, the doyen of modern translation efforts, published his first book on translation theory and practice. This is important, since Nida stands today as one of the foremost figures in translation theory, particularly concerning translation of the New Testament. I will say more about Nida below. Nevertheless, what makes Nida's work on translation so important is not only that subsequent generations of translators, whether biblical or secular, continue to respond to it but also that he attempted to take the kinds

---

99. This may provide a way forward in talking about the use of the Old Testament when it is cited in the New Testament. Rather than vexing oneself over whether an instance is an echo, or an allusion, or a quotation, perhaps in many instances we simply have sense-based translation rather than literalism. This merits further exploration by those interested in translation theory and biblical interpretation.

of thoughts and impressions noted above and develop some formal structures around them, putting them into a system by which translations could be evaluated and, more importantly, by which the process of the creation of translations could be implemented. The comments above by a number of writers through the centuries make it clear that the complexity of translation has been realized, if not fully appreciated or systematically analyzed, by literate people. In this section I will examine the major approaches to translation theory today, especially as they are related to continuing translation efforts of the New Testament, in an attempt to move beyond the simple opposition between literal and dynamic equivalence.[100] As I proceed, some may think that the approaches less resemble translational methods than theories about translation and understanding. In a sense, this is true. There are those who are calling for a greater semiotic and communicative awareness among translators, so that they are cognizant of what is implied by translation within their symbolic world.[101] There is also the sense that most of these approaches are focused upon textual and receptive dynamics rather than formal structures, even if there is rejection of what some of this implies. One limitation to discussion of several of these approaches is that they have not been as fully utilized in Bible translation as have the formal and dynamic

100. The following material draws directly upon two of my essays. See Stanley E. Porter, "Some Issues in Modern Translation Theory and Study of the Greek New Testament," *CurBS* 9 (2001): 350–82; "Assessing Translation Theory: Beyond Literal and Dynamic Equivalence," in *Translating the New Testament: Text, Translation, Theology*, ed. Stanley E. Porter and Mark J. Boda, MNTS (Grand Rapids: Eerdmans, 2009), 117–45. For similar sets of classifications, see Jeremy Munday, *Introducing Translation Studies: Theories and Applications* (London: Routledge, 2001); Aloo Osotsi Mojola and Ernst Wendland, "Scripture Translation in the Era of Translation Studies," in *Bible Translation: Frames of Reference*, ed. Timothy Wilt (Manchester: St. Jerome, 2004), 1–25, esp. 13–25; and now Roy E. Ciampa, "Approaching Paul's Use of Scripture in Light of Translation Studies," in *Paul and Scripture: Extending the Conversation*, ed. Christopher D. Stanley, Early Christianity and Its Literature 9 (Atlanta: Society of Biblical Literature, 2012), 293–318.

101. See, for example, Ubaldo Stecconi, "A Map of Semiotics for Translations Studies," in *Similarity and Difference in Translation: Proceedings of the International Conference on Similarity and Translation, Bible House, New York City, May 31–June 1, 2001*, ed. Stefano Arduini and Robert Hodgson Jr. (Rimini: Guaraldi, 2004), 153–68; Timothy Wilt, "Translation and Communication," in Wilt, *Bible Translation*, 27–80. For a handy guide to some of the literature, see Paul Cobley, ed., *The Communication Theory Reader* (London: Routledge, 1996).

equivalence models, and hence there are inherent limitations in their exposition. Nevertheless, there is in fact much more that can be said about translation theory than has been said, especially recently, in some biblical studies circles.

### Literal/Formal Equivalence Translation

Literal or formal equivalence translations[102] typically try to emphasize one-to-one correspondence between the source and target languages, fidelity to the wording of the source text, consistent rendering of similar lexical and grammatical items, and recognition of genre or literary-type considerations, such that there is a correspondence between lexical items and grammatical features, so far as this is possible and still makes sense. More than that, retaining features such as stylistic characteristics and word order is emphasized, and stilted or even unnatural language is often seen as a hallmark if not a virtue of such translation because it maintains the biblical translation tradition (the Great Tradition) or what a translation should "sound" like.[103] In the English-speaking world the Authorized Version is usually seen as the paragon of literalistic translation.[104] Today, in large part because

102. Some want to distinguish between these two. For example, Wayne Grudem ("Are Only *Some* Words of Scripture Breathed Out by God? Why Plenary Inspiration Favors 'Essentially Literal' Bible Translation," in Grudem et al., *Translating Truth*, 19–56, esp. 20) rejects the term "formal equivalence" because it suggests adherence to the form of the source text, something that he claims to reject, while at the same time endorsing the idea of "word-for-word" translational technique. Grudem's stance is highly reactive.

103. Few writers define a literalistic or formalistic translation and how to create it. Even those who purport to be doing so present their definition more by way of negation of other forms of translation, especially dynamic equivalence. See, for example, Ryken, *Word of God*, 67–119, where he has three sets of fallacies about the Bible, translation, and Bible readers; see also Ryken, "Five Myths about Essentially Literal Bible Translation," in Grudem et al., *Translating Truth*, 57–76; *Understanding English Bible Translation: The Case for an Essentially Literal Approach* (Wheaton: Crossway, 2009), which is not about how to translate but an extended assertion that the literal approach is correct, to the point of identifying dynamic equivalence as paraphrase (103–6). In many ways, Eugene Nida's definition of formal equivalence (*Toward a Science of Translating: With Special Reference to Principles and Procedures Involved in Bible Translating* [Leiden: Brill, 1964], 159) is a more concise and better definition than I have found elsewhere (and is the basis for mine above).

104. For example, Ryken, *Word of God*, 157–72; *Understanding*, 47–55; *The ESV*, 17–27.

of Nida's work, literalist or formalist translation of the New Testament is not as widely assumed (or even endorsed) as it once was, but a few scholars have recently attempted to revive it, often by appealing to features and characteristics of the Authorized Version itself.[105] This theory reflects the purported desire to be faithful to and consistent with the original text of the New Testament. The translation is often seen to provide a regulative guide to how and how well the translator understood the original by the characteristics of the rendering. Besides the Authorized Version, a number of translations would consider themselves or want to be seen as literal or formal equivalence versions, including the Revised Standard Version and New Revised Standard Version, New American Standard Bible (and 1995 revision), English

105. Ryken (*Word of God*) attempts to define (or at least summarize) "essentially literal Bible translation." A distillation of his principles (provided in his conclusion, 287–93) includes accuracy, fidelity to the original words, effective diction, theological orthodoxy, preservation of multiple meanings, retention of the full exegetical potential of the source text, expectation of reader competence, transparency to the Bible's original context, translational ethical honesty, respect for poetry, rhythmic excellence, and dignity and beauty. On several of these principles, who could object? All Bible translators want accuracy, effective diction, respect for the original context, and so forth; the question is how to achieve this (see Ryken, *Understanding*, 72–78). Other principles are more problematic. Accusing some translators of ethical dishonesty because of their approach is unwarranted. Also, several red herrings are dragged across the argument—for example, regarding fidelity, orthodoxy, and reader competence. Most problematic, I think, is Ryken's adherence to a word-based rather than meaning-based approach linked to preservation of theological orthodoxy (pursued more rigorously by Grudem ["Are Only *Some* Words?" 25–45], who associates inspiration with the translation of individual words). This comes perilously close to equating words and concepts, as well as letting theology drive translation and exegesis. Whereas words do have meanings, they do not transmit them on their own, and so I would have thought that propositionalists (such as, I assume, Ryken, Grudem, and others are) would want to endorse the clause as the minimal unit of meaning for translation. Ryken is (unintentionally?) most persuasive that, rather than take the risk of mistranslation, we should all learn the ancient languages, so as to be able to deal with all of the words; however, this also involves interpretation and reformulation. See, in Scorgie, Strauss, and Voth, *Challenge of Bible Translation*, the critique offered by Moisés Silva, "Are Translators Traitors? Some Personal Reflections," 37–50, showing how important context and previous knowledge are; and the reminders by Herbert M. Wolf, "Translation as a Communal Task," 143–57. I also share the concerns voiced by D. A. Carson regarding what he terms the "rise of linguistic conservatism" in translation ("The Limits of Functional Equivalence in Bible Translation—And Other Limits, Too," in Scorgie, Strauss, and Voth, *Challenge of Bible Translation*, 65–113). At the end of the day, no real translational method is proposed by Ryken and others.

Standard Version based upon the RSV (of 1971), and, in some ways, Holman Christian Standard Bible.[106]

Several observations are to be made regarding a literal or formal equivalence translation. First, no such translation can be as formal or literal as some would ideally like; there is always the caveat that it must still make sense in English. Otherwise, such a rendering would resemble an interlinear version, where there is word-for-word alignment and substitution. If one were to take John 1:1 as an example, a literal word-for-word rendering would read as follows (assuming that these are even the correct translational equivalents to use for the individual words):[107]

In – beginning – was – the – word – and – the – word – was – toward – the – god – and – god – was – the – word.

This makes some sense (though, realistically, only if one knows what it "should" say), but clearly it is not serviceable English even for the strictest literalist. Some English speakers say "in hospital," but few say "in beginning." The preposition "toward" does not sound like idiomatic English, and the word order, if it were not the familiar John 1:1, would be unusual if not unusable, apart from the last clause, which misrepresents the Greek syntax (the syntax should have "the word" as the subject of the clause). There is also the question, for literal and other translations, of whether "word" is the right rendering for λόγος, *logos*. I could raise questions about other words as well. So, even a simple passage like this makes strict formalism difficult if not impossible; there is always the need for accommodation to the fact that the source and target languages, because they are different and distinct language systems, are not equivalent, and so adjustments in lexis and syntax are required.

106. There have been various attempts to categorize translations. See Porter, "Modern Translations," 134–47; Grudem, "Are Only *Some* Words?" 22; C. John Collins, "What the Reader Wants and the Translator Can Give: First John as a Test Case," in Grudem et al., *Translating Truth*, 82, 84; Ryken, *Understanding*. I note that most of these discussions simply differentiate between formal and dynamic equivalence.

107. See David Alan Black, *Linguistics for Students of New Testament Greek: A Survey of Basic Concepts and Applications* (Grand Rapids: Baker Academic, 1988), 138, where his possible alternative translation "the treasurer was in the midst of a body of troops" (for "in the beginning was the word") shows the difficulties of restriction to word-for-word equivalence.

A second observation, often overlooked in discussion of translation theory in general and particular translations specifically, is that such literalism (and what we now see as awkwardness) was never intended by those who were responsible for the Authorized Version in the first place. The Authorized Version was originally commissioned to be as "consonant" with the biblical languages as it could be.[108] Further, the guidelines to be followed by the translators indicated that biblical names were to be those commonly used, not literalistic renderings of Hebrew or Greek. Thus, "Isaac" was used, not "Izhák" as in the Geneva Bible or "Isahac" as in the Bishops' Bible. The translators went so far as to render "Joshua" as "Jesus" in two places in the New Testament (Acts 7:45; Heb. 4:8), and not keep continuity with the Old Testament.[109] The translators also used intentionally ecclesial language (departing from Tyndale), so they employed "baptism" rather than "washing," and "church" rather than "congregation."[110] They did not purposefully translate the same source word with the same target word. In Romans 5:2, 3, 11 the same Greek word (καυχάομαι, *kauchaomai*) is rendered in the Authorized Version "rejoice," "glory," and "joy."[111] The Authorized Version also employs prose rhythms, such as in Psalms and elsewhere, that are based upon English poetic conventions and expectations rather than those of Hebrew.[112] Finally, the translation is admittedly based upon previous translations, including the Bishops' Bible, with all of their own characteristics.[113] The major translation relied upon and used 90 percent of the time, as already noted above, is Tyndale's. Tyndale's style is characterized by straightforward language used for everyday communication,[114] especially by the reader whom Tyndale mentions in his famous statement: "If God spare my life, ere many years I will cause a boy that driveth the plough shall know more of the Scripture than thou dost [referring to the Pope]."[115] This

108. Bruce, *History of the Bible*, 96.

109. Ibid., 98.

110. Ibid., 98, 105.

111. Ibid., 105.

112. Ibid., 109.

113. See ibid., 99.

114. Daniell, introduction to Tyndale, *Tyndale's New Testament*, xxiii. Contra Ryken (*The ESV*, 22), who says that the statement is not about social class but about widespread availability. I think that it is about both.

115. Bruce, *History of the Bible*, 29.

idiomatic character can be seen in the fact that the Revised Version, though it attempted to revise the Authorized Version in more literalistic ways, such as using the same word in the target as in the source language, was generally rejected by readers for the older Authorized Version. Later updatings of the Authorized Version, such as the New King James Version, show increasing tendency to move further away from literalism, using language that eliminates archaisms and instead employs contemporary English words.[116]

I equate formal equivalence translation with the word group (or phrase) as the minimal translational unit—protests regarding individual words notwithstanding—because it seems to be at this level that much of the translational work is being done.

### Dynamic/Functional Equivalence Translation

Dynamic or (more lately) functional equivalence translation is usually the alternative translational approach when translational models are discussed, especially in biblical studies. As the quotations above from numerous historical figures illustrate, one may well argue that such an alternative between formalist or literalist translation and dynamic or functional equivalence[117] has defined translation from the beginning of reflective thought on the process. In many ways, this is correct. However, even though many were intuitively aware of the dynamic nature of all translation, the explication of a coherent theory of dynamic or functional equivalence translation fell to Eugene Nida.[118]

116. See Farstad, *New King James Version*, 120–21. Farstad calls the technique of the New King James Bible (NKJV) "complete equivalence"—literal translation that benefits from linguistic analysis (124–25). This is a problematic description; as we have seen above, there is no such thing as complete equivalence.

117. Some want to argue that functional has replaced dynamic equivalence, necessarily and not merely terminologically (e.g., Carson, "New Bible Translations," 38; "Limits of Functional Equivalence," 65), but others question the shift. See Nigel Statham, "Dynamic Equivalence and Functional Equivalence: How Do They Differ?" *BT* 54, no. 1 (2003): 102–22; "Nida and 'Functional Equivalence,'" *BT* 56, no. 1 (2005): 29–45. Statham argues that in the adoption of functional equivalence something has been lost.

118. His first book was Eugene A. Nida, *Bible Translating: An Analysis of Principles and Procedures, with Special Reference to Aboriginal Languages* (New York: American Bible Society, 1947). This was followed by *Toward a Science of Translating*

Because he could not find a book that laid out such a theory, as he once told me, Nida took it upon himself to formulate and disseminate the principles of Bible translation that he articulated in the course of his work in translation, with organizations such as the Summer Institute of Linguistics (1937–1953) and the American Bible Society (1946–1984), and well past his retirement. In the course of doing so, "he did more than any other person in the twentieth century to change the way that Bible translation is carried out"; he literally "brought about a revolution in translation."[119] These ideas developed into several major works on translation, including both theoretical and practical studies. The first explicitly created translation that demonstrated the principles of dynamic equivalence was the Good News Translation (originally Today's English Version). However, as we have seen above, there are translators who were thinking of dynamic equivalence long before Nida formulated the theory for it, and this was reflected in some earlier translations as well, such as John Wesley's. Wesley contended that he wrote his translation in "common English." As he admits, it is capable of "being brought, in several places, nearer to the original," but he chose not to do so.[120] Thus, his rendering of John 1:1–3: "In the beginning existed the Word, and the Word was with God, and the Word was God. The same was in the beginning with God. All things were made by him; and without him was not one single thing made that was made." Other dynamic translations include the New Revised Standard Version in some of its elements, Contemporary English Version, New International Version (as well as TNIV), New Living Translation, and perhaps, in some ways, Holman Christian Standard Bible.

---

(1964); with C. R. Taber, *The Theory and Practice of Translation* (Leiden: Brill, 1969); and with Jan de Waard, *From One Language to Another: Functional Equivalence in Bible Translating* (Nashville: Nelson, 1986). The last three remain his major contributions to translation theory.

119. Philip C. Stine, review of *Fascinated by Language*, by Eugene A. Nida, *BT* 56, no. 1 (2005): 58, 59. For several tributes and recountings of Nida and his influence, see Matthew Black and William A. Smalley, eds., *On Language, Culture, and Religion: In Honor of Eugene A. Nida*, Approaches to Semiotics 56 (The Hague: Mouton, 1974); Wendy J. Porter, "Life and Works of Eugene Albert Nida," *BT* 56, no. 1 (2005): 1–8; Philip C. Stine, *Let the Words Be Written: The Lasting Influence of Eugene A. Nida*, BSNA 21 (Atlanta: Society of Biblical Literature, 2004).

120. John Wesley, *Explanatory Notes upon the New Testament* (London: Epworth, 1929), 6.

Nida's dynamic equivalence model begins with a number of assumptions regarding the target language (he uses the term "receptor language"): (1) each language has its own distinctive characteristics; (2) these characteristics must be respected rather than altered; (3) what can be said in one language can be said in any other; (4) the content of the message must be preserved even if the form must be changed.[121] He continues with assumptions regarding the source language: (1) the biblical languages are languages like any other languages, with their own limitations; (2) the biblical writers expected to be understood; (3) a translation should reproduce the meaning of a given passage according to the understanding of the writer.[122] As a result, Nida posits that (1) a translation must aim primarily at reproducing the message of the source language; (2) a translation is to seek equivalence of the message rather than conserve the form of the utterance; (3) the closest natural equivalent is to be used; (4) meaning is given priority over structure; (5) style, though secondary to content, must be preserved.[123] Much in Nida's own definition is unique to dynamic equivalence, such as the priority of the message over the form, but there are also elements similar to formal equivalence, such as using the closest natural equivalent and preserving style.

Nida develops his theory of kernel sentences as a means of putting his principles to work, differentiating between the surface structure of any language and the underlying kernel sentences.[124] Differing underlying kernels may be beneath the same surface structures. An example is the English surface structure expression "the will of God,"

121. Nida and Taber, *Theory and Practice*, 3–6.
122. Ibid., 6–8.
123. Ibid., 12–14.
124. Ibid., 33–55; cf. Nida, *Science of Translating*, 9, where he acknowledges his indebtedness to Noam Chomsky. The similarity of Nida's kernel sentences with Chomsky's use of this notion in phrase structure grammar is noteworthy. See Eugene A. Nida, "A New Methodology of Biblical Exegesis," *BT* 3, no. 3 (1952): 97–111, which was published five years before Chomsky's *Syntactic Structures* (The Hague: Mouton, 1957), which uses the term "kernel" from p. 46 on. In this article Nida uses as his primary example Mark 1:4, and analyzes it not in terms of kernels (he still uses some of the language of Bloomfieldian immediate constituent analysis) but in terms of a distinction between surface or word meanings and underlying meanings, which govern the objects, processes, and abstract features of nonrelational units. Those noting that Nida preceded Chomsky include W. Porter, "Life and Works," 4; Stine, *Let the Words Be Written*, 39.

which has an underlying kernel "God wills." This is different from the surface structure "Jesus of Nazareth," which has an underlying kernel "Jesus comes from Nazareth." According to Nida, one first analyzes a surface structure source-language construction into its underlying kernel, then one transfers this kernel into the equivalent kernel in the target language, and one renders this kernel into the appropriate surface structure of the target language. Nida has continually used the example of Mark 1:4 to illustrate how this works.[125] John preached literally "a baptism of repentance for the forgiveness of sins." Nida posits that there are five basic kernels that make up the phrase in Mark 1:4: (1) "John preached X" ("in which X stands for the entire indirect discourse"); (2) "John baptizes the people"; (3) "the people repent"; (4) "God forgives X" (where the goal of X is the people's sin); (5) "the people sin."[126] Nida determines a number of meaning relations among the five kernel sentences,[127] and then he proposes two means of rendering the phrase as a result of his kernel analysis. For languages that do not have passive-voice formations, a rendering might be "I will baptize you" or "You will receive baptism." For languages that do have passive formations, of which English is one, a rendering might be "John preached, 'Repent and be baptized, so that God will forgive the evil you have done.'"[128]

125. Eugene A. Nida, *God's Word in Man's Language* (New York: Harper & Row, 1952), 33–34; Nida and Taber, *Theory and Practice*, 44, 51–53; Nida, *Good News*, 99–101; and lectures delivered at Roehampton Institute London in September 1995. For my assessment of Nida's kernels, in particular with reference to this verse, see Stanley E. Porter, "Mark 1.4, Baptism and Translation," in *Baptism, the New Testament and the Church: Historical and Contemporary Studies in Honour of R. E. O. White*, ed. Stanley E. Porter and Anthony R. Cross, JSNTSup 171 (Sheffield: Sheffield Academic Press, 1999), 81–98.

126. Nida and Taber, *Theory and Practice*, 51.

127. Nida finds the following relationships: First, the goal of kernel 1 is kernels 2–5, with the result that, in many languages, he believes, it is appropriate to render indirect discourse into direct discourse. Second, "Kernel 3 precedes kernel 2 in time, as two related events combined by *and*. This set of kernels is equivalent to the expression 'repent and be baptized'" (ibid., 51–52). Third, "Kernel 5 is the goal of the verb of kernel 4," and fourth, apparently on the basis of the Greek preposition εἰς, *eis*, "Kernel 4 (with its goal, kernel 5) is the purpose of kernels 3 and 2. That is to say, *the forgiveness of sins* is not related merely to *repentance* but to the combined expression 'repent and be baptized'" (ibid., 52).

128. Ibid., 52. The above is also found in Porter, "Issues in Modern Translation Theory," 354–56.

Several responses must be made regarding Nida's proposal.[129] First, there is a particular hermeneutical stance that he takes on the relationship between the author and interpreter, in which the author's intentions are clearly apprehendable.[130] This constitutes a necessary assumption that leads to the utilization of Nida's kernel theory in which kernel sentences reflect the authorial intention of the surface structure. There is little question by Nida whether such apprehension is possible or likely, especially in a given context. A second response concerns the theory of kernel sentences. Similar in many ways to early forms of Chomskyan linguistics, Nida's kernel structures have not undergone the kind of theoretical advancement that has occurred in Chomskyan linguistics. A number of linguists are highly skeptical that the recovery of meaning of the deep structure is even possible, even if it has not been overtly disproved.[131] A third response concerns the practical issue of Nida's use of his kernel relations themselves. Although his system of analysis is internally consistent, Nida provides no further theoretical or practical support for his major formulations. Thus, there is no defense of why kernel 3 should precede kernel 2 where there is no temporal indicator, or why kernel 5 should be the goal of kernel 4 without goal-oriented language in the passage, and the like.[132]

Equally problematic for dynamic equivalence translation is the fact that when we examine various dynamic or functional equivalence translations, we recognize that there are many similarities that they have with what have often been identified as formal or literal equivalence translations. Even the example of Mark 1:4 is often rendered similarly in the two major types of translations. The rendering of this verse with "a

129. There is a growing body of literature in response to Nida even within the Bible Society community—that is, those translators connected with the various national Bible societies such as the American Bible Society. For a recent summary and assessment, see Stephen Pattemore, "Framing Nida: The Relevance of Translation Theory in the United Bible Societies," in Noss, *History of Bible Translation*, 218–63, esp. 220–50.

130. Brook W. R. Pearson, "Remainderless Translations? Implications of the Tradition concerning the Translation of the LXX for Modern Translational Theory," in Porter and Hess, *Translating the Bible*, 84. See also Y. C. Whang, "To Whom Is a Translator Responsible—Reader or Author?" in Porter and Hess, *Translating the Bible*, 46–62.

131. Jean Aitchison, *The Articulate Mammal: An Introduction to Psycholinguistics* (London: Hutchinson, 1976), 175. See also Randy Allen Harris, *The Linguistic Wars* (New York: Oxford University Press, 1993), 80–89.

132. Porter, "Issues in Modern Translation Theory," 356.

baptism of repentance for the forgiveness of sins" is found in Tyndale's New Testament of 1534 (with "remission" instead of "forgiveness"), Authorized Version (and New King James Version), Revised Standard Version (and New Revised Standard Version), New American Standard Bible, New International Version (and Today's New International Version), Jerusalem Bible, NET Bible, Holman Christian Standard Bible, and, indeed, even the English Standard Version. In other words, the same syntax and virtually same wording is found from Tyndale to the present, including in both supposedly more literalistic and more dynamic translations. This should not be surprising, given the discussion above, as the dynamic equivalence translation has several features in common with the literalistic translation, so much so that some of these dynamic translations retain many similar distinguishing characteristics of literalistic renderings. The formalist and dynamic equivalence methods have much in common theoretically (e.g., Nida's kernel model) and practically. The emphasis of formalist equivalence was on the word or, better, the word group, although the practical outworking, as we saw in the example of John 1:1, is the clause, and the major units of analysis of dynamic equivalence are the word group (often seen as correlating with the kernel) or, perhaps more accurately, the clause. Thus, both translational methods are tied to the lower syntactical levels of language usage, especially the word group (or phrase) and the clause.

### Functionalist Translation

Functionalist translation, not to be confused with functional equivalence advocated by Nida and others, draws heavily upon an early form of what has been called "scale and category grammar."[133] This translation theory was first developed in the 1960s by the linguist J. C. Catford and continues to be used and developed.[134] The fundamental assumption of functionalist translation is the concept

133. Scale and category grammar is attributable to M. A. K. Halliday, "Categories of the Theory of Grammar," *Word* 17, no. 3 (1961): 241–92; repr. in Halliday, *On Grammar*, ed. Jonathan Webster (London: Continuum, 2002), 37–94.
134. J. C. Catford, *A Linguistic Theory of Translation* (London: Oxford University Press, 1965), further developed by Peter Newmark, *A Textbook of Translation* (New York: Prentice-Hall, 1988); Mona Baker, *In Other Words: A Coursebook on Translation* (London: Routledge, 1992). Cf. now also Erich Steiner, "Halliday and Translation Theory: Enhancing the Options, Broadening the Range and Keeping the Ground," in

of defined levels of language usage, and the resultant differentiation within these levels between form and substance. According to Catford, when language is employed, three levels of abstraction can be exemplified: grammatical/lexical form, consisting of grammar and lexis; medium form, consisting of phonology (spoken) and graphology (written); and medium substance, consisting of phonic substance and graphic substance. These exemplifications occur within a situation (or situation substance) and context, which he defines as interlevels among the three levels already noted. Most theories of translation are concerned with the meanings of grammatical/lexical forms, while Catford contends that meaning is larger than such a limited notion. He identifies a hierarchical scale of grammar that exists on five levels, from the largest unit to the smallest: sentence, clause, group, word, and morpheme, where the smaller units function as exponents of the larger units (the smaller units make up the larger units), or larger units may shift to lower levels.[135]

Catford defines translation as "the replacement of textual material in one language (SL [source language]) by equivalent textual material in another language (TL [target language])."[136] He identifies various levels of translational equivalence. Catford is not concerned with formal equivalence, but rather with what he calls "textual equivalence." Textual equivalence is defined as the target language material being the equivalent of the source language material. In this context, meaning is defined in terms of the situation and context in which the translation is used, with a target language text being meaningful within its context as it is used according to the code of that language.[137]

There is no New Testament translation I know of that utilizes the functionalist approach. Some might say that this is understandable, as one respondent to Catford's theory accused it of having "no connection with applied linguistics, either in theory or in practice."[138] I am not as skeptical, although I must admit that, within the current

*Continuing Discourse on Language: A Functional Perspective*, ed. Ruqaiya Hasan, Christian Matthiessen, and Jonathan J. Webster (London: Equinox, 2005), 1:481–500.

135. Munday, *Translation Studies*, 60–62.

136. Catford, *Linguistic Theory*, 20 (italics removed).

137. Ibid., 43.

138. Antoine Culioli, response to J. C. Catford, "Translation and Language Teaching," in Council for Cultural Co-Operation, *Linguistic Theories and Their Application* (Strasbourg [?]: AIDELA, 1967), 146.

environment of formal versus dynamic equivalence, it is hard to see whether other translational models will emerge. Nevertheless, in some instances the Contemporary English Version and the New Living Translation might come close. The CEV indicates with asterisks where it has either combined verses together or reorganized material in a way that departs significantly from a word-for-word rendering. Presumably, the translators are saying by this that their rendering, in a given context, is the functionalist equivalent of the language of the source text. Despite there not being a single functionalist translation, there are individual translational instances that illustrate this approach. One example is the translation of the Greek masculine singular pronoun (i.e., "he"). English no longer uses the masculine singular pronoun inclusively of men and women, as it was clearly used in Greek. This results in various English expressions that are not the "same" as (i.e., formally equivalent to) the original literal (formal) Greek, such as the use of "they" to translate the Greek masculine singular pronoun.[139] Even more important, perhaps, are issues related to translation of Greek verbal aspect (tense-forms) and causality (voice-forms), where there is not iconicity or one-to-one correspondence with English.[140] Various synthetic aspects in Greek are expressed with differing English analytic realizations (the Greek present tense-form, a single word, is rendered by the English composite present progressive [e.g., "am going"]), or the Greek middle voice is captured by an English paraphrase [e.g., "the door 'opened on its own'"]).[141]

139. The issue of gender and translation has aroused disproportionately large reaction, with accusations being thrown (mostly from one side) regarding the emasculation of the Bible. This is unfortunate, with often more heat than light being produced. Some of the recent evangelical debate is captured in D. A. Carson, *The Inclusive-Language Debate: A Plea for Realism* (Grand Rapids: Baker Academic, 1998); Mark L. Strauss, *Distorting Scripture? The Challenge of Bible Translation and Gender Accuracy* (Downers Grove, IL: InterVarsity, 1998); Vern S. Poythress and Wayne A. Grudem, *The Gender-Neutral Bible Controversy: Muting the Masculinity of God's Words* (Nashville: Broadman & Holman, 2000); and Strauss's response, "Current Issues in the Gender-Language Debate: A Response to Vern Poythress and Wayne Grudem," in Scorgie, Strauss, and Voth, *Challenge of Bible Translation*, 115–42.

140. On the Greek aspectual system, see Porter, *Verbal Aspect*, esp. 75–108; *Idioms of the Greek New Testament*, 2nd ed. (Sheffield: Sheffield Academic Press, 1994), 20–49.

141. See Matthew Brook O'Donnell, *Corpus Linguistics and the Greek of the New Testament*, NTM 6 (Sheffield: Sheffield Phoenix Press, 2005), 367. The middle

Thus, in rendering the Greek ἀδελφοί, *adelphoi*, whereas a formalist might argue for the use of "brothers" in order to retain word-for-word equivalence, a functionalist might argue for "brothers and sisters" in a given context. Such a situation, such as a letter of Paul addressed to churches with both men and women, would warrant the use of "brothers and sisters" because the textual equivalence for the original hearers is best captured in English by the inclusive term. A more extended example is the New Living Translation's rendering of Mark 1:4, a passage often used in such discussions: John the Baptist "was preaching that people should be baptized to show that they had turned from their sins and turned to God to be forgiven." Whereas Nida recommended "Repent and be baptized," which alters the word order and creates two clauses, the NLT goes even further. The two major clauses regarding repentance and baptism are expanded and related conceptually so that one explains the other: baptism is an illustration of turning from sin. More than that, Nida's "so that" clause, which preserves the syntactical differentiation of the prepositional phrase, becomes a second explanatory clause. The major changes have reached to the clause complex level.

Despite these positive features, Catford recognizes a number of restrictions upon a functionalist approach to translation. One is that there are limits to the possible sources of a translation where there is a crossing of significant boundaries, such as a difference in medium (intersemiotic translation). Another is that having linguistic pertinence is not the same as having functional pertinence; translation is concerned with the latter and may restrict the former. A third restriction is linguistic untranslatability. Rejecting the hard form of this theory (that items cannot be translated from one language to another),[142] Catford does note that there are circumstances that limit translatability. An example of this is when there is the same formal realization for differing features, such as lexical polysemy, where a simple word may have multiple genuine meanings.

Although Catford mentions the context of situation in his translation theory, when it comes to actually analyzing examples of how

---

voice grammaticalizes semantic features not found in the English causality (voice) system and thus requires interpretive translation to capture its semantics function.

142. This theory has persisted in some forms of literary criticism, especially those associated with the New Criticism, but is not meant for general extension.

translation is done, he confines himself to the clause complex as the largest category for treatment. He limits the theory to dealing with the linkage of individual clauses into larger units, with the orientation focused upon the function of the units within the target language.

## Discourse Analysis (Text-Linguistics)–Based Translation

Discourse analysis, or text-linguistics as it is still sometimes called in Europe, is a composite, and hence not precisely defined, method that encompasses various forms of linguistic analysis in the study of entire texts or discourses.[143] Discourse analysis that works from the "bottom up" makes this especially clear, since smaller linguistic units provide the foundation for building larger discourse structures (e.g., word groups make up clauses, which in turn make up paragraphs, etc.). The importance of discourse analysis for general translational theory has only fairly recently been articulated, and its promise for biblical studies is yet to be realized. However, a discourse-based translational approach provides unique opportunities that go beyond other forms of translational theory already discussed because the Bible, after all, is a discourse that contains a variety of individual and discrete (sub)discourses.[144] Discourse analytical translation theory has been influenced by functionalist methodologies and builds on some of the same linguistic principles. Two major books on discourse-based translation, both by Basil Hatim and Ian Mason, bring together discussion of various individual linguistic elements and place them in the context of how discourse considerations affect translational practices.[145] There are two major results. The first is that discourse-based analysis is primarily concerned with elements

143. Two excellent introductions to discourse analysis are Gillian Brown and George Yule, *Discourse Analysis*, CTL (Cambridge: Cambridge University Press, 1974); Alexandra Georgakopoulou and Dionysis Goutsos, *Discourse Analysis: An Introduction*, 2nd ed. (Edinburgh: Edinburgh University Press, 2004).

144. Opportunities for correlation with other areas of biblical studies, including canonically based methods, biblical theology, and the like, are readily apparent, though most of these approaches have lacked the critical rigor of discourse analysis.

145. Basil Hatim and Ian Mason, *Discourse and the Translator* (London: Longman, 1990); *The Translator as Communicator* (London: Routledge, 1997). See also Roger T. Bell, *Translation and Translating: Theory and Practice* (London: Longman, 1991), esp. 161–97.

that are beyond the level of the clause or clause complex, which can include both formal structures and, perhaps more importantly, means by which texts are organized and structured (e.g., information flow, cohesion, etc.). The second is that functionalist linguistics has had a large influence upon such model-building, especially in its attention to levels of language. One of the direct applications of this approach is appraisal theory, pioneered in translation theory by Jeremy Munday.[146] Assuming a discourse perspective, and realizing that the use of language involves evaluation, Munday examines the translation process, as well as the means by which the author's attitude and speaker's engagement are evaluated and how this influences translation (e.g., lexical choice, evaluative words, syntax, etc.). The discourse analytical treatment of translation, therefore, encompasses further, and I would say necessary, developments and extensions of the functionalist model discussed above.

There is, to date, no explicitly discourse-based translation of the New Testament.[147] If such a translation were to be created, there would need to be the kind of level-based analysis that functionalist translation theory has articulated as a necessary foundation. However, there would also need to be more attention to higher discourse structures, such as paragraphing and subparagraphing, discourse boundaries, cohesion, the ordering and highlighting of information, and textual types. For example, within a Gospel a discourse analyst would need to ask whether a passage is a parable, or some other literary type, or a subtype within a larger discourse type. Information from lower levels of analysis would need to be considered, such as lexical forms to determine subject, participants, and the types of expression (e.g., participant name versus reduced forms), and types of cohesion used to establish bounded units. With named participants, there is the

---

146. Jeremy Munday, *Evaluation in Translation: Critical Points of Translator Decision-Making* (London: Routledge, 2012), 12. Munday is clear that he draws on a systemic-functional approach as found in Michael A. K. Halliday, *Introduction to Functional Grammar* (London: Arnold, 1994; 4th ed., with Christian M. I. M. Matthiessen, 2004); and James Martin and Peter White, *Language of Evaluation: Appraisal in English* (London: Palgrave, 2005).

147. However, there has been an attempt to use discourse analysis as a means of evaluating translations. See Stanley E. Porter and Matthew Brook O'Donnell, "Comparative Discourse Analysis as a Tool in Assessing Translations, Using Luke 16:19–31 as a Test Case," in Porter and Boda, *Translating the New Testament*, 185–99.

possibility of a historical rather than a fictional account, and necessary adjustments would need to be made in the translation to reflect the historicality of the narrative world. The discourse structure, on the basis of connective words (e.g., conjunctions), verb-form shifts (e.g., tense-forms, mood, causality), and other boundary words and cohesive devices, would need to be established, especially in terms of the participants and their interaction.

Translations into English have often included headings to indicate discourse units, even if they have not dealt consistently with such issues as paragraphing or larger discourse features. Headings may not in themselves seem important, or even integral to a translation, especially as they are not part of the original text. However, they exercise an important discourse function, in that they guide the reader's set of expectations by dividing and labeling the text. Not all translations always get this correct, and their mistakes illustrate the importance of sensitivity to such discourse features. In one humorous example, the 1717 edition of the Authorized Version gave the heading for Luke 20 as "Parable of the Vinegar" (rather than "Vineyard").[148] Of standard edition Bibles—not counting study Bibles—one of the most elaborate schemes of discourse identification is that of the Contemporary English Version. It has a brief introduction to each biblical book, an outline that is used throughout the text of the particular book, and then running headings in the margins to mark divisions.[149] It also uses a portion of the biblical book itself as a title, as in John 1:1 and possibly 1 John 1:1a[150] (but not Mark 1:1).

Discourse-based translational theory takes up a variety of issues that have not usually been discussed in traditional formal or dynamic

148. Bruce, *History of the Bible*, 108–9.
149. If I read correctly the bibliographical information page in one edition of the Contemporary English Version, the introductions and outlines are produced by the translators, but the other running heads in the translation are by the publisher (*The Contemporary English Version* [Nashville: Thomas Nelson, 1995], iv).
150. There seems to be a discrepancy between editions that inevitably shapes the discourse differently in each. One edition that I have has the first part of the verse isolated, and the rest in poetic lines but attached to the main text (*The Contemporary English Version*, 1480). Another has the two parts displayed as two separate poetical units (*Holy Bible with Deuterocanonicals/Apocrypha: Contemporary English Version* [New York: American Bible Society, 1999], 1607). These differences are bound to affect the reader's interpretation and understanding.

equivalence treatments of translation, whether literalistic or dynamic, because many of these discourse issues are concerned with language levels beyond the clause or sentence. Sometimes this extension beyond the sentence goes quite a bit beyond, even beyond an individual discourse itself. Thus, in their treatment of discourse-based translation, Hatim and Mason recognize general issues of translation—such as questions of objectivity and subjectivity, liberal and free translation, form and content, and author- and reader-centered translation, issues often associated with more general literary concerns—before discussing how to handle the major discourse-based translational issues. They contend that models such as dynamic equivalence as proposed by Nida, which is reflective of Chomskyan notions of deep structure, have moved translation away from concern for communication.[151] They want to focus upon the communicative function of discourse and the major features that make this possible. As a consequence, they are concerned with the pragmatic dimension of language, and the way that pragmatics relates to communication and semiotics.[152] The result is attention to the complex interplay of language as it is used in entire discourses, not as random or chaotic individual elements but as structured and intentional uses.[153] These larger patterns of usage that create structure in texts and give texture to discourses are important parts of the meaning in context. In fact, Hatim and Mason want to go beyond the text to include intertextuality within the scope of issues that a full discourse analytical translational model discusses, since these intertextual references are part of the communicative intent of the discourse. One area to note is that discourse analysis provides a means for quality assessment of translation, in which focus is not simply on "mistakes" in translation (a common area of discussion and evaluation, especially highlighted in disputes between formal and dynamic equivalence), but on a variety of higher-level features that allow assessment of translational effectiveness.[154]

151. Hatim and Mason, *Discourse*, 32.
152. Pragmatics is a branch of linguistics, often distinguished from semantics. Two major works on pragmatics are Stephen Levinson, *Pragmatics*, CTL (Cambridge: Cambridge University Press, 1985); Jacob L. Mey, *Pragmatics* (Oxford: Blackwell, 1993).
153. Hatim and Mason, *Discourse*, 107–8.
154. See Christoph Gutknecht and Lutz J. Rölle, *Translating by Factors* (Albany: State University of New York Press, 1996); Malcolm Williams, *Translation Quality*

The development of suitable tools for translation quality assessment may well offer much future promise for evaluating the qualities of various biblical translations.

## Relevance Theory

As mentioned above, with the passing of Eugene Nida from the scene, there is renewed discussion of the best model for Bible translation. This discussion will no doubt continue for some time, especially with a wide range of possible approaches available. In some Bible translation circles, especially those connected with the United Bible Societies, there is serious discussion of relevance theory becoming the driving model of translation,[155] just as Nida's model of dynamic equivalence once dominated Bible translation in the past.[156]

Relevance theory as a translational model develops out of a critique of two major linguistic concepts. The first, which is relevant to both formal and dynamic equivalence models of translation, is a critique of the code theory of language, which claims that language can be described as a systematically organized code, apart from its speakers. The linguists Dan Sperber and Dierdre Wilson,[157] the major intellectual forces behind development of relevance theory, contend that the code theory of language—the dominant theory behind most linguistic models—does not satisfactorily answer the question of

---

*Assessment: An Argumentation-Centred Approach* (Ottawa: University of Ottawa Press, 2004).

155. See Pattemore, "Framing Nida," 251–62. However, he admits that relevance theory "is really a move beyond linguistics proper" (241n97). See also Stephen Pattemore, *Souls under the Altar: Relevance Theory and the Discourse Structure of Revelation*, UBSMS 9 (New York: United Bible Societies, 2003), 193, where he still notes that "our theories of translation rightly emphasize the priority of function and meaning over surface form," which sounds like the old opposition between formal and dynamic equivalence.

156. Timothy Wilt's edited book is designed to replace Nida and Taber's *Theory and Practice* as the guide for translation. See Timothy Wilt, introduction to Wilt, *Bible Translation*, xii. I doubt that this will happen, as it has neither the same unified focus as do the individual works of Nida nor the dominating personality to guide adoption. For comparison within a larger context, see Paul Ellingworth, "Translation Techniques in Modern Bible Translations," in Noss, *History of Bible Translation*, 307–34, esp. 324–34.

157. Dan Sperber and Dierdre Wilson, *Relevance: Communication and Cognition*, 2nd ed. (Oxford: Blackwell, 1995).

how communication takes place, since there remains an unbridgeable gap between linguistic expression and meaning, a point that formal equivalence (and other) theories purportedly neglect. In other words, most theories of language, especially the ones that Sperber and Wilson are most readily responding to,[158] are focused upon issues of syntax rather than semantics and especially pragmatics. This is seen particularly when contextless individual or hypothetical sentences are created and then examined. In the sentence "I will see her next Thursday," the general semantic sense of "I" as including a singular speaker does not, according to Sperber and Wilson, provide adequate information that can only be gained by knowing the "I" in a specific context. The same can be said of "her." Similarly, reference to "next Thursday" communicates only if one knows the day today, rather than simply knowing that Thursday is after Wednesday. Code theories of language have clearly dominated both major forms of translational theory—the formalist and the dynamic equivalence models—and have, so it is claimed, led to a division between the form of language and its meaning or communicative abilities. Instead, Sperber and Wilson believe that language always invokes much beyond the words themselves, and as a result they look to cognitive linguistics in a revised and streamlined form, which they call "relevance theory," as a model of communication to develop the notion of inference further.

Their second critique is of Paul Grice's implicatures of conversation.[159] Grice, a philosopher of language whose work has direct relevance for linguistics, developed his conversational maxims to describe what is implicated (or implied or assumed) when conversation occurs. These include maxims of quantity, quality, relation, and manner. Grice's maxims have been both severely criticized and strongly embraced as the foundation of a more robust set of generalized conversational implicatures.[160] Some of the criticisms pertinent

---

158. Relevance theory is in many ways the "pragmatic" descendant of Chomskyan-based cognitive linguistic models. Cognitive linguistics is, of course, a huge and growing area of exploration. See Vyvyan Evans and Melanie Green, *Cognitive Linguistics: An Introduction* (Edinburgh: Edinburgh University Press, 2006).

159. Paul Grice, "Logic and Conversation" (1967), repr. in *Studies in the Way of Words* (Cambridge, MA: Harvard University Press, 1989), 22–40, along with other important essays on this topic.

160. See Stephen C. Levinson, *Presumptive Meanings: The Theory of Generalized Conversational Implicature* (Cambridge, MA: MIT Press, 2000). Levinson, however,

to translation should be noted. The first is that Grice's implicatures are particularly well suited to English conversational communication because they emphasize brevity, sincerity, and relevance, among others.[161] Other cultures, whether ancient or modern, may emphasize other values in conversation not captured by Grice's maxims. Furthermore, some implicatures are of less pertinence or explicit content than others, especially when examined closely. Thus, the "maxim of relation," which is based upon intuitive subjective analysis, rather than objective analysis, is less stringent or useful.[162] Sperber and Wilson, therefore, reassess Grice's maxims with regard to the concept of ostensive-inferential communication, working within the overarching notion of situational relevance. Ostention and inference make clear that certain information is being put forward as constituting the assumptions for communication within a given situational context. This is then evaluated in terms of relevance.

Despite the claims made for it, and some of the developments in translational theory and practice, relevance theory does not itself provide a robust theory of translation, but attempts to provide a theory of cognition, especially as it relates to language. Ernst-August Gutt, who as a linguist and Bible translator has directly applied the theories of Sperber and Wilson to translational issues, states, "The central claim of relevance theory is that human communication crucially creates an expectation of optimal relevance, that is, an expectation on the part of the hearer that his attempt at interpretation will yield *adequate contextual effects at minimal processing cost.*"[163] In other words, there should be maximal un-

---

offers a devastating critique of Sperber and Wilson's relevance theory (55–59). He contends that it uses deduction improperly, and that it is unable to make accurate (or possibly any) predictions.

161. Baker, *In Other Words*, 237.

162. Ibid., 236, citing Sperber and Wilson, *Relevance*, 36.

163. Ernst-August Gutt, *Translation and Relevance: Cognition and Context* (Oxford: Blackwell, 1991), 20, cited in Mojola and Wendland, "Scripture Translation," 20–21. Besides some mentioned above, see Ernst-August Gutt, *Relevance Theory: A Guide to Successful Communication in Translation* (Dallas: Summer Institute of Linguistics, 1992); Stephen Pattemore, *The People of God in the Apocalypse: Discourse, Structure and Exegesis*, SNTSMS 128 (Cambridge: Cambridge University Press, 2004); Ernst-August Gutt, "Translation, Metarepresentation, and Claims of Interpretive Resemblance," in Arduini and Hodgson, *Similarity and Difference*, 93–101; Ronald J. Sim, "Modeling the Translation Task: Taking Luke 2:27–38 as a

derstanding with minimal effort on the part of the hearer. Further, when a reader engages in more effort, the expectation is that there will be a commensurably larger amount of understanding to warrant the effort. Otherwise, there is material that is not relevant that is being processed.

The Contemporary English Version has been used by Aloo Mojola and Ernst Wendland as an example for discussion of translation theory and translation,[164] not because it was written with relevance theory in mind, but because it was translated in an effort to minimize processing (on the basis of its use of contemporary English, attention to the biblical translational tradition, etc.) and maximize understanding. A good example is found in how the Contemporary English Version renders the opening of the parable of the rich man and Lazarus in Luke 16:19–20: "There was once a rich man who wore expensive clothes and every day ate the best food. But a poor beggar named Lazarus was brought to the gate of the rich man's house." The use of "once," instead of "certain" (as in "a certain rich man") found in other translations, infers from the context an example held up to others as relevant, rather than making the man himself either specific or generic and hence descriptive. The reference to being at the gate of the rich man's house appears at the end of the verse in the Contemporary English Version. One further notices that there is no reference in verse 20 to the poor man having sores. Instead, this phrasing is moved to verse 21: "He was happy just to eat the scraps that fell from the rich man's table. His body was covered with sores, and dogs kept coming up to lick them." The catalogue of elements is brought together to provide a cumulative description of the poor man. A number of features of the Contemporary English Version are clearly utilized to optimize relevance in the posited situational context of the parable.

---

Case Study," in Arduini and Hodgson, *Similarity and Difference*, 103–24; Gene L. Green, "Relevance Theory and Biblical Interpretation," in *The Linguist as Pedagogue: Trends in the Teaching and Linguistic Analysis of the Greek New Testament*, ed. Stanley E. Porter and Matthew Brook O'Donnell, NTM 11 (Sheffield: Sheffield Phoenix Press, 2009), 217–40; Margaret G. Sim, *Marking Thought and Talk in New Testament Greek: New Light from Linguistics on the Particles* ἵνα *and* ὅτι (Eugene, OR: Pickwick, 2010).

164. Mojola and Wendland, "Scripture Translation," 21.

## Descriptivist Translation

Much Bible translation has traditionally (and, one might argue, legitimately and of necessity) focused upon linguistic matters and the translational processes themselves. These are often treated as if translation occurs without reference to larger nonlinguistic issues, such as the role of the translator.[165] The descriptivist approach to Bible translation instead focuses upon describing the specific (literary) situational context of a translation, rather than prescribing what such a translation should be like.[166] The descriptivist approach is part of a wider effort to recognize the contextual nature of translation. With a background in literary translation and both its source and target cultures, descriptivists view both formalist and dynamic equivalence translational theories (much to the horror of advocates of each) as prescriptive; these prescriptive approaches are concerned to formulate rules and guidelines for translation, and they develop practical means to make a translation. A descriptivist translational approach is concerned with the general principles governing and even surrounding translation and the manifestation of these principles. Theo Hermans, a major advocate of descriptivist translational theory (as are Stuart Campbell and Susan Bassnett-McGuire),[167] states that descriptivists are much more concerned with the theory of translation than with its activity. They have a "view of literature as a complex and dynamic system; a conviction that there should be a continual interplay between theoretical models and practical case studies; an approach to literary translation which is descriptive, target-oriented, functional and systemic; and an interest in the norms and constraints that govern the production and reception of translations, in the relation between translation and other types of text processing, and in the place and role of translations both within a given literature and in the interaction between literatures."[168] The major issue with all literary

165. See Stuart Campbell, *Translation into the Second Language* (London: Longman, 1998), 3–4.

166. See Mojola and Wendland, "Scripture Translation," 17–19; cf. Munday, *Translation Studies*, 119–21; also 108–19.

167. Susan Bassnett-McGuire, *Translation Studies*, rev. ed. (London: Routledge, 1991).

168. Theo Hermans, *Translation in Systems: Descriptive and System-Oriented Approaches Explained* (Manchester: St. Jerome, 1999), 32, cited in Mojola and Wendland, "Scripture Translation," 17–18. See also a number of the essays in Theo Hermans,

translations is how the text is perceived as literature within different cultures, not what constitutes literature in and of itself—something that, interestingly enough, formal equivalence translators sometimes claim to be interested in. In other words, literature in a culture is based upon the culture in which it is found, not on any inherent features of the text. The conclusions of descriptivism are significant. By virtue of translation, virtually any text is going to be seen as (at least to some degree) a literary text in a target culture, and thus it will be expected to follow the patterns of similar literary texts within that culture. It is this reception that establishes the guidelines for a given translation.

A descriptivist translational approach would want to begin by asking questions about the comparative literary quality of the translation, especially in terms of the context's available literary types. It is worth observing that the Authorized Version is often hailed as a great literary work. This is especially the claim of many recent formal equivalence advocates who wish to preserve in modern translations some of the features that they believe distinguish the literary qualities of the Authorized Version. I do not want to dispute that analysis here or whether it constitutes sufficient grounds for the type of translation that they advocate. Neither would a descriptivist. However, when the Contemporary English Version was published, the translators tried to position it not as attempting "to *retain the form* of the King James Version," as had some other previous translations, but rather as seeking "to *capture the spirit* of the King James Version by following certain principles set forth by its translators in the document 'The Translators to the Reader.'"[169] They then excerpt wording from that document to help describe their new translation. A descriptivist might well say that the literary forms used in the Contemporary English Version are intentionally chosen so as to find the contemporary equivalent, not for the individual books in the original language, but for the Authorized Version. Whether it has succeeded in doing that I cannot say, although I have some questions about gearing the Contemporary English Version to the Authorized Version rather than to the original ancient context.

---

ed., *The Manipulation of Literature: Studies in Literary Translation* (London: Croom Helm, 1985).

169. *The Contemporary English Version*, vii. See Porter, "Contemporary English Version," 20–22.

Like relevance-based translational theory, the descriptivist approach attempts to describe the context in which translation occurs rather than being an approach to translational procedure. Descriptive translational theory functions within the context in which the source text is rendered into the target language.

## Cultural/Postcolonial Theory

As one reviewer of previous work on this topic has observed, in my treatment of topics such as relevance theory and descriptivism I have clearly gone beyond the traditional confines of translation theory as discussed within biblical studies and entered the broader realm of translation studies.[170] This is intentional on my part, as I want to see translation of the Bible within the larger context of general linguistic and translational theory, and not be confined by what I see as the largely stagnant debate between formal and dynamic equivalence theories. In this final category, in some ways, I go to the furthest lengths in such exploration. Cultural ideology can and does play a role in most kinds of translation, although until recently it has not often been explicitly noticed.[171] One of the major reasons for this is that a number of models of translation—including the formalist and dynamic equivalence models, but others as well, including functionalist, discourse analytical, and even relevance theory—purport to provide objectivist translational methods, even when there are subjective factors involved. As noted above, these approaches to translation

170. Robert Hodgson Jr., review of *Translating the New Testament: Text, Translation, Theology*, ed. Stanley E. Porter and Mark J. Boda, *CBQ* 72 (2010): 879.
171. See Hatim and Mason, *Translator*, 143. I include here what Mojola and Wendland ("Scripture Translation," 24–25) label as foreignization versus domestication. See also Munday, *Translation Studies*, 126–61; in a biblical context, Richard L. Rohrbaugh, "Foreignizing Translation," in *The Social Sciences and Biblical Translation*, ed. Dietmar Neufeld, SBLSymS 41 (Atlanta: Society of Biblical Literature, 2008), 11–24. See also the essays by Simon Crisp, Lamin Sanneh, and Jeremy Punt, as well as their respondents, in Brenner and van Henten, *Bible Translation*, 36–49, 70–85, 94–124; and the essays by K. K. Yeo and Elsa Tamez in Porter and Boda, *Translating the New Testament*, 271–304, 314–23. See also Christiane Nord, "Similarity and Strangeness in the Translation of New Testament and Early Christian Texts," in Arduini and Hodgson, *Similarity and Difference*, 293–307; Bai Liping, "The Identity of the Language in Translation: A Case Study at the Level of Lexicon," in Arduini and Hodgson, *Similarity and Difference*, 383–403.

focus upon the process, not the product, with the explicit purpose of providing rigorously defensible translations. However, there has been a recent reaction against the formal and dynamic equivalence models in particular, and questions have been raised about the translation process itself. These come not just from those, like the descriptivists, who wish to place the translational product within its proper context, but from those who want to question the entire nature of translation, especially where the Bible is concerned.

The English literature scholar and translator Lawrence Venuti, who has become identified with such an approach to translation, and to Bible translation in particular, has specifically criticized the dynamic equivalence model of Nida from an ideological point of view.[172] Reflecting a culturally based approach, Venuti claims that Nida's translational method imposes a cultural hegemony of the target language upon the source text itself,[173] since a dynamic equivalence translation is meant to be fluent and fully comprehensible in the target language, while neglecting the character and context of the original source text.[174] Venuti argues instead for foreignizing translations that restrain what he calls "the ethnocentric violence of translation," which attempts to exert hegemonic control over the translated text.[175] Venuti, perhaps not surprisingly, sees this translational hegemony in Anglo-American culture as a whole, and in translational practice in particular. He claims that such translational practice is dominated by "domesticating theories" that strive to produce fluent translations, but in which an "illusion of transparency" masks that the translation can only be a "partial interpretation."[176] In this critique, Nida's emphasis upon "naturalness of expression"[177] in the target language involves subor-

---

172. Lawrence Venuti, *The Translator's Invisibility: A History of Translation* (London: Routledge, 1995); *The Scandals of Translation: Towards an Ethics of Difference* (London: Routledge, 1998).

173. For example, Venuti, *Translator's Invisibility*, 21–23.

174. See Jonathan M. Watt, "Eugene A. Nida's Contributions to Sociolinguistics," *BT* 56, no. 1 (2005): 19–29.

175. Venuti, *Translator's Invisibility*, 20. For an attempt to address some of the issues of foreignizing Bible translations, see Andy Cheung, "Foreignising Bible Translation: Retaining Foreign Origins when Rendering Scripture," *TynBul* 63, no. 2 (2012): 257–73. He argues that sometimes foreignizations should be used and other times rejected depending on the basis of the purpose of the translation.

176. Venuti, *Translator's Invisibility*, 21.

177. Nida, *Science of Translating*, 159.

dination and domestication of the source text, with unrecognizable source-language features being replaced by understandable ones in the target language.[178] Nida's argument for translational accuracy is, according to Venuti, a warrant for creating the same effect in the target-language readers as was produced in the source-language readers. In other words, the differences in language and culture that separate the two are overcome by forcing the one (the source) to submit to the other (the target). Venuti claims, however, that this results in a translation that enshrines "target-language cultural values while veiling this domestication in the transparency evoked by a fluent strategy."[179] Going further, Venuti claims that Nida does not take into account "the ethnocentric violence that is inherent in every translation process."[180]

Venuti, unrelenting in his critique, attributes Nida's position to a number of different but related factors. One of these is what Venuti claims is Nida's "transcendental concept of humanity as an essence that remains unchanged over time and space."[181] Venuti recognizes that this perspective is related to what he labels as Nida's Christian evangelism and cultural elitism, two characteristics that he conveniently links. Venuti sees these as going together, in that Nida wants to promote a translated text that is "centred in Christian dogma" and that "seeks to impose" a "specific dialect of English as well as a distinctly Christian understanding of the Bible."[182] Venuti's solution, a foreignizing translation, while not immune to its own cultural and political agendas, "resists dominant target-language cultural values so as to signify the linguistic and cultural difference of the foreign text."[183] In other words, the issues are larger than simply the technical dimensions of translation. Even if Nida were to argue for a change in the rendering of a particular problematic word in a translation, according to Venuti, Nida would not have addressed the cultural, social, and political issues that have been raised. According to Venuti, Nida creates

178. Venuti, *Translator's Invisibility*, 21.
179. Ibid., 22.
180. Ibid.
181. Ibid.; cf. Nida, *Science of Translating*, 2.
182. Venuti, *Translator's Invisibility*, 23. One might well wonder what understanding of the Bible Nida, an active Christian (and even ordained Baptist minister), might otherwise have.
183. Ibid.

only a partial translation. However, the same could be argued for any translation, admittedly including the kind of foreignizing translation for which Venuti argues. Venuti recognizes that there are ideological and cultural (read also political) issues at stake in such a debate. Venuti is not suggesting a corrective that creates a theory-neutral or value-free translational model. There is not only a recognition that Nida's model is not neutral, but also an outright acknowledgment and endorsement of a competing translational ideology.

Related to the ideological critique by Venuti is the issue of post-colonialism in translation. Not only has the translation process itself been the target of much postcolonialist theory, but the concept of translation itself has also been subjected to criticism.[184] The positional basis for such criticism is that translation never occurs apart from a particular context but is always linked to the forces of empire, power, wealth, cultural domination, colonialization, indoctrination, dilution of native cultures, and the like—elements of which have come into contact with translations of the Bible and with those making them. Translations are, so the critique goes, made by those in power at the expense of the disenfranchised. Thus, translation is accused of becoming an insidious colonizing tool of those wishing to extend their power and influence and dominate those unable to resist. Translations as part of this process do much more than simply render a text into the language of an indigenous people; translations become the tools of domination by others, since the translations themselves end up reflecting and even imposing the viewpoint and will of the dominant culture. Those who sponsor such a colonizing translation end up helping to perpetuate their domination through the translation itself, rather than simply communicating as equals with those with whom they have contact. This is supposedly seen to be at its worst in terms of Christianity using translation as a means of evangelizing, for the purpose of conversion, those for whom the translation is accomplished. There may be individual translational choices that are questionable when specifics are examined, but from a postcolonial

---

184. Mojola and Wendland, "Scripture Translation," 22–23. Others who have recognized the political dimensions of translation include contributors to these collections: Palma Zlateva, ed., *Translation as Social Action: Russian and Bulgarian Perspectives* (London: Routledge, 1993); Susan Bassnett and Harish Trivedi, eds., *Post-Colonial Translation: Theory and Practice* (London: Routledge, 1999).

theoretical standpoint the problem is the much larger one that transla-tion is taking place from a standpoint or viewpoint of power. This approach to translation—ideological including postcolonial—is not so much an approach to translation as a critique offered of other approaches to translation. This demonstrates that the level of engagement with translation itself is minimal, and the level of com-ment is related to the context of culture rather than even a particular context of situation or particular linguistic entities. As a result, that translation is merely an ideological conflict, or a set of competing claims, is merely another ideological assertion. Whether this is true or not, translation occurs and will continue to occur—and should occur. There is little doubt that there is some value in being reminded of the difficulty of translation, the need to respect and recognize the context in which the text was written and the context into which one translates, the integrity of the form and meaning of the source text, various differentials of power, and the like. However, as the history of Bible translation indicates, the translation of the Bible into other languages as missionary purposes dictated has been a feature of the spread of Christianity from the start, even when Christianity was not in a position of cultural or political influence or power. No doubt this has not always been done in the most contextually sensitive way. However, making the Christian message known in the language of the local people has been a staple of the Christian missionary move-ment since its inception, beginning with Pentecost and continuing with Paul's missionary journeys.

### Assessment of Translational Models

There are many ways of analyzing translations. I have attempted here to move significantly beyond the simple opposition between formal and dynamic equivalence translation. One of the distinguish-ing features of varying translational models is that they often end up addressing differing issues. Formalist models tend to function at the word-group level and are concerned with issues that tend not to go higher than the clause. The word is purported to be the maximal unit of concern, when in reality the clause probably should be the minimal unit of concern and meaning. In that case, such a model can use differing individual words, and even alter the constituents of word groups, while maintaining a theory of formalism, because larger units remain unaltered and as close to the original as possible. It may come as a surprise to realize that dynamic equivalence models also function maximally at the level of the clause. Nida's model of kernel structures is a sentence- or clause-based model (or in some instances of minimal kernels it is word-group based), in which the major points of contrast with formal equivalence revolve around changes to clause component order rather than simply focusing on individual words or vocabulary. Although these two models of translation are often played off against each other, they have much more in common than ways in which they differ. As a result, despite the rhetoric and even vitriole, it is often difficult to tell the difference between formal and dynamic translations. Functionalist models also have much in common with formal and dynamic equivalence models because they differentiate several distinct functional levels of language, and hence they include at least the same basic linguistic structures focused upon by formal and dynamic equivalence models. Functionalists take discussion up another linguistic level, however, to the clause complex as the highest unit in which major discussion occurs. Discourse-based translational models are purportedly concerned with the entire discourse, although, as is inherent with any discourse model, they encompass the discrete linguistic units below the discourse level as well. In this sense, discourse-based translation is an extension of the functionalist model, and the two translational theories have much in common. Several other models of translation also are proposed, but these, I believe, serve less well as models of translation than they do as theories of how one approaches larger levels of nonformal linguistic elements, such as context and culture. Relevance theory potentially has much to offer as a cognitive theory of pragmatics (although certainly there are some problems to work out in its relation to generalized conversational implicature), and it addresses the notion of situational context—that is, the context in which particular linguistic elements are used for their pragmatic value. In order to become a serviceable theory of translation, relevance theory will need to encompass a model of translation that deals with lower linguistic levels of exponence, such as the clause and word group—some recent efforts are moving in this direction. Descriptivist linguistics likewise addresses the question of context, specifically describing how the context of culture is enshrined in a particular literary context. As opposed to prescriptive methods of translation, descriptivism is concerned not with the process of translation, but with the translational product and its evaluation. Ideological/postcolonial models are less theories of translation than they are (often strong) commentaries on cultural contexts and those who function within them. Their reminders may be useful, but they must be recognized for the sometimes offensive political statements that they are.

The relations among translational models that I have discussed may be displayed in the following way:[185]

| Cultural Context | Cultural/Postcolonial Theory |
|---|---|
| Situational Context | Relevance Theory; Descriptivist Approach |
| Discourse | Discourse Analysis |
| Paragraph | |
| Clause Complex (Sentence) | Functionalist Translation |
| Clause | Dynamic/Functional Equivalence Translation |
| Word Group | Literal/Formal Equivalence Translation |
| Word | |
| Morphology | |

Note: I designate the word group (or phrase) as the minimal unit of meaningful translation. See further discussion in the text.

This chart correlates the levels of language and context (admittedly in a simplified form) with various approaches to translation, with the recognition that the categories are not absolute. The word group (or phrase) is the minimal unit of meaningful translation, since one must have some minimal context (or, better, cotext) for determination of meaning. Formal equivalence translation functions at this level as its minimal level of translational meaning. As noted above, there probably should be more effort to work at the clause level for formal equivalence translation, or at least recognition of the significance of

185. I have changed the linguistic units in the following chart from the one used in Porter, "Assessing Translation Theory," esp. 142, but elsewhere also, for a number of reasons. The major one is that I want to clarify some of the categories so that they are more understandable to readers of this volume, and to eliminate categories that have not proven useful in the discussion.

this level for translational practice. Dynamic equivalence, with its reliance on kernels, functions at the word group or, better, clause level. As we can see, in that sense, formal and dynamic equivalence are more closely related to each other and have much more in common, given their dealing with the lower levels of language, than do some other translational models. Functionalist translational models attempt to deal with the clause complex (or sentence), while discourse-based translation functions at the discourse level. Both relevance theory and descriptivist translational models are situationally oriented, with relevance theory focusing on situationally imposed constraints of relevance, and descriptivism focusing on literary context. Cultural or postcolonial translational critique addresses the cultural context in which translation occurs.

I am not advocating here for a particular translational model, although I hope that my comments are helpful as we think more about translation itself. I believe that the debate over formal versus dynamic equivalence has, or at least should have, run its course, so that we can learn from our accomplishments and move to the next level of translational theory and practice. I believe that this probably will involve some type of functionalist and/or discourse-based translational theory. In other words, I believe that the next stage—and it will be a difficult stage to move to because it requires that we move outside of our long-standing translational comfort zones—is to explore levels of language use that move beyond the clause all the way to the discourse level, to see how these various levels open up and yet constrain translational possibilities. This will probably require development of new translational tools for New Testament scholars as various linguistic elements not previously considered enter into the discussion. One brief example illustrates what I am saying. Organization of information flow in a Greek discourse revolves around thematic and rhematic (or given and new) material. Greek has particular ways of organizing such information. All clauses have a primary and secondary element to them—that is, a first element and subsequent elements—but not all fully grammaticalize the thematic material in such a form as an explicit subject (noun group) or place it first in the clause. Some clauses are dependent upon previous clauses' thematization. In any case, this organization of information is not the same as in English, yet it demands an appropriate rendering into English in order to capture how these higher-level elements function. I think that there are a number of potential and exciting opportunities in the area of New Testament translation if such areas are fully explored. Such opportunities might include translations that integrate their visual display more fully with their theory of translation, translations that consider it part of the translational task to indicate units of meaning and structure within the text more clearly, and translations that offer renderings with a view to the overall discourse function rather than paying overly close attention to local meaning or wording. There are no doubt other potential areas of exploration as well. All of these are the logical and, in some ways, inevitable next step in a history of productive and developing translation of the New Testament, from the earliest centuries of Christianity to the present.

## Conclusion

If every translation is a betrayal, as the Italian aphorism *traduttore, traditore* ("translator, traitor") states,[186] then what hope is there for conveying accurately the meaning of the source text in our modern target versions? Not only is there a reasonable hope on the basis of the continuous work of those who are dedicated to Bible translation, but one can also find hope in the continuing history of accomplishment in Bible translation, which has been an important dimension of Christianity almost since its earliest days. Bible translation has been an important part of the discussion of the text and transmission of the New Testament, just as the question of which text to translate and the transmission of the text both through time and across cultures remain important. As a result, various translations of the New Testament have played important roles in the development of Christianity, especially and most recently in the English-speaking world. In the course of the production of English and other translations, those involved have of necessity reflected on the translational process and have come to recognize many of the major problems that continue to vex Bible translators. Despite all of this important preliminary work,

---

186. It has been noted that this phrase itself is difficult to translate. See Silva, "Are Translators Traitors?," 37n2.

it is only within the last century that the most important theoretical research on translation has occurred. The result has been the articulation and development of a variety of translational models, several of them with more in common than is often realized. While a number of these models will continue to be used, there is also scope for development and refinement of further translational models, some as primary models for translation, and others as a means of assessing and evaluating the translations of others. In this sense, the translation of the New Testament, along with the text and transmission of the New Testament, is integral to how we got the New Testament, and where it will continue to go.

# Conclusion

We have now completed this brief but significant journey through issues surrounding the text, transmission, and translation of the New Testament in an attempt to describe "how we got the New Testament." This is not a simple or straightforward issue to address, and is an even more difficult one to describe. The difficulties stem from the lack of direct information during some of the crucial times in the New Testament's history. This is what makes acts of reconstruction such necessary and promising avenues of exploration. I have ventured into this territory on several occasions in the previous three chapters. I have done so never with the idea of creating lines of connection that do not exist, but rather with the expectation of teasing out a number of areas that remain troublesome for those who take a high view of Scripture.

As a result, I have explored three major areas of New Testament study: text, transmission, and translation. Each of these areas deserves its own separate monograph exploring the various interpretive and historical problems concerned. Some of these monographs have been written, although none that I know of take the approach offered here. In chapter 1 I examined the nature of establishing the text of the New Testament. We saw the importance of the text of the New Testament, especially the importance of the traditional, even if recognizably difficult, goal of discovering the text as it was put forth by the author (or "published" by the author). There have been many recent attempts to call this goal into question and to propose other goals. Some of these goals are linked to recent methods of doing textual criticism. Many of these goals, however, appear to be either ill conceived or simply badly defined, as they end up attempting to achieve the traditional goal, even if under a new or different name. The development of the modern printed Greek text of the New Testament has, for the most part, been a reflection of the goal of producing as close to the original text as possible. However, even with the goal of seeking the original text, we recognize that the limits of achievement of this goal demand that we perhaps revise our expectations when it involves creating an eclectic text that admittedly never existed as a biblical text in the ancient world. This is where the single-manuscript text has a legitimate place in New Testament studies, because it is an acknowledged early text that was actually used by early Christians rather than being simply a product of recent scholarship, as venerated as that might be.

In chapter 2 I discussed the transmission of the text of the New Testament. Once I had established the importance of the early text, I used our knowledge of the text to see how it had been transmitted to us in various ways and forms. Transmission of the text of the New Testament involves several dimensions. One of these is the kinds of manuscripts that developed as the tradition was transmitted, and what these contained and how they were written. Another is how we can use these manuscripts, which are the product of textual transmission, to reconstruct how the New Testament itself developed. The major codex manuscripts, one of the great early steps in textual transmission, not only represent a significant milestone in the development of the text but also provide a turning point in textual transmission. We can work back from the major codexes to earlier stages in textual transmission by paying close attention to manuscript and other evidence, even if slight, that is available to us. Not all sections of the New Testament evidence the same developmental speed. Nevertheless, the major codexes also are crucial to this textual transmission and give us clearer insight than we had perhaps earlier realized about the status of the New Testament as a whole by the time of the fourth and fifth centuries. Other types of manuscripts, such as the papyri and lectionaries, also play an important role in chronicling this development. As a result, I propose that there is a better way to categorize the manuscripts used in textual criticism that preserves their integrity and the clarity of the transmissional process.

In chapter 3 I discussed the translation of the New Testament. Some readers perhaps did not think that translation fit within the scope of understanding the topic of how we got the New Testament, because it seems as though a major leap has been made from the New Testament itself—that is, its text and transmission—to its rendering in other languages. I hope to have dispelled any doubts regarding the importance of translation of the New Testament by showing how translation has been, and in fact remains, integral to the use and transmission of the New Testament. Translations of the New Testament have been integral to what it means to read and understand the New Testament from its earliest days. After tracing the major ancient versions, I also discussed a number of important English translations from the time of Wycliffe and Tyndale to the present. Most debate over translation of the New Testament has focused on the opposition between formal and dynamic equivalence translations. Because this simple opposition has, I think, hindered the translational opportunities for the New Testament, in this chapter I introduced other approaches to translation in vogue in translation studies as an attempt to widen our translational horizons and suggest new avenues for further exploration. These translational models deal with different levels of the text, and in so doing, they address differing issues regarding the text, including what it is that culturally is being implied by doing translation at all.

I would be naïve to believe that I have answered all of the most important pressing questions regarding the text, transmission, and translation of the New Testament. Discussion of these topics will continue because the New Testament will continue to occupy its central theological, intellectual, and linguistic place within scholarship concerned with early Christianity. More than that, the origins and development of the New Testament remain vital topics for Christians who seek greater understanding of the foundational text of their faith.

# Index of Ancient Sources

## Old Testament

**Genesis**
1:1–5 145
1:1–46:28 125

**2 Samuel**
2:5–67 125
10–13 125

**1 Kings**
22:38 165

**Psalms**
33:2–34:16 122
90:1 143
91:5 163
105:27–137:6 125
119:89 55
119:161 165

**Ecclesiastes**
11:1 163

**Isaiah**
40:8 55

**Daniel**
3:51–53 145
3:55 145

## New Testament

**Matthew**
1:1 143
1:1–25:6 128
3:6 105
3:7–17 140
3:9 95

3:14 145
3:15–16 92
3:15 145
3:16 92
3:16–17 92
3:17 145
3:25 95
4:5 91, 92
4:23–24 143
4:23–5:12 140
5:9 163
5:13 162
5:14 92
5:17–18 55
5:27–32 30
6:9 143
6:9–13 30
6:13 30, 43
6:33–34 144
7:7 162
7:12 144
7:13–20 140
8:2–3 104
8:4 92, 104
9:35 140
9:37 102
10:16 102
10:37–42 140
11:25–30 145
15:7–9 105
16:3 162
17:1–3 143
17:6–7 143
17:21 52
18:11 52
18:15–17 143
18:19 143
18:20 162
18:32–34 145

19:1–3 145
19:3–9 30
19:5–7 145
19:9–10 145
19:21 158
19:26 162
20:4 18
20:20–23 101
22:16 105
23:14 52
23:24 164
23:35 92
24 86
25:8–10 143
26:7–8 95
26:30–34 102
26:41 162
27:10 95
27:14–15 95
27:22–23 95
27:31–33 95
27:51 92
27:56–57 93, 145
27:62–64 143
28:1 100
28:2–5 143
28:9–10 100
28:18–20 101
28:19 101

**Mark**
1:1 143, 193
1:4 184–86, 190
1:5 105
1:11 21
1:40–42 104
1:41 68
1:43 69
1:44 104

2:7 22
3:1 91
5:41 85
6:18–29 140
7:6–7 105
7:16 52
7:27 165
9:44 52
9:46 52
10:2–12 30
10:32–40 101
11:26 52
12:14 105
12:26 22
14:26–30 102
15:28 52
15:34 70
15:40 93, 145
15:42 93, 145
16:1–8 31, 100
16:2 100
16:8 31
16:9 100
16:9–10 18, 31
16:9–20 67, 133, 139, 153, 166
16:10 100, 101
16:11 101
16:12 101
16:12–13 101
16:13 101
16:14 100, 101
16:15 101
16:15–17 101
16:16 100, 101
16:17 101
16:18 101
16:19 100, 101
16:20 100, 101

214

**Luke**
1:28 139
1:54–55 145
1:58–59 95
1:62–2:1 95
2:1–20 141
2:6–7 95
2:10 105
2:29–31 145
3:8–4:2 95
3:22 21
4:28–31 92
4:29–32 95
4:30 104
4:34–35 95
5:3–8 95
5:12–13 104
5:30–6:16 95
6:46 105
7:22–26 143
7:36–45 143
7:50 143
8:35 162
9:1–2 101
10:1 101
10:2 102
10:3 102
10:17 101
10:17–18 101
10:38–42 143
11:2–4 30, 139
11:27–32 141
12:4–5 102
12:19 162
16:18 30
16:19–20 198
16:20 198
16:21 198
17:3–4 91
17:14 104
17:36 52
18:19 105
20 193
20:21 105
22–24 22, 25
22:14 22
22:16 22
22:17 71
22:17–19 71
22:17–20 71
22:19 71
22:19–20 22, 71, 72
22:20 71
22:35–37 22
22:43–44 21, 22, 68
22:47 22
22:49–51 22

22:62 22
23:1–5 22
23:17 22, 52
23:32–24:1 22
23:43 92
23:48 92
23:49–51 93, 145
23:54 93, 145
24:1 100
24:3 22
24:4–5 155
24:6 22
24:10 101
24:11 101
24:12 22
24:13–35 101
24:33–35 101
24:36 22, 101
24:36–38 141
24:36–43 101
24:39 92
24:40 22
24:43 22
24:51 22, 101
24:52 22

**John**
1:1 143, 180, 187, 193
1:1–3 183
1:5–6 143
1:18 70
1:23 143
3:2 105
3:18 101
3:36 101
5:3–4 19, 52, 159, 166
5:20 163
5:39 104
5:45 104
6:11–15:11 159
6:50–8:52 128
7:1–13 137, 138
7:14–30 138
7:30 104
7:31–36 138
7:37–46 138
7:42 159
7:44 104
7:52 31
7:53–8:11 18, 31, 43, 65, 67, 159, 166
7:53 139
8:39 159
8:59 104
9:3–4 143
9:29 104

10:8–14 143
10:23 144
10:25 105
10:31 104
10:35 55
10:39 104
12:12–15 143
12:16–18 143
12:24 105
14:9 22
18:31–35 86
18:35–38 86
19:38 93, 145
20:1 100
20:1–18 141
20:11–18 100
20:18 101
20:19 101
20:24–27 141
20:26 101
21 31, 35

**Acts**
1:2 101
1:9 101
2:4 101
7:45 181
8:26–32 143
8:37 19, 38, 43, 52
9:5–6 38
9:17 101
9:18 162
10:26–31 143
10:46 101
15:34 43, 52
17:28 162
19:6 101
20:18–35 114
24:6–8 52
28:3–5 101
28:8 101
28:29 52

**Romans**
1:1–7 144
1:29–32 112
2:14 162
5 108
5:1 56, 67
5:2 181
5:3 181
5:11 181
6:1 112
13:1 162
14:23 29
14:33 52
15:33 29
16 28, 29, 112

16:24 52
16:25–27 29, 52

**1 Corinthians**
1:11–13 112
1:17–20 73
6:13–15 73
6:16–18 73
7:3–4 73
7:10–11 73
7:12–14 73
7:17 113
11:24–25 72
12:12 112
13:4–7 112
14:33–36 67
15:20 112
15:36–37 112
16 143
16:4–7 143
16:9–10 143

**2 Corinthians**
3:1 113
3:18 112
4:13–12:6 128
5 143
5:18–19 143
5:19–21 143
10:9–10 113

**Galatians**
2:9 112
3:1 112

**Ephesians**
1:1 29
1:11–13 107
1:18 112
1:19–21 107
4:4–6 112
4:18 112

**Philippians**
1:27 112
2:9 22
4:15 112

**Colossians**
1:12–13 112
4:16 112, 114

**1 Thessalonians**
5:27 114

**2 Thessalonians**
1:4–5 108
1:11–12 108

2:2 113
3:13 162
3:17 113

1 Timothy
1:17 112
3:16 19, 68
6:12 162

Titus
2:4–5 112
2:21 112
3:1 112
3:17 112

Hebrews
1:1 144
1:1–14 112
2:3–4 101
2:4 101
2:9 69
2:14 119
2:14–5:5 119
4:8 181
9:14 125
10:8–22 119
10:29–11:13 119
11:28–12:17 119
12:2 162
13:22–25 120

James
1:10–12 123
1:15–18 123
3:13–4:4 123
4:9–5:1 123
5:11 162

1 Peter
1:23–25 55

2 Peter
1:1 22

1 John
1:1 193
4:3 21
5:7 166
5:7–8 39, 43, 52

2 John
1–9 121

Jude
4–5 143
7–8 143

Revelation
1–3 111
1:17 102
2:12–13 145
3:20 162
7:17 162
11:7 163
15:9–16:2 145
22:16 38
22:17 38
22:18 38
22:19 38
22:21 38

Old Testament
Pseudepigrapha

Odes of Solomon
11 122

Dead Sea Scrolls
7Q5 145

Philo

Moses
2.26–44 150

Josephus

Ant.
12.11–118 150

Ag. Ap.
2.45–47 150

Early Christian
Literature

1 Clement
2:1 112
2:7 112
3:4 112
5:2 112
5:5–7 114
21:2 112
24:1 112
24:4 112
24:4–5 112
33:1 112
35:5–6 112
36:2 112
36:2–5 112
37:5 112
38:1 112
46:6 112

47:1 112
47:1–2 112
49:5 112
59:2 112
59:3 112
61:2 112

Eusebius
Epistula ad
Carpianum
1 91

Hist. eccl.
2.15.1 77
3.39.14–15 77
3.39.16 85
4.29.6 91
6.14 120

Praep. ev.
13.12.1–2 150

Vit. Const.
4.36–37 126

Irenaeus
Haer.
3.10.6 100
28.2 94

Jerome
Epistula ad
Algasiam
6 91

Justin Martyr
1 Apol.
45 100

Tertullian
Marc.
4.2 94
4.5 94
5.21 110

Praescr.
27.2 111

Greco-Roman
Literature

Cicero
Att.
13.6.3 115

Fam.
7.18.1 115
9.26.1 115

Horace
Ars Poetica
125 174

Papyri

0145
144

0153
145

0210
144

Austrian National
Library Suppl.
Gr. 106 3
Gr. 121 (0105) 137

𝔓¹
141

𝔓²
81, 141, 143

𝔓³
141, 143

𝔓⁴
95–99, 158

𝔓⁷
144

𝔓⁹
141

𝔓¹⁰
144

𝔓¹¹
23

𝔓¹²
81, 144

𝔓¹³
81, 119, 120

𝔓¹⁴
23

𝔓¹⁷
141

𝔓¹⁸
81, 141

𝔓¹⁹
141

𝔓²⁰
141

𝔓²¹
141

𝔓²³
123, 141

𝔓²⁵
145

𝔓²⁶
141

𝔓²⁸
141

𝔓³⁰
109

𝔓³¹
141

𝔓³²
141

𝔓³⁴
143

𝔓³⁵
141

𝔓³⁷
141

𝔓³⁸
63

𝔓³⁹
141

𝔓⁴²
145

𝔓⁴³
81, 145

𝔓⁴⁴
143

𝔓⁴⁶
69, 70, 72, 75, 108–
10, 113, 116–20,
158

𝔓⁴⁸
63, 141

𝔓⁵⁰
143

𝔓⁵¹
141

𝔓⁵²
86, 87, 141, 158

𝔓⁵³
99

𝔓⁵⁵
144

𝔓⁵⁶
141

𝔓⁵⁷
141

𝔓⁵⁹
23, 144

𝔓⁶⁰
23

𝔓⁶¹
23

𝔓⁶²
145

𝔓⁶³
144

𝔓⁶⁴
95–99, 158

𝔓⁶⁶
62, 64, 67, 70, 72, 98

𝔓⁶⁷
95–99, 158

𝔓⁶⁸
23, 141

𝔓⁷¹
141

𝔓⁷²
26, 75, 122, 145

𝔓⁷⁴
123

𝔓⁷⁵
62, 64, 67, 70, 71,
95, 98–100, 106

𝔓⁷⁶
144

𝔓⁷⁸
143

𝔓⁸⁰
144

𝔓⁸¹
141

𝔓⁸²
141

𝔓⁸³
23

𝔓⁸⁴
23

𝔓⁸⁵
141

𝔓⁸⁶
141

𝔓⁸⁷
109, 141

𝔓⁸⁸
141

𝔓⁸⁹
141

𝔓⁹⁰
141

𝔓⁹¹
141

𝔓⁹²
107, 109

𝔓⁹³
141

𝔓⁹⁴
141

𝔓⁹⁵
141

𝔓⁹⁶
141

𝔓⁹⁷
141

𝔓⁹⁸
141

𝔓¹⁰⁰
123

𝔓¹⁰¹
141

𝔓¹⁰²
141

𝔓¹⁰³
141

𝔓¹⁰⁴
141

𝔓¹⁰⁵
141, 143

𝔓¹⁰⁷
141

𝔓¹⁰⁸
141

𝔓¹⁰⁹
141

𝔓¹¹⁰
141

𝔓¹¹¹
141

𝔓¹¹² 141

𝔓¹¹³ 141

𝔓¹¹⁴ 141

𝔓¹¹⁶ 141

𝔓¹¹⁷ 141

𝔓¹¹⁸ 141

𝔓¹²⁰ 141

𝔓¹²¹ 141

𝔓¹²² 141

𝔓¹²³ 141

𝔓¹²⁴ 141

𝔓¹²⁵ 141

𝔓¹²⁶ 141

P.Aberd.
3 145
4 145
5 145
6 145

P.Amh.
III[a] 145
III[b] 145
III[c] 145

P.Barcelona
1 95

P.Berl.
11710 4

P.Bodmer
VII 122
VIII 123

P.Chester Beatty
1 (𝔓⁴⁵) 15, 29, 61,
72, 87–89, 99,
106

P.Egerton
2 (= P.Lond.Christ.
1) 4, 86, 103–5,
144

P.Köln
VI 255 4, 103

P.Merton
II 51 104

P.Oxy
II 210 3, 4, 104, 144
IV 840 80, 144
VIII 1077 143
XV 1786 136
XVII 2110.15 2
LX 4009 102

P.Ryl.
III 464 4

PSI
1200bis 102
VI 719 143

P.Vindob.
G 2325 102, 144
G 26225 3
G 29831 143

Major Codexes
and Majuscules

015
125

016
125

0171
99

0212 (Dura
Parchment)
93, 94

0232
121

0243
69

Alexandrinus
40, 42, 88, 119, 122,
123, 128–31,
133–35

Bezae
14, 19, 21, 25, 27,
31, 40, 41, 43,
46, 47, 62, 63,
68, 71, 88, 134,
135, 155

Claromontanus
41, 43, 46, 117–20,
129, 135

Ephraemi
Rescriptus
46, 70, 115, 119,
123, 128, 129

Freer Gospel
(Washingtonianus)
61, 88

Fuldensis
88, 90

Gigas
155

Glazier
159

Koridethi
61, 139

Regius
46

Scheide
159

Sinaiticus
14, 15, 17, 22, 25,
44, 46, 52, 62,
63, 67, 69, 70,
74, 75, 88, 95,
99, 106, 115,

119, 122–27,
129–35, 139,
156, 159

Vaticanus
12, 13, 22, 25, 39,
43, 46, 52, 62–
64, 67, 69, 70,
74, 75, 88, 95,
99, 106, 115,
117, 119, 122–26,
130, 133, 139,
159

Minuscules
1 138, 139
5 118, 125
13 139
61 39, 40
69 139
88 40
118 139
124 139
131 139
174 139
209 139
230 139
346 139
543 139
629 40
788 139
826 139
828 139
983 139
1079 12
1582 139
1689 139
1709 139
1739 69, 70
1957 126
2814 38, 139
2815 38, 139
Family 1 61, 139
Family 13 61, 139
Tischendorf ω
110 40

Lectionaries
1043 140, 141, 143
1604 140

# Index of Modern Authors

Ackroyd, P. R., 81
Adams, A. W., 70, 88, 153
Aitchison, J., 186
Aland, B., 12, 16, 24, 28, 36,
    49, 50, 52, 57, 58, 72,
    80, 87, 123, 138, 140–42,
    145, 152
Aland, K., 12, 16, 24, 32, 36,
    48–50, 52, 58, 72, 73,
    80, 96, 121, 123, 140–42,
    145, 152
Alford, H., 18, 166
Allen, W. C., 154, 164
Allert, C. D., 89, 91, 92
Amos, F., 175
Amphoux, C.-B., 3, 144
Andorlini, I., 3, 104
Archer, R. L., 115
Arduini, S., 177, 197, 198, 201

Baarda, T., 89
Bagnall, R. S., 80
Baker, D., 87
Baker, J. A., 110
Baker, M., 187, 197
Barclay, W., 172
Barker, K. L., 170
Barnard, R. K., 170
Barns, J. W. B., 64
Barrera, J. T., 150, 151
Barrett, D. P., 64, 69, 87, 95,
    96, 98, 103, 108, 109,
    119, 121–23, 158
Bartoletti, V., 119
Barton, J., 110
Bassnett-McGuire, S., 199,
    204
Bauckham, R. J., 3
Bauer, W., 20

Baur, F. C., 20, 86, 107
Bedard, Ş. J., 6
Bell, H. I., 103
Bell, R. T., 191
Bengel, J. A., 42, 43
Bengel, M. E., 42
Bernhard, A., 3
Betz, H. D., 84
Beza, T., 41, 47
Biddle, M. E., 150
Biguenet, J., 174
Bird, M. F., 111
Birdsall, J. N., 16, 153
Black, D. A., 22, 23, 27, 180
Black, M., 183
Blass, F., 62
Boda, M. J., 4, 5, 177, 192,
    201
Boismard, M.-E., 62
Bonus, A., 154
Borkowski, Z., 103
Böttrich, C., 45, 127
Bover, J. M., 24, 48, 49
Bovon, F., 80
Bowman, A. K., 23
Bowyer, W., 43
Brake, D. L., 55, 161
Bratcher, R., 169
Brenner, A., 169, 201
Brock, S., 154, 155
Brower, R. A., 147, 148, 174
Brown, D., 5
Brown, G., 191
Brown, J., 9–11, 13
Bruce, F. F., 39, 89, 110,
    113, 118, 160–62, 164,
    181, 193
Burgon, J. W., 18, 153, 154
Burke, D. G., 151, 164

Burns, D., 150
Burns, R., 174

Cadwallader, A., 166
Campbell, S., 199
Carlson, S., 28
Carson, D. A., 54–56, 60,
    61, 86, 118, 165, 179,
    182, 189
Cassirer, H. W., 172
Catford, J. C., 187, 188, 190
Chadwick, O., 152
Charlesworth, S. D., 12,
    96, 97
Cheung, A., 202
Childs, B. S., 113
Chilton, B., 2
Chomsky, N., 184, 186, 194,
    196
Ciampa, R. E., 177
Clarke, A. D., 62
Cobley, P., 177
Cockerell, D., 131
Coles, R. A., 102
Collins, C. J., 172, 180
Colwell, E. C., 19, 26
Comfort, P. W., 19, 35, 57,
    60, 64, 69, 72, 82, 87,
    95, 96, 98, 103, 108,
    109, 119, 121–23, 149,
    158, 161
Conington, J., 175
Conybeare, F., 154
Coogan, M. D., 7
Coverdale, M., 163
Cowper, B. H., 128, 130,
    133, 134
Cowper, W., 175
Crisp, S., 201

Cross, A. R., 4, 185
Crystal, D., 164
Culioli, A., 188
Daniell, D., 162, 163, 181
de Hoop, R., 4
de Waard, J., 183
Deines, R., 150
Deissmann, A., 145
Delobel, J., 28, 57, 63
Dentan, R. C., 168
Dines, J. M., 151
Dodd, C. H., 168
Dodson, J. R., 111
Driver, G. R., 168, 169
Dryden, J., 174
Duff, J., 109

Edie, W., 15
Ehrman, B. D., 6, 7, 13, 16,
    20–23, 25, 26, 29, 33, 34,
    49, 52, 57, 60, 63, 65–72,
    76, 77, 82, 90, 102, 122,
    123, 138, 152
Ellingworth, P., 195
Elliott, J. K., 3, 16, 49, 125,
    126, 142, 144
Elliott, W. J., 50
Ellis, E. E., 115, 118
Epp, E. J., 20, 23, 27, 29, 33,
    34, 36, 44, 60, 62, 63,
    72, 140
Erasmus, D., 13, 18, 37, 38,
    39, 40, 52, 55, 61, 67,
    139, 161, 172
Estienne, R. (Stephanus),
    40, 41
Evans, C. A., 1, 2, 67, 85, 87,
    100, 101, 111, 129, 149
Evans, C. F., 81
Evans, V., 196
Ewert, D., 161, 162, 163,
    168

Farmer, W. R., 85
Farstad, A. L., 48, 52, 56,
    182, 165
Fassberg, S. E., 85
Fee, G. D., 36, 44, 60, 61, 63,
    64, 72
Fell, J., 41
Fischer, B., 157
Fitzmyer, J. A., 118
Förster, H., 21, 97, 98
Foster, P., 86
Fuller, D. O., 18, 55
Funk, R. W., 5

Gaebelein, F. E., 86
Gagos, T., 96
Gallazzi, C., 108
Gamble, H. Y., 110, 113
Gardthausen, V., 126
Gathercole, S., 91
Georgakopoulou, A., 191
Giannakis, G., 150
Goodacre, M. S., 94
Goodrich, R. J., 51
Goodrick, E., 51
Goodspeed, E. J., 111, 112,
    116, 167
Gössner, A., 45
Goutsos, D., 191
Grant, F. C., 175
Grant, R., 33
Green, G. L., 198
Green, M., 196
Greenlee, J. H., 16
Gregory, C. R., 14, 17, 73,
    95, 143–45
Grenfell, B. P., 119, 123, 144,
    145
Grice, P., 196, 197
Griesbach, J. J., 18, 27, 43, 46
Gronewald, M., 103
Grudem, W., 172, 178–80,
    189
Guthrie, D., 114, 115
Gutnecht, C., 194
Gutt, E.-A., 197
Gwilliam, G. H., 154

Hahneman, G. M., 109,
    110, 129
Haines-Eitzen, K., 123
Halliday, M. A. K., 187, 192
Handley, E. W., 143
Hannah, D. D., 55
Harding, M., 12
Harnack, A., 86
Harpur, T., 6
Harrington, D. S., 166
Harris, J. R., 18–20, 117
Harris, R. A., 186
Harrison, W., 168
Hasan, R., 188
Haslam, M. W., 123
Hatim, B., 191, 194, 201
Head, P. M., 26, 62, 95, 97, 99
Headlam, A. C., 154
Heath, G. L., 20
Heide, K. M., 24
Hengel, M., 64, 150
Hennecke, E., 105
Hermans, T., 199

Hess, R. S., 4, 75, 170, 186
Hill, C. E., 4, 63, 89, 103,
    159
Hill, J. H., 93
Hodges, Z., 48, 52, 56
Hodgson, R., 177, 197, 198,
    201
Hoffmann, S., 128
Holmén, T., 85
Holmes, M. W., 26–29, 32,
    33, 36, 49–52, 60, 74, 82,
    90, 138
Hoover, R., 5
Horsley, G. H. R., 143
Hort, F. J. A., 14, 17, 18, 22,
    23, 26, 45, 46, 48, 49,
    52, 53, 57, 60, 62–64,
    67, 71–75, 153, 154, 166,
    167, 173
Horton, C., 87, 92
Huleatt, C., 95
Hunt, A. S., 119, 123, 143–45
Hunt, G., 168
Hurtado, L. W., 19, 61, 130
Husselman, E. M., 159
Hyatt, J. P., 73

Ingrams, L., 143

Jakobson, R., 148
Jarick, J., 75
Jeffrey, D. L., 164
Jeremias, J., 105
Jobes, K., 37
Jongkind, D., 126, 131
Jowett, B., 175

Kasser, R., 64, 159
Keck, L. E., 111
Kee, H. C., 106, 165
Keith, C., 31
Kelhoffer, J. A., 31
Kenyon, F. G., 15, 70, 87–90,
    108, 109, 125, 126, 128,
    139, 153, 156–59
Kilpatrick, G. D., 49
Kim, Y. K., 109
Knibb, M. A., 151
Knox, J., 111, 112
Koch, D.-A., 63
Koester, H., 88, 89
Kohlenberger III, J., 51
Korpel, M. C. A., 3, 4
Köstenberger, A. J., 20
Kraeling, C. H., 93
Kraft, R., 20
Kramer, B., 3, 143

Kraus, T. J., 2, 4, 103, 105, 141
Krodel, G., 20
Kruger, M. J., 4, 20, 63, 84, 89, 103, 105, 144
Kubo, S., 161
Kümmel, W. G., 106

Lachmann, K., 44, 46, 58
Lake, H., 70, 125
Lake, K., 15, 16, 18, 19, 70, 110, 125
Lamouille, A., 62
Land, C. D., 120
Lanier, S., 175
Lattimore, R., 172
Legg, S. C. E., 50
Levinson, S. C., 196, 194
Lewis, C. S., 167
Lewis, M. P., 7, 147
Lieu, J. M., 4, 41, 164
Liping, B., 201
Lona, H. E., 112
Longenecker, R. N., 63, 113
Lovering, E. H., 63
Lührmann, D., 102
Luijendijk, A., 144
Lukaszewski, A. L., 51
Lupas, L., 164
Luther, M., 162

Mace, D., 42
Mai, A., 125
Marguerat, D., 86
Markschies, C., 4
Martin, J., 192
Martin, V., 64
Martyn, J. L., 111
Mason, I., 191, 194, 201
Matthew, T., 163
Matthiessen, C., 192
McDonald, L. M., 85, 107, 110, 118, 124, 129, 130, 134
McKendrick, S., 3, 75, 141
McKnight, S., 12
McRay, J., 82
Merk, A., 24, 47, 49
Merrell, J., 98
Metzger, B. M., 13, 16, 22, 27, 36, 38–41, 53, 57, 60, 70, 71, 77, 80, 89, 92, 126, 134, 149, 152, 153, 155–61, 168
Mey, J. L., 194
Mill, J., 41, 42, 65–66
Miller, B. V., 16
Miller, E., 154

Milligan, G., 110
Milne, H. J. M., 78, 131–34
Min, K. S., 26
Mink, G., 27, 32–34, 59
Mitton, C. L., 113
Moffatt, J., 120, 124, 167, 173
Moir, I., 16
Mojola, A. O., 177, 197–99, 201, 204
Morgan, B. Q., 174
Moule, C. F. D., 114
Munday, J., 177, 188, 192, 199, 201
Murphy-O'Connor, J., 115–18

Nash, R. N., 161
Neill, S., 152
Nestle, Eberhard, 15, 48, 49, 73, 74, 173
Nestle, Erwin, 48
Neufeld, D., 201
Newman, B. M., 169
Newmark, P., 187
Newton, B. W., 45
Nicklas, T., 2, 3, 63, 103, 105, 141
Nicolson, A., 164
Nida, E. A., 49, 147, 148, 169, 176, 178, 179, 182–87, 190, 194, 195, 202–204, 206
Niebuhr, R., 33
Nobbs, A., 12
Nongbri, B., 86
Nord, C., 201
Norsi, M., 119
North, J. L., 154
Noss, P. A., 151, 186, 195

Oates, J. F., 143
O'Donnell, M. B., 2, 5, 189, 192, 198
Oesch, J. M., 3, 4
Ogden, C. K., 172
Osborne, G. R., 12
Osburn, C., 138
O'Sullivan, O. A., 3, 75, 141

Paine, G. S., 164
Palme, B., 2, 3, 136, 144
Palmer, E., 166
Parker, D. C., 29, 30–35, 50, 57, 59, 76, 77, 80, 82, 94, 99–101, 124, 126, 127, 131–33, 135
Parker, M., 163
Parsons, P. J., 23, 98, 143

Pattemore, S., 186, 195, 197
Pearson, B. W. R., 186
Perrin, N., 91
Pervo, R., 113, 114
Peters, C., 92, 145
Petersen, W. L., 27, 28, 60, 73, 88–92
Peterson, E., 172
Petzer, J. H., 57, 61, 62
Phillips, C. A., 91, 92
Phillips, J. B., 167
Pickering, W. N., 18, 55
Pierpont, W. G., 24, 48, 51–53, 56, 57
Pisano, S., 13, 125
Pitts, A. W., 4, 86, 120, 137, 158
Plumley, J. M., 160
Plunkett, M. A., 68
Pöhlmann, E., 136
Porter, J. S., 13, 14
Porter, S. E., 1–3, 20, 102–4, 107, 111, 114, 118, 120, 137, 140–46, 150, 158, 161, 164–66, 170–72, 175, 177, 180, 185, 186, 189, 192, 198, 200, 201, 207
Porter, W. J., 2–4, 87, 102, 136–38, 140–43, 145, 183, 184
Postgate, J. B., 175
Poythress, V. S., 172, 189
Punt, J., 201

Quinn, J. D., 109, 110

Ralston, T. J., 61
Reed, J. T., 118
Rhodes, E. F., 12, 80, 152, 164
Richards, E. R., 115
Rieu, C. H., 172
Rieu, E. V., 172
Roberts, C. H., 81, 86, 95, 96, 121
Robertson, A. T., 9, 11, 13, 167
Robertson, E. H., 161
Robinson, J. M., 123
Robinson, M. A., 24, 48, 51–54, 56, 57, 72
Roca-Puig, R., 95, 96
Roche, O. I. A., 166
Rogerson, J. W., 4, 41, 150, 164, 165, 169
Rohrbaugh, R. L., 201
Rölle, L. J., 194

Römer, C., 145
Royse, J., 26, 27, 71
Ryken, L., 171, 172, 178–81
Samuel, A. E., 143
Sanday, W., 89, 154
Sanders, H. A., 108
Sanders, J. A., 110
Sanneh, L., 201
Sanz, P., 97
Scheil, V., 95
Schlarb, E., 102
Schmid, U. B., 50
Schmithals, W., 117
Schnabel, E. J., 12, 33
Schneemelcher, W., 105
Scholz, J., 43
Schonfield, H., 172
Schopenhauer, A., 175
Schröter, J., 4
Schulte, R., 174
Scorgie, G. G., 170, 179, 189
Scrivener, F. H. A., 14, 135, 164, 166
Semler, J. S., 43
Sheeley, S. M., 161
Silva, M., 22, 27, 37, 179, 209
Sim, M. G., 198
Sim, R. J., 197
Skeat, T. C., 81, 96, 97, 103, 126, 131–34
Smalley, W. A., 183
Souter, A., 15, 47, 129
Specht, W., 161
Sperber, D., 195–97
Stamps, D. L., 2
Stanley, C. D., 177
Stanton, G. N., 96
Statham, N., 182
Steane, W., 45
Stecconi, U., 177
Steely, J. E., 117
Stegmüller, O., 145
Steiner, E., 187
Steudel, J., 42
Stewart, R. B., 24, 67
Stine, P. C., 183, 184
Störig, H. J., 174
Strachan, L. R. M., 145
Strauss, M. L., 170, 179, 189
Streeter, B. H., 58, 61
Strutwolf, H., 32, 34
Sturz, H., 54, 55

Swete, H. B., 152
Sysling, H., 151
Taber, C. R., 183, 184, 185, 195
Talmon, S., 129
Tamez, E., 201
Tasker, R. V. G., 49, 168, 173
Taylor, D. G. K., 94, 154
Taylor, K., 172
Tenney, M. C., 63, 113
Testuz, M., 122
Thackeray, H. St. J., 151
Thiede, C. P., 95, 97
Thomas, J. D., 143
Thompson, E. M., 128, 133, 134
Thompson, H., 159
Tilly, M., 3, 63
Tischendorf, C., 14, 18, 23, 44, 45, 48, 49, 71, 73, 74, 125–28, 132, 135
Tov, E., 1, 111, 149
Tregelles, S., 13, 14, 18, 38–40, 44, 45
Trivedi, H., 204
Trobisch, D., 27, 28, 110, 115–20, 128, 135
Tuckett, C., 63
Turner, E. G., 98, 103
Tyndale, W., 157, 161–65, 181, 187, 213
Tyson, J., 111
Tytler, A., 174

Vaganay, L., 16
van der Louw, T. A. W., 151
van Haelst, J., 64, 87, 142
van Henten, J. W., 169, 201
Venuti, L., 174, 202–4
Vogels, H. J., 24, 47, 49
von Campenhausen, H., 110
von Harnack, A., 113, 129
von Humboldt, W., 175
von Soden, H., 24, 47, 49, 56, 167, 173
Voth, S. M., 170, 179, 189

Wachtel, K., 32, 33, 36, 138
Walker, J. F., 120
Wallace, D. B., 52, 54–56
Walton, B., 40, 41
Walton, S., 114
Warfield, B., 14, 15

Wasserman, T., 122, 123
Watson, W. G. E., 150
Watt, J. M., 202
Webster, J. J., 187, 188
Webster, N., 166
Weigle, L. A., 167
Weiss, B., 46, 48, 73
Wellecz, E., 137
Welles, C. B., 143
Wells, E., 42
Wendland, E., 177, 197–99, 201, 204
Weren, W., 63
Wesley, J., 166, 183
Wessely, C., 78, 140
West, M. L., 58, 136
Westcott, B. F., 14, 17, 18, 22, 23, 26, 45, 46, 48, 49, 52, 53, 57, 60, 62–64, 67, 71–74, 75, 92, 113, 153, 154, 161, 166, 167, 173
Westerholm, S., 114
Westfall, C. L., 67
Wettstein, J., 42, 43
Weymouth, R., 48, 73, 167, 173
Whang, Y. C., 186
Whitby, D., 42
White, P., 192
Wikgren, A., 71
Wilamowitz-Moellendorff, U., 175
Wilcken, U., 109
Willard, L. C., 117
Williams, M., 194
Williams, T. B., 100
Wilson, D., 195–97
Wilson, R. McL., 105
Wilt, T., 177, 195
Winter, B. W., 62, 172
Woide, C. G., 128
Wolf, H. M., 179
Wood, J. H., 90
Wooden, R. G., 149
Wycliffe, J., 161, 213

Yeo, K. K., 201
Yule, G., 191

Zaharova, A. V., 45
Zahn, T., 113
Zlateva, P., 204
Zuntz, G., 70, 109, 110, 119